BORIS JOHNSON

Also by Andrew Gimson:

The Desired Effect

Boris:
The Making of the Prime Minister

Gimson's Kings & Queens:
Brief Lives of the Monarchs Since 1066

Gimson's Prime Ministers:
Brief Lives From Walpole to Johnson

Gimson's Presidents:
Brief Lives From Washington to Trump

BORIS JOHNSON

*The Rise and Fall of a Troublemaker at
Number Ten*

ANDREW GIMSON

**SIMON &
SCHUSTER**

London · New York · Sydney · Toronto · New Delhi

First published in Great Britain by Simon & Schuster UK Ltd, 2022

Copyright © Andrew Gimson, 2022

The right of Andrew Gimson to be identified as the
author of this work has been asserted in accordance
with the Copyright, Designs and Patents Act, 1988.

3 5 7 9 10 8 6 4

Simon & Schuster UK Ltd
1st Floor
222 Gray's Inn Road
London WC1X 8HB

www.simonandschuster.co.uk
www.simonandschuster.com.au
www.simonandschuster.co.in

Simon & Schuster Australia, Sydney
Simon & Schuster India, New Delhi

The author and publishers have made all reasonable efforts to contact
copyright-holders for permission, and apologise for any omissions or errors
in the form of credits given. Corrections may be made to future printings.

A CIP catalogue record for this book is available from the British Library

Hardback ISBN: 978-1-3985-0279-6
eBook ISBN: 978-1-3985-0280-2

Typeset in Perpetua by Palimpsest Book Production Ltd, Falkirk, Stirlingshire

Printed in the UK by CPI Group (UK) Ltd, Croydon, CR0 4YY

MIX
Paper from
responsible sources
FSC
www.fsc.org
FSC® C171272

For Eliza, Clive and Katy

CONTENTS

Contents

Contents

'He is late, rushed, chaotic, uncollegiate, unstrategic, some-times inaccurate. But he is also a bit of a genius.'

Charles Moore, *Daily Telegraph*, 11 August 2018

'I would rather prefer my cat to be leader of the Conservative Party. Mr Pumpkin is more trustworthy than Boris.'

Keith Simpson, Conservative MP, 15 December 2018

'Success is the child of Audacity.'

Benjamin Disraeli, prime minister in 1868 and from 1874 to 1880, in *The Rise of Iskander*, published in 1833

DEATH OF A PRIME MINISTER

On the morning of Tuesday 7 April 2020, I was commissioned by the *Daily Mail* to write Boris Johnson's obituary. At 7 p.m. on Monday evening the prime minister had been admitted to the intensive care unit at St Thomas' Hospital, and nobody knew whether he would pull through. Death laid its icy hand on him, and opinion polls show he received greater public approval and sympathy than at any time before or since. For a few days Johnson was no more the hated Brexiteer, unscrupulous populist and brazen liar, but a fellow human being, equal with any other victim of the pandemic, mortal like the rest of us.

Your eye may have slid smoothly over the last phrase, but you, dear reader, will die soon enough, as will the author of this book. The glories of our blood and state are shadows, not substantial things. So says the poet, and I have tried while writing about Johnson, as insatiable a glory-seeker as our times can show, to bear in mind that he is also a man.

But an extraordinarily difficult man to write about. When I asked my children, then aged twenty-five, twenty-one and nineteen, if I could dedicate this book to them, provided I put in a line about their having slight reservations about Johnson, one of them replied: 'Only if you say we think he's a vile, disgusting human being.' Boris Johnson inspires in many people a profound and implacable aversion; in many others the warmest affection and support. I do not aspire to change anyone's mind about him:

that would be a vain endeavour. But I do hope, perhaps just as presumptuously, to write a book which partisans on both sides will reckon is fair, and can read with amusement.

A great, maybe insoluble problem at once arises. As soon as I start to explain why Johnson has not, at certain times in his career, been a total failure, I open myself to the charge of seeking to ignore or extenuate his faults. But any sympathy that I extend to him (and I do not think he can be understood without a degree of sympathy) is liable to be dismissed by his admirers as pitifully inadequate.

There was no time to worry about all that while writing his obituary for the *Daily Mail*, which at a time of national shock and mourning would expect, I assumed, an account which at least ended on a relatively favourable note. This, roughly speaking, is what I sent them:

> Boris Johnson loved the Chumbawamba song, 'I get knocked down, but I get up again. You're never going to keep me down.' He was often knocked down, but until his life was cut short by Covid-19 always got back up again. Johnson was far less cautious than the usual run of career politician, took risks which onlookers regarded as mad, but came back from blows which would have crushed a less resilient figure.
>
> On entering the Commons in 2001 as MP for Henley, he decided, in defiance of all prudent advice, to remain editor of *The Spectator*. Senior politicians and pundits warned him that riding two horses was bound to end in tears. He defied their predictions, and at first all went well. He became more and more famous, and at the start of September 2004, *Vanity Fair* billed him as 'the Tory MP who could one day be Britain's prime minister'.

Michael Woolf, who wrote that magazine's profile, likened him to two famous actors who had gone into politics: 'He is, it occurs to me, as he woos and charms and radiates good humour, Ronald Reagan. And Arnold Schwarzenegger . . . He is, I find, inspirational.' No other Conservative MP could have been compared to Reagan, one of the most successful (though at first derided) post-war American presidents, or to Schwarzenegger, then serving as governor of California. Johnson had an astounding ability to connect with the wider public. He had star quality, and the Conservatives began to think he might be the leader who could end Labour's decade of success under Tony Blair.

In the summer of 2004 I started work on my first volume about Johnson, published in 2006 and updated in 2007, 2008, 2012 and 2016. As recounted in the introduction to that work, he was at first tremendously keen on the idea of a book all about him ('Such is my colossal vanity that I have no intention of trying to forbid you'), but then got cold feet ('Anything that purported to tell the truth really would be intolerable') and offered me £100,000 to abandon the project, which I, annoyed by his assumption that I could be bought, turned down.

In October 2004, *The Spectator* published an editorial in which it abused the people of Liverpool and made several atrocious mistakes about the Hillsborough disaster. There was uproar, and Michael Howard, the Conservative Party leader, who was a Liverpool fan, was warned that the next time he went to a game he would be booed. Howard was furious and ordered Johnson to go and apologise to the people of Liverpool, speaking only to the local media. This Johnson did, but the national press were determined to cover the story too, and during his visit to the city a media scrum developed which amused the watching nation, but made Howard look ridiculous.

Worse soon followed. Johnson dismissed press reports of his affair with Petronella Wyatt as 'an inverted pyramid of piffle', the press proved he was lying and Howard, who had only a few months previously promoted him to the post of shadow arts spokesman, now sacked him. By the end of 2004, Johnson's political career lay in ruins. Many of his fellow Tory MPs, jealous of his fame and angered by his neglect of parliamentary duties, had concluded he was hopelessly dishonest and unreliable.

So when Howard lost the 2005 general election to Blair, and resigned the Tory leadership, Johnson was in no fit state to mount a bid for the vacant post, and instead supported David Cameron, who came through and won. Cameron had been junior to him at Eton, junior to him at Oxford, had a less original mind and, until becoming leader, was less famous than Johnson, who had reached the wider public by giving a series of brilliantly amusing performances on *Have I Got News For You*.

The next ten years belonged to the prudent and professional Cameron, not the reckless and frivolous Johnson, who had to content himself with the junior post of shadow spokesman for higher education. In 2006, at the launch party for a book he had written about ancient Rome, Johnson said in his speech, 'I occasionally wonder what people like me are doing in public life,' and went on: 'It is because we hope to become shadow spokesman for higher education.'

This was funny because it was such obvious nonsense. Johnson yearned to become prime minister, but knew he was going to get nowhere much at Westminster as long as Cameron was in charge. Mary Wakefield, who worked at *The Spectator*, was among those who suggested Johnson should instead take on Ken Livingstone, mayor of London, in the elections to be held in May 2008. The problem was that Livingstone was reckoned to be invincible. The advantage was that Johnson would be entering a popularity contest, in which his ability to reach the wider public, including those who hated conventional politicians, might be a trump card.

Johnson dared take on the mighty Livingstone, something no other prominent Conservative was prepared to do, and came through and won, whereupon he resigned his parliamentary seat. He had proved himself as a campaigner, and soon he started to prove himself an ambassador for London, who would stand up for the metropolis against central government. He employed gifted individuals such as Simon Milton to do the administrative work for which he himself was temperamentally unsuited. In May 2012, Johnson beat Livingstone again, and that summer he welcomed the world to London for the Olympics.

The media, and many Londoners, expected the Games to be an embarrassment, with the trains and buses unable to cope with so many visitors. Johnson insisted the Games would be a triumph, and was proved right. He proceeded to dominate every joint appearance he made with Cameron, who since 2010 had served as prime minister.

During the Games Johnson got stuck on a zipwire, a mishap which made him even more popular. On another celebrated occasion, carried away by his own competitiveness, he rugby-tackled a German player while taking part in a charity football match – the sort of thing most people would never think of doing, let alone actually do. On yet another occasion, he flattened a Japanese child while playing rugby. Johnson's behaviour was an affront to serious-minded people's idea of how politics should be conducted.

At the general election of 2015, Johnson returned to Westminster, sitting now for Uxbridge, in west London, so able to claim he was representing the city for which he would remain mayor until the following year. It was not at first clear what use there would be at Westminster for Johnson's gifts as a campaigner. Cameron, to widespread surprise, had managed to gain a narrow overall majority for the Conservatives at the 2015 general election, without any special help from Johnson. But Cameron had only been able to hold the Tory Party together, and to blunt the threat posed by the UK Independence Party, by promising that if he won the election, he would hold a referendum on Britain's membership of the European Union.

Here was Johnson's opportunity. With his mastery of political theatre, he wavered between Leave and Remain, admitted he was 'veering all over the place like a supermarket trolley', even let it be known he had written two opposing columns for the *Daily Telegraph*, one in favour of staying in the EU and one in favour of leaving. At teatime on the afternoon of Sunday 21 February 2016 he emerged from his handsome Georgian house in Islington and announced to the excited mob of journalists which had gathered outside – throughout his career he had a genius for fomenting a media scrum – that he would be joining the Leave campaign. Johnson took on Cameron, becoming

the voice of Britain's Eurosceptic voters who felt themselves scorned and ignored by the pro-European
Establishment. He showed again his abilities as a campaigner
who, unlike just about every other British politician, could
enter a dreary shopping centre on a Wednesday afternoon
and bring the place alive.

On and on the obituary rolled. The *Daily Mail* was calling
for my copy, determined to have the piece ready for publication
the moment the prime minister died. By now I had managed
to get him into Downing Street. A few moments later he was
consigned to the grave:

Then came the pandemic. It required a change in tone:
Johnson had to curb his natural ebullience. This he did,
and demonstrated he was working night and day with his
team to bring the nation through the danger, regardless
of any risk to his own health. His career has been cut
cruelly short at a point when he had just achieved his
greatest successes – Brexit and the election victory of
December 2019 – and seemed set for many years at the
top in which to develop his vision of One Nation conservatism. Many who had never warmed to him realised at
the end that this man who had long seemed to them a
mere joker was in reality a statesman of astonishing political gifts, the most brilliant communicator of his generation,
impelled not only by a burning thirst for fame but by a
deep love of his country and a determination to serve it
to the uttermost of his powers.

CAVORTING CHARLATAN

Johnson did not die, and his enemies, some of whom were surprised to find when he was at death's door that they had tender feelings for him, soon reverted to likening him to Hitler (as a celebrated Hampstead thinker remarked to me in a tone which brooked no contradiction), or to King John, conventionally regarded as the worst monarch in English history (this option proposed on Twitter by Ivo Dawnay, Johnson's brother-in-law).

No politician of this century has so often been written off. As early as 2006, Simon Heffer declared of Johnson that 'a man blessed with high intelligence and great abilities has, through moral failure and self-indulgence, now largely ceased to be taken seriously in public life'. Nor has any politician so often been denounced as a liar. This charge will be examined later in the book, but is not the place to start, for once he is convicted of lying, we cease to consider whether he ever tells the truth. As a result of his lies many refused to accept Johnson as a legitimate player of the political game, and the reasons why he has quite often won it went unexamined.

Distinguished liberal-conservative pundits such as Max Hastings and Matthew Parris proceeded on the assumption that Johnson is 'a cavorting charlatan' (Hastings) whose 'shamelessness shames Britain' (Parris). They were sure he cheated his way to the top and would soon be found out. But meanwhile these commentators under-estimated his chances of success, which became inexplicable unless one held that the British people wanted to vote for a scoundrel, or were too stupid to detect one.

Johnson's uncle on his mother's side, Edmund Fawcett, who worked for many years for *The Economist* and has described himself as 'a left-wing liberal', in 2020 brought out *Conservatism: The Fight for a Tradition*, an account of conservative thought in Britain, France, Germany and the United States over the past two centuries. He suggested in his introduction that readers on the left could get from it 'a view of their opponent's position, which they are prone, like rash chess players, to ignore', and went on to put 'in comradely spirit' this question to them: 'If we're so smart, how come we're not in charge?' The same question might be put to Johnson's critics, whether on the left or the right. They were brilliant at abusing him, but hopeless at working out how to beat him, so for long periods were reduced to waiting for him to beat himself.

Their abuse had the paradoxical effect of strengthening Johnson's claim to be an outsider, which further infuriated them, for how could someone with his privileged education at Eton and Balliol be an outsider?

This volume takes on, roughly speaking, from July 2016, the point at which the last update of my first volume about him ended.

THE GILDED CAGE

On Wednesday 13 July 2016, Theresa May became prime minister and summoned Johnson to Downing Street. 'Crikey, I'm the foreign secretary,' he texted one of his advisers after meeting her. 'Holy fuck,' the adviser replied. For although the PM was clearly trying to bind a potentially dangerous opponent into the government, there had been no expectation on Johnson's part that she would invite him to enter such a gilded cage, the grandest that Whitehall affords.

Once people had recovered from their astonishment, the general feeling was that he was lucky to have been awarded this glittering consolation prize. Only a fortnight earlier, he had been down and out, having withdrawn from the Conservative leadership race once Michael Gove – his comrade-in-arms in the Leave campaign which triumphed in the EU Referendum on 23 June – declared him unable to 'provide the leadership or build the team for the task ahead'.

The knifing, as it was referred to in Johnson's circle, meant he did not become prime minister in 2016. Many Remainers already believed he was a contemptible opportunist who had only backed Leave because he calculated that it gave him his best chance of reaching the top. Now Gove had demonstrated that even some influential Leavers thought he was not up to it.

Senior officials at the Foreign Office shared this low view of

Johnson. They had committed their entire careers to the cause of Britain in Europe, first adopted in the early 1960s by Harold Macmillan, prime minister from 1957 to 1963. Soon after Johnson became foreign secretary, a British diplomat said to me, 'I'd push him off his bike if I saw him in the street.'

Professional diplomats accused him of 'lack of self-discipline', 'lack of content in his vapid assurances', 'insistence on seeing foreigners as raw material for jokes', 'the belief that he can bullshit because he's very bright', and 'irresponsibility for drawing up no plan for Brexit'. Remainers accused him of stirring up 'the ignorant, racist hooligans of the north'.

In Oxford, the professor of French history, upon bumping into my younger brother, who lives there, told him to punch me on the nose, after I said a few words in defence of Johnson on Radio 4, where I usually found myself put up – the BBC being committed to a doctrine of balance – to debate against some outspoken critic of Johnson. For most of the time, I kept quiet about my opinions, for I had not entirely worked out what I thought. I could see that Johnson had grievous weaknesses as well as formidable strengths, and I did not want to annoy the devout Remainers in my immediate circle.

I myself voted Remain, in part because I was worried about the irreparable damage which might be done to the Union with Scotland and with Northern Ireland if Britain left the EU. Before the referendum I went round London saying David Cameron had been rather clever: he had told the Tory Eurosceptics they could have their referendum, but that he was going to win it. When Leave won, I was shocked, and felt a fool for failing to see this coming. But I was not bereaved in the way many Remainers were, and I knew my lack of bereavement was tactless, so I shut up about it. In families up and down the land the whole thing was not just political, but personal. The nation was split down the middle, and so was the Conservative Party.

Theresa May, who during the referendum campaign had been a silent Remainer, sought to reunite the party, and reassure Tory Brexiteers, by appointing three of their most senior figures – Boris Johnson, David Davis and Liam Fox – to Cabinet posts. Some of Johnson's supporters believed that if he had fought on against May in the leadership campaign, he would have won. It was a striking idea to send her most dangerous rival to the Foreign Office. Perhaps she was going to be a more imaginative prime minister than anyone had expected.

LIBERAL COSMOPOLITAN

Almost no one supposed it was worth paying attention to whatever general opinions the new foreign secretary had expressed in the past about foreign affairs, although his journalistic works were combed for the rude things he had said about various foreign leaders, and for words which could be construed as racist. But the general assumption prevailed that he had nothing which could be dignified by the term *Weltanschauung*, nothing in the way of a world view. After all, Johnson had been the most prominent figure in the Leave campaign, and that campaign had won, many Remainers thought, by appealing to xenophobes, racists and Little Englanders.

So the passage in his speech on 9 May 2016 about the liberal cosmopolitan case for voting Leave attracted little notice. He did not pretend this was the only reason to vote Leave. Taking back control of laws and preventing unrestricted immigration from the European Union were important too: there were things in this speech of which the xenophobe and the Little Englander could approve, and the press reported that he had attacked David Cameron for failing to obtain concessions from the EU.

But Johnson began by saying that someone had insulted him the other day 'in terms that were redolent of 1920s Soviet Russia – he said that I had no right to vote Leave, because I was in fact a "liberal cosmopolitan".' In his peroration, by far the most heartfelt part of the speech, he went on to accept this description of himself, and to contest its implications:

I am a child of Europe. I am as I say a liberal cosmopolitan, my family is the genetic equivalent of a UN peacekeeping force.

I can read novels in French, I think I've even read a novel in Spanish, I can sing the Ode to Joy in German [cry of 'go on then']. I will, if you keep accusing me of being a Little Englander I will. [Sings in a deep voice] *Freude, schöner Götterfunken* . . . Anyway you know it, you know it. Both as editor of *The Spectator* and as mayor of London [jabs the lectern with his finger] I have promoted, promoted actively, the teaching of modern European languages in our schools, French and German – which are dying out by the way at the moment, dying out under this government of Remainers – and I have dedicated much of my life to the study of the common origins [hits the lectern again], the common origins of our European civilisation [thump, thump, thump] in ancient Greece and Rome.

So I find it offensive, insulting, irrelevant and positively cretinous to be told – sometimes by people who can barely speak a foreign language – that I belong to a group of small-minded xenophobes; because the truth is that it is Brexit that is now the great project of European liberalism, and it is leaving the EU, it is we who want to leave the EU who are the idealists. I am afraid that it is the European Union – for all the high ideals with which it began – that now represents the ancien régime.

It is we who are speaking up for the people, and it is

they who are defending an obscurantist and universalist system of government that is now well past its sell-by date and which is ever more remote from ordinary voters.

It is we in the Leave camp, we who vote Leave – not they – who stand in the tradition of the liberal cosmopolitan European enlightenment – not just of Locke and Wilkes, but of Rousseau and Voltaire; and though they are many, and though they are well-funded, and though we know that they can call on unlimited taxpayer funds for their leaflets, it is we, we few, we happy few Leavers who have the inestimable advantage of believing strongly in our cause, and that we will be vindicated by history; and we will win for exactly the same reason that the Greeks beat the Persians at Marathon – because they are fighting for an outdated absolutist ideology, and we are fighting for freedom.

This passage could not be fitted into the news agenda, so was ignored or ridiculed. Here is the Politico website's report: 'In a bizarre twist, Johnson stressed his love of Europe and attempted to demonstrate this by singing "Ode to Joy" in German.'

It is possible, he contends, to love Europe and to wish to leave the EU. One may question, of course, whether Johnson's argument is correct. It is also possible to contend that Brexit, far from being, as he asserts, 'the great project of European liberalism', happened for illiberal reasons and will have illiberal consequences. But it would be wrong to doubt Johnson's sincerity when he made this argument. One hears it in his voice, especially when he touches on the origins of European civilisation in Greece and Rome.

CAKEISM

On Saturday 1 October 2016 Johnson told readers of the *Sun*, in his first newspaper interview since becoming foreign secretary, that Britain would take back control of immigration while maintaining free trade with the EU: 'Our policy is having our cake and eating it. We are Pro-secco but by no means anti-pasto.'

For ten years he had set out at the start of each October to steal the Conservative leader's thunder. 'Look at me,' he would tell the Tories as they gathered for their annual party conference, 'you'd be feeling more cheerful if I was your leader. I would make you feel good about being Conservative. I want us all to enjoy the good things of life, including cake.'

According to the French, *'On ne peut avoir le beurre et l'argent du beurre'* – one can't have the butter and the money from selling the butter. The Germans declare, *'Man kann nicht auf zwei Hochzeiten gleichzeitig tanzen'* – one can't dance at two weddings at the same time. The English have long said, 'You can't have your cake and eat it.'

Johnson insisted, on the contrary, that you can do both, and in not much more than a year the term 'cakeism' entered the language of diplomacy, to describe the pursuit of Brexit objectives which were dismissed by the EU as mutually incompatible. At the end of a report on 3 March 2018 on Theresa May's negotiating position, we find the first use of the word in *The Times*: 'Brussels officials were negative in private, however.

"This is still in the world of cakeism," said one diplomatic source.'

Brussels, and British Remainers who hoped to overturn the referendum result, strove to gain the upper hand by declaring in an expert tone that the Brexiteers were making impossible demands, so deserved to be written off as a bunch of cakeists. It was unreasonable to treat May in this dismissive fashion: any impartial person could see she was a conscientious woman who was doing her best. Brussels and the Remainers were so intent on winning, they gave little thought to who they might get instead of May, if they refused to reach a reasonable compromise with her.

That Johnson is an incorrigible cakeist cannot be denied. Early evidence of this is found in the summer of the year 2000, when he was editing *The Spectator* and had just been selected as the Conservative candidate for Henley, despite having promised his proprietor, Conrad Black, that he would not run for Parliament. Johnson rang Charles Moore, editor of the *Daily Telegraph*, to ask for advice about how to handle Black.

Moore at length wearied of Johnson's indecision and said: 'Look, Boris, what do you want?'

'I want to have my cake and eat it,' Johnson replied.

Examine any election manifesto, by any party, and one will find traces of cakeism, or often great slices of the stuff: huge, implausible, mutually contradictory promises. In his book about Winston Churchill, Johnson remarks of the Balfour Declaration of 1917, in which the then foreign secretary, Arthur Balfour, said the British government favoured 'the establishment in Palestine of a national home for the Jewish people', as long as it was 'clearly understood that nothing shall be done which may prejudice the civil and religious rights of existing non-Jewish communities in Palestine': 'Another way of putting it might have been that the British government viewed with favour the eating of a piece of cake by the Jewish people, provided nothing should be done to prejudice the rights of non-Jewish communities to eat the same piece of cake at the same time.'

But although cakeism has been around for millennia, the actual word has not, and political commentators soon decided that, as Gideon Rachman put it in the *Financial Times* on 15 July 2019, if Johnson's name 'is ever linked to a political idea, it is likely to be "cakeism" – the notion that it is possible to govern without making hard choices'. Jonathan Freedland, writing in the *Guardian* of 22 November 2021, declared in a stern tone: 'The government has adopted Johnson's notorious attitude to cake – wanting to have it and to eat it – and made cakeism its defining creed.' Rafael Behr agreed, in the same newspaper on 22 December 2021, and concluded: 'Cakeism is not a formula that works in government because, in reality, the cake has to be rationed and people notice.'

Life is real! Life is earnest! So the moralists insist. And yet within fallen humanity there is also a craving for the frivolous, the fantastical, the purely entertaining. How grateful we are when we find ourselves amused by something political. Satirists and political cartoonists try to meet this need for laughter, which is not always incompatible with self-improvement. 'EAT OUR CAKE AND HAVE IT' is, by the way, one of the slogans found on the outside of Clark's Bakery in *Palmy Days*, one of the most popular films of 1931, starring Eddie Cantor, with dances by a troupe of young bakers arranged by Busby Berkeley.

OFF MESSAGE

A foreign secretary's most significant relationship is not with some foreign power, but with the prime minister. After all, if May did not treat Johnson as a valued ally, why should anyone else? For the period from July 2016 to April 2017, she dominated British politics. Older and less patrician than her predecessor, David Cameron, she promised on entering Downing Street to help those who were 'just about managing', and to do so in a calm, competent, understated way: 'I know I'm not a showy politician. I don't tour the television studios. I don't gossip about people over lunch. I don't go drinking in Parliament's bars. I don't often wear my heart on my sleeve. I just get on with the job in front of me.'

This holier-than-thou rebuke to the political class struck many people as a change for the better. May turned her unglamorous sense of duty – no boozing, gossiping or displays of emotion, but conscientious hard work – into a strength. Her obstinately virtuous character meant she could not approve of Johnson. During her six years at the Home Office, she was a solitary figure, who treated with frigid hostility any incursion on that department. In the summer of 2011, when she was home secretary and Johnson mayor of London, she deserted him during an appearance they had made to try to reassure people during the London riots: when Johnson got the tone wrong, she moved out of camera shot. More recently, she had publicly humiliated him by refusing to allow the use of three second-hand water cannon he had bought from Germany for the Metropolitan Police.

At the Conservative Party conference of 2015, Johnson complimented her as she returned backstage – 'Really nice job, Theresa' – and she responded with a look so frosty it said: 'I don't believe a word that comes out of your mouth.' And yet by the party conference the following year, she had promoted Johnson to a splendid post, which he described with evident pleasure in his speech, knowing his listeners would enjoy this evocation of imperial glory tempered by a self-mocking reference to reality TV:

> Every day I go to an office so vast that you could comfortably accommodate three squash courts and so dripping with gilt bling that it looks like something out of the Kardashians. And I sit at the desk of George Nathaniel Curzon, and I sometimes reflect that this very seat I occupy was once the nerve centre of an empire that was seven times the size of the Roman empire at its greatest extent under Trajan, or was it Hadrian, I can't remember, and when I go into the Map Room of Palmerston I can't help remembering that this country over the last two centuries has directed the invasion or conquest of 178 countries – that is most of the members of the UN – which is obviously not a point I majored on in New York at the UN General Assembly.

Johnson proceeded to insist that although the British Empire is no more, we are now 'a soft-power superpower', and such were his oratorical gifts that he persuaded the conference to applaud the BBC, 'no matter how infuriating and shamelessly anti-Brexit they sometimes can be', as 'the single greatest and most effective ambassador for our culture and our values'.

Two days later, May began her final speech to the conference by saying: 'When we came to Birmingham this week some big questions were hanging in the air. Do we have a plan for Brexit? We do. Are we ready for the effort it will take to see it through? We are.'

These assurances were, by the way, untrue. Cameron had allowed no planning to be done for Brexit. Britain was pitifully unprepared for what was bound to be a difficult negotiation with the EU, and Cameron himself, who had promised to stay on whatever the outcome of the referendum and who could at least have presided over an initial study of the various possible ways to approach Brexit, had instead jumped ship within a few hours. But such thoughts were averted by the gale of laughter which greeted May's next words: 'Can Boris Johnson stay on message for the full four days?'

Johnson – sitting between Philip Hammond, chancellor of the exchequer, who laughed uproariously, and Amber Rudd, the home secretary, who was scarcely less amused – gave a thumbs up, smiled in a good-natured way and shouted through the applause, 'Slavishly!' and 'Religiously!'

'Just about?' the prime minister went on, with tremulous hand gestures to indicate it was touch and go whether Johnson had stayed on message.

May was in charge, and had taken this opportunity to humiliate Johnson in front of the whole party. She had an overwhelming lead in the polls, and at prime minister's questions faced Jeremy Corbyn, leader of the Labour Party, who looked like a superannuated geography teacher. He had been an independent-minded backbencher for over thirty years, with no responsibility for anything but his own opinions, many of which he had learned at the knee of the late Tony Benn and had seen no need to modify since entering the Commons in 1983. In 2015 he was unexpectedly elected party leader as a kind of belated revenge by left-wingers on Tony Blair, who during his dozen years running the party had treated them with contempt.

Corbyn was a weak performer at the despatch box, and infuriated his MPs by playing almost no part in the EU Referendum; their suspicion being that although he claimed like most of them to be a Remainer, he was at heart still a Leaver, just as Benn had been. After the referendum, Labour MPs rebelled and declared by 172 votes to 40 that they had no confidence in Corbyn, but in the resulting leadership election the wider membership reaffirmed its support for him.

So Corbyn was the lamest of lame ducks, a man his own MPs did not consider fit to be PM, and May had no difficulty walking all over him in the Commons. The bigger and trickier question for her was how to manage the Conservatives. At the start of the party conference she told them she could be depended upon to carry out the will of the people, as declared in the referendum, during which she herself had been a shy Remainer, not lifting a finger to help Cameron. She declared that 'Brexit means Brexit': a meaningless tautology, but the Brexiteers were in ecstasy, one veteran Eurosceptic remarking to me after she had spoken that this was the first time he had heard a speech by a Conservative Party leader in which he agreed with every word.

Hammond, the Oxford contemporary whom she had appointed chancellor, was less impressed, saying in an interview after they had both left office: 'My assessment of Theresa May's prime ministership, in terms of Brexit, is that she dug a 20-foot hole in October 2016 in making that speech and, from that moment onwards, cupful by cupful of earth at a time, was trying to fill it in a bit so she wasn't in such a deep mess.'

The Foreign Office was from the start cut out of the Brexit negotiations: these were in theory to be handled by the new Department for Exiting the European Union, led by David Davis, with the task of negotiating trade deals given to the new Department for International Trade, led by Liam Fox. The three Brexiteers were put in the Cabinet to reassure everyone that May really meant it, but in practice she was going to run Brexit herself.

PUT DOWN BY MAY

At the *Spectator* Parliamentarian of the Year Awards, a convivial occasion held on 2 November 2016, Johnson was declared winner in the Comeback of the Year category, created in recognition of his return 'from the political dead'. In his acceptance speech, Johnson referred to Kim, an Alsatian dog belonging to Michael Heseltine's mother. Heseltine had recently told *Tatler* that when Kim attacked him, he brought the dog under control by strangling it with its choke collar until it went limp, after which a vet put the dog down. Johnson said:

> What an extraordinary year it has been, and I have to admit there have been times when like the loyal and faithful hound Kim . . . like the loyal and faithful Alsatian belonging to Michael Heseltine, there have been moments since June the 23rd when I have genuinely feared in those very grim days . . . I genuinely feared that I might be strangled by Craig's pop-eyed Europhile Remainers [a reference to Craig Oliver, David Cameron's director of communications]. And like Kim the Alsatian therefore I am absolutely thrilled to have had this reprieve . . . I hope, obviously, that my bounce, my comeback will be a bit longer than Kim the Alsatian's . . .

Theresa May, speaking last after receiving Politician of the Year, capped this: 'I feel I just have to make a comment or an intervention on a previous speech. Boris, the dog was put down [laughter] when its master decided it wasn't needed any more [whoops of laughter].'

Very funny, but from Johnson's point of view, not very funny. The prime minister had just declared, in front of his home crowd from *The Spectator*, that once she decided he wasn't needed any more, she would have him put down.

James Landale, the BBC's diplomatic correspondent, who had known Johnson since they served together as correspondents in Brussels, felt moved to write after this:

Now every government has a court jester and Boris Johnson will never be able to escape that title. But his role in this government is crucial. He is there to convince the international community that Britain is not turning its back on the world post Brexit, that Britain has a positive role to play in global affairs.

And to do that he needs to be taken seriously. Many foreign politicians and diplomats that I speak to tell me they are pleasantly surprised when they meet the foreign secretary for the first time. They talk of the man behind the caricature – the cultured, over-educated intellectual who often speaks a bit of their language and who can be thoughtful when he is not gripped by banter.

The problem is that many others – who have not met the foreign secretary in person – often still see him as a kind of upmarket Nigel Farage, a Eurosceptic clown with clout. So to do his job, Britain's diplomat-in-chief needs every bit of credibility he can lay his hands on. He is already the butt of many jokes. The last thing he needs is his prime minister adding to the mirth.

In circumstances where another Englishman would sit tight and think there was nothing to be done to mend a broken relationship, Johnson generally attempts without delay to mend fences. He feels a compulsion to do this, and has quite often found that the personal touch mollifies even those who are infuriated by him. His cavalier treatment of Conservative MPs was based on the assumption – not, in the end, justified – that he could always make things up with them.

When it was put to him that however rude May had been to him, it would be a good idea to ask her and her husband Philip to dinner, he did so. He and his wife, Marina Wheeler, invited the Mays to the foreign secretary's official residence in Carlton Gardens, which they had moved into at the end of October. At their previous house in Colebrooke Row, Islington he had been abused by furious Remainers the moment he opened the front door, and it was in any case too far from the office.

Johnson had once accused the Romans of introducing 'a scourge that has never vanished from these islands – *elegantia conviviorum* – dinner parties'. He cannot bear being stuck next to the same people for hours, which is one reason he usually arrives late at any meal where he is to give a speech, but this was not a workable solution for a dinner he and his wife were hosting. He reported that the evening was 'a bloody disaster'. There is a zany element in Johnson's conversation. He likes to follow unexpected flights of fancy, often ending in humiliation for himself and for others. The mighty are cast down by comedy. He is a debunker. Perhaps that was why May had felt such an urge to debunk him in her recent speeches. She wanted to show she could beat him at his own game. But this was not her natural bent, and in truth she could not bear his impious sallies, his love of lowering the tone. As one of his advisers said later of her: 'She never really understood him or got him.'

TRUMP, TRUMP, TRUMP

Donald Trump's victory in the American presidential election held on Tuesday 8 November 2016 inflicted acute pain on liberals the world over. They bewailed the triumph of a tawdry and mendacious populist, which few pundits and pollsters had seen coming. What a falling off there was from Trump's predecessor, Barack Obama, a brilliant orator who could on any occasion strike the sublime note, again and again gratifying the desire of his supporters to treat the story of the republic as a morality tale, an example to the world, 'a city upon a hill', words used by the Puritan leader John Winthrop when he preached to his followers as they sailed from England to Massachusetts in 1630, and quoted by John F. Kennedy in January 1961 in his address to the Massachusetts General Court before departing for Washington to be inaugurated as president.

Senior Republicans had denounced Trump, before he defeated fifteen other candidates to win their party's nomination, as 'a pathological liar', 'race-baiting' and 'xenophobic', 'utterly amoral', a 'terrible human being' who had made 'disgusting and indefensible' comments about women, and a 'narcissist at a level I don't think this country's ever seen'. There were fears this could be the end of the Western alliance, for Trump was an isolationist who intended to bring American troops home and was on suspiciously friendly terms with the Russian leader, Vladimir Putin.

'I keep finding myself singing "Nellie the elephant" who, packing her trunk and saying goodbye to the circus, went off "with a trumpety-trump, trump, trump, trump",' Alexander Chancellor, a British journalist who had lived and worked for long periods in America, wrote in what turned out to be his last piece for *The Spectator*, published on 26 January 2017, six days after Trump's inauguration. 'I'm hoping against hope,' Chancellor went on, 'that Donald Trumpety-Trump will also say goodbye to the circus in Washington and return to the jungle whence he came; for irrespective of whatever he does in government, even if some of it proves to be beneficial, he is unworthy to be president.' He added that Trump was 'a liar on a Hitlerian scale, fomenting distrust and hatred of groups that bear no blame for the popular grievances that brought him to power'.

Johnson, speaking in Belgrade after talks with the Serbian president Aleksandar Vučić, struck a more optimistic note in a message about Trump for his 'beloved European friends and colleagues': 'I think it's time we snapped out of the general doom and gloom about the result of this election and the collective whinge-arama that seems to be going on in some places.' The foreign secretary pointed out that the president elect had already had 'a very very good conversation with Theresa May', and 'is after all a deal maker', who 'wants to do a free-trade deal' with the United Kingdom. Johnson did not attend the meeting of EU foreign ministers which had been called to discuss Trump's victory. His priority was to get as close as possible to the new president, and he was soon in New York, meeting Trump's people and getting on well with them.

Less than a year before, when Trump called for a blanket ban on Muslims entering the United States, Johnson, as mayor of London, had retorted, 'I think Donald Trump is clearly out of his mind.' Trump said there were areas of London so radicalised that the police feared to go there – a claim which betrayed, Johnson said, 'a quite stupefying ignorance that makes him, frankly, unfit to hold the office of president of the United States. I would invite him to see the whole of London and take him around the city except that I wouldn't want to expose Londoners to any unnecessary risk of meeting Donald Trump.'

As recently as March 2016, Johnson had said he was 'genuinely worried' that Trump could become president: 'I was in New York and some photographers were trying to take a picture of me and a girl walked down the pavement towards me and she stopped and she said, "Gee, is that Trump?" It was one of the worst moments.'

But Trump as dark-horse candidate making crass remarks about London was a different proposition to Trump as victor extending the hand of friendship to the UK. For while moralists yearn to see politics as a question of espousing timeless verities, and sticking to them through thick and thin, realists reckon circumstances determine how practical it is to stick to any verities one may happen to have discovered, and that 'timeless' is the wrong term to use, since times change.

What mattered more than Johnson, along with many others, trying to work out how to get along with the new president was the widespread assumption that Trump and Johnson were pretty much identical. Here, people pointed out, were two disreputable fair-haired populists, willing to say anything to get elected, and revelling in baiting the Establishment.

The awkward question of why anyone might vote for Trump or Johnson was not at this stage much asked by their critics.

The moral imperative was to demonstrate that no one had any right to vote for Trump or Johnson. On an occasion like this it becomes, as Gwendolen puts it in *The Importance of Being Earnest*, 'more than a moral duty to speak one's mind. It becomes a pleasure'. Denouncing Trump or Johnson induced warm feelings of self-righteousness. In the bad old days, an uptight schoolmaster with a penchant for corporal punishment could reassure himself that the more he beat his pupils, the more virtuous he was, and the better it would be for them too. In modern times, such punitive urges could be indulged by denouncing Trump and Johnson. The more one went for them, the better one felt oneself to be.

In the United States, the *New York Times* and other bastions of liberalism compiled authoritative catalogues of Trump's lies, published before the election, but for some reason having no apparent effect on the result. In 2016 in the United Kingdom, the claim on the side of the Vote Leave bus that Britain sent £350 million a week to Brussels was again and again held up as a shameless lie perpetrated by Johnson and his allies. But, once again, Vote Leave still won.

Part of the trouble was that, to the wider public, these denunciations could seem a bit exaggerated, even a bit hysterical. Anyone could see that Trump and Johnson were flawed: that much was obvious. But were Trump and Johnson wrong 100 per cent of the time? Maybe the destruction of great swathes of manufacturing industry, the loss of millions of skilled jobs to competitors such as China, was something the politicians should stop treating as inevitable. Maybe the welfare of American and British workers should matter a bit more, and the moral causes so dear to the liberals should matter a bit less.

Trump, the liberals shuddered to say, was a nationalist. This was true, but not the conclusive point for which they took it.

The question for any American president is not whether to be a nationalist, but what kind of nationalist to be; how best to uphold the national interest; how, in the language some prefer, to be a true patriot. One could believe, as the Washington foreign policy establishment had since the Second World War, that taking the lead in international alliances was in the American interest. But there is a powerful isolationist tradition in America, which is why the United States was so slow to enter the First and Second World Wars, and did so only under intense provocation. Both Woodrow Wilson and Franklin Roosevelt had to promise, in order to get re-elected during those conflicts, that as the latter put it in October 1940, 'Your boys are not going to be sent into any foreign wars.'

George Washington put this question to his compatriots in his tremendous Farewell Address of 1796, just before he stepped down as president: 'Why, by interweaving our destiny with that of any part of Europe, entangle our peace and prosperity in the toils of European Ambition, Rivalship, Interest, Humour or Caprice?' Compared to Washington, Trump was an oaf. This did not, however, mean he was unable to express various sentiments which he knew would appeal to middle America. In 2016, he became middle America's chosen instrument of revenge on the prosy, priggish, liberal hypocrites who were lined up behind the uninspiring figure of Hillary Clinton.

At the end of January 2017, May became the first world leader to meet Trump at the White House. The president disconcerted her by holding her hand while they were walking along in full view of the cameras, and by asking her, during lunch, 'Why isn't Boris Johnson the prime minister? Didn't he want the job?' According to the American notes of this conversation later obtained by Ben Riley-Smith, US editor of the *Daily*

Telegraph, May explained that Johnson had withdrawn after losing the support of Michael Gove.

Trump responded: 'Oh, so you were drafted, like in baseball. But I really think you were plotting this all along.'

ON THE ROAD TO MANDALAY

After serving for eight months in 1955 as foreign secretary, Harold Macmillan remarked on the difficulties faced by the holder of that post: 'Nothing he can say can do very much good and almost anything he may say may do a great deal of harm. Anything he says that is not obvious is dangerous; whatever is not trite is risky. He is forever poised between the cliché and the indiscretion.'

The press was confident Johnson would err on the side of the indiscretion, or gaffe as it is today more often called, and vast resources of time and energy were devoted to catching him out. Channel 4 sent Lottie Gammon, a gifted young film-maker, to follow him round the globe for sixteen months, for, as she remarked when I spoke to her in 2021, 'in the back of everyone's mind was the thought that he might be PM'.

'It's extraordinary the charisma he has,' she said, and explained what she means by people with charisma: 'They walk in the room and it's like the sun comes out. Everyone turns towards them.' In December 2016 she followed him to Belgrade and filmed him with the Serbian edition of his book about Churchill, bearing the Serbian version of his name, Boris Džonson: 'If I may say so,' he remarked, 'I think my name looks much better in Serbian.' Not long afterwards, the *Guardian* suggested he had used his official visit to Belgrade to promote the book. The next time Gammon saw him, in London, at

Hillingdon in his constituency, he accused her of giving the story to the *Guardian*, which she denied. Gammon said: 'He has a nasty side. In Hillingdon, he was quite physically imposing, he was smiling but he was jabbing at me, I was quite frightened. He's not very tall but he's a big man. You see the Jekyll and Hyde character. There's a very charming Boris, and moments when he's riled and pissed off.'

In January 2017 she and her producer, Tamanna Rahman, followed him to India, where they received a tip-off from a local journalist that he was going on to Myanmar. They obtained the necessary visas, waited for him at the Shwedagon Pagoda, the most sacred site and main tourist attraction in Yangon, also known as Rangoon, and were rewarded with some remarkable footage. The dialogue went as follows:

Johnson [in explanation to the British Ambassador to Myanmar, Andrew Patrick]: 'My friends from Channel 4.'

Gammon: 'Good evening. How are you, Boris?'

Johnson: 'How are you doing?'

Gammon: 'I'm very well.'

Johnson: 'Nice to see you.'

Gammon: 'Nice to see you. Last saw you in Hillingdon.'

Johnson [having walked past, in view from the back]: 'Some Channel 4 guys who've been stalking me for months.'

Gary Gibbon [political editor of Channel 4 News, providing voiceover]: 'Boris Johnson is being chaperoned by the British ambassador.'

Johnson [on being shown a colossal bell]: 'Forty-two tons!'

He strikes the bell with a clapper which has been handed to him and begins to recite:

'"The temple-bells they say,
Come you back you English soldier . . ."'

'Remember that?

'"The wind is in the palm trees, the temple-bells they say . . ."'

Ambassador [looking and sounding frightfully uptight]: 'On mike. Probably not a good idea.'

Johnson: 'What, "The Road to Mandalay"?'

Ambassador: 'No, not appropriate.'

Rudyard Kipling's poem, written in 1890 and later set to music and performed by such singers as Peter Dawson (warmly recommended) and Frank Sinatra, evokes the hopeless longing for the East felt by those who had served there:

By the old Moulmein Pagoda, lookin' eastward to the sea,
There's a Burma girl a-settin', and I know she thinks
    o' me;
For the wind is in the palm-trees, and the temple-bells
    they say:
'Come you back, you British soldier; come you back
    to Mandalay!'
Come you back to Mandalay,
Where the old Flotilla lay:
Can't you 'ear their paddles chunkin' from Rangoon
    to Mandalay?
On the road to Mandalay,
Where the flyin'-fishes play,
An' the dawn comes up like thunder outer China
    'crost the Bay!

Johnson knows reams of poetry, which he loves to find occasion to recite, but this particular verse was deemed 'not appropriate' by the Foreign Office. Wasn't Kipling some kind of colonialist? And didn't he write about a love affair between a British soldier and a Burmese woman? No matter that she is

35

compared favourably to women in London, being described as 'a neater, sweeter maiden in a cleaner, greener land'. The urge to suppress any aspects of British culture that might cause offence had kicked in.

Johnson appeals to those who abominate this self-censorship, the suppression of all voices from the past which offend against the morality of the present day. We see him being bolder, and as a result more offensive, than the official class is prepared to be. He flirts with a danger round which the poor ambassador is determined to tiptoe. We watch a foreign secretary make fun of his dutiful, inhibited minder, and naturally this episode has been watched a great many times on YouTube: Gammon has never yet shot a more popular scene. Johnson dramatised the clash of culture, not between Britain and Myanmar, but within the British ruling class. He had the guts or tastelessness to turn the volume up for a second or two, and to become box office in a way that few foreign secretaries since Ernest Bevin and Anthony Eden have been.

Some of the younger diplomats loved working for Johnson, with his unstuffy appreciation of talent wherever it was found, and his openness to unconventional modes of thought. 'I know that a lot of people in the Foreign Office really liked him,' Gammon said. 'He got to know the cleaners.' Any decent person ought to get to know the cleaners, but not many important people do.

This is Johnson the democrat, talking to people who do not belong to the Establishment, and who would otherwise be ignored. The danger of antagonising senior officials, and ignoring their understanding of how to do things, was not yet apparent.

THE DUNCAN INDEX

Alan Duncan, appointed a Foreign Office minister at the same time as Johnson, had ample opportunity to observe how his boss conducted himself. Here are a few of the entries in the index to Duncan's diaries, published in 2021 and covering the period January 2016 to January 2020:

> Johnson, Boris: lack of seriousness and application, 4, 134, 140, 160, 163–4, 171, 178, 202, 217, 299, 383, 508; manoeuvrings for leadership, 4, 19, 22, 40, 223, 224, 225–8, 234, 272, 325–6, 331–2, 334, 420, 445; self-serving ambition, 22, 40, 43, 200, 227–8, 285, 321–2, 331–2, 336, 348, 402–3, 420, 465; lack of grip on detail, 140, 200, 217, 264, 296, 506; bluff-and-bluster routine, 163–4, 173, 180, 264, 268, 489; anti-May manoeuvres, 223, 224, 225–8, 234, 265–6, 272, 325–6, 331–2, 334; disloyalty of, 227, 235, 272, 325–6, 333–4, 351, 371, 402–3, 410, 514; facile reasoning on Brexit, 227, 267–8, 348, 358, 372, 383; Hunt as much more grown up than, 317, 344, 363, 493; refers to the French as turds, 492.

Duncan is frequently scandalised by Johnson. But that is only part of the story. In some ways, Duncan's complimentary remarks about Johnson are even more telling, for they indicate the latter's astonishing capacity to win round, even impress, people who have lost all patience with him. In his introduction, Duncan writes of Johnson:

I despaired of his lack of seriousness and refusal to apply himself properly, but he is no fool, and when he focuses on an issue he can be genuinely impressive. I was angered by his nakedly ambitious manoeuvrings for the leadership, but it is undeniable that he brings a rare energy and spark to politics. The problem for me was that the spark too often lit a fuse that ignited an unplanned media explosion.

What frustrated me most of all, and still does, is that he has the makings of an exceptionally good politician – one with moderate, liberal instincts and a gift for rallying an audience. If he could channel his energies into devising a compelling and optimistic vision of the future direction of the country, and use it to consign the unpleasant divi-siveness of Brexit to the past, he would be a formidable prime minister. I still hold out hope.

This is the language of a school report. It recalls what Martin Hammond, Johnson's housemaster at Eton, wrote about him in a report in April 1982, words first printed in my earlier volume and since quoted everywhere from the *New Yorker* to Russia Today, and even read by Rory Stewart in the Royal Albert Hall: 'Boris sometimes seems affronted when criticised for what amounts to a gross failure of responsibility (and surprised at the same time that he was not appointed Captain of the School for next half): I think he honestly believes that it is churlish of us not to regard him as an exception, one who should be free of the network of obligation which binds everyone else.'

After this penetrating observation, Hammond offered hope of redemption: 'I'm enormously fond of Boris, and saddened that he should have brought upon himself this sort of report. All is not lost, by any means: he can easily effect a full return to grace by showing obvious commitment next half.'

In some of his critics, Johnson inspires such fondness, and the hope that he will do better next time. Duncan expresses this hope in his diaries. On 12 March 2018, the Russian ambassador, Alexander Yakovenko, was summoned to the Foreign Office to be addressed by Johnson, in the presence of Duncan and one British official, about the Salisbury nerve gas attack, which had occurred eight days before:

> Yakovenko and his deputy came in, all jaunty and smiling as if nothing had happened. Boris and I were suitably severe. We all remained standing up, on facing sides of the foreign secretary's large office table.
>
> 'Ambassador. Two people have been poisoned on UK soil in Salisbury. One is in a critical condition and might die. His daughter and a policeman are in hospital. Our laboratory has established beyond doubt that the poison used was a banned military-grade nerve agent called Novichok. We know that this was made in Russia, and can only have been handled by the Russian state. Either the Russian state did this or it has lost control of its Novichok stocks. You have until midnight tomorrow to let us know which.'
>
> And then he raised his tone and with fabulous indignation verging on anger, told him in no uncertain terms how unacceptable it was to violate our security, try to murder someone on British soil, breach a highly important international convention, etc. It was a deliciously delivered dressing down, in response to which the dumb-struck Yakovenko couldn't say anything, and just left.

Well done, Boris! I felt genuinely proud of him. Perhaps it worked so well because he was not larking about and playing to the gallery – he spoke from the heart and meant what he said. It was a magic moment, which shows that little can beat Boris at his best.

A striking testimonial, from a witness who at other times remained among Johnson's fiercest critics. Duncan would say if he thought the foreign secretary was a lost cause, but instead records the violent fluctuations which are such a mark of Johnson's career. If this politician has the talents needed to develop into a statesman, why is he so erratic at using those gifts? His worst is criminally unprofessional, but as the diarist also says, 'little can beat Boris at his best'. It is tempting, in the interests of simplicity, to conclude that Johnson is either good or bad. He is actually both. One thinks of the cricketer David Gower coming to the crease, playing some wonderful strokes no one else could have played, impelling spectators to hurry to the ground or turn on the telly, and then getting himself out before he has amassed a serious score. Was Johnson a serious competitor, or would he always get himself out?

CALAMITOUS SELF-HARM

In her speech at Lancaster House on 17 January 2017, Theresa May promised to 'take back control of our laws and bring an end to the jurisdiction of the European Court of Justice in Britain'. She added that 'Brexit must mean control of the number of people who come to Britain from Europe', and declared: 'we will pursue a bold and ambitious free trade agreement' with the EU, which 'cannot mean membership of the single market'. For that would mean accepting the EU's 'four freedoms' of goods, capital, services and people, and complying with the rules and regulations which support those freedoms, 'without having a vote on what those rules and regulations are'.

She also said she was not going to provide a running commentary on how the negotiations were going: 'however frustrating some people find it, the government will not be pressured into saying more than I believe it is in our national interest to say. Because it is not my job to fill column inches with daily updates, but to get the right deal for Britain. And that is what I intend to do.'

It was, however, the job of hundreds of journalists to fill column inches with daily or even hourly updates, and for the whole of May's premiership, as well as for some time afterwards, the papers and websites were filled with detailed accounts of how Brexit was going, with rival experts offering their definitive views about the correct way to proceed, and predicting disaster if their advice was not followed. On no topic were these technocrats better informed than the immediate future, which would only be bright if their instructions were heeded.

But what if the prime minister proved unable to attain her ambitious, and still distinctly Eurosceptic, objectives? What if the EU just said 'No'? At the end of her speech, she worked round to this tricky question via a series of platitudes:

> So I believe the framework I have outlined today is in Britain's interests. It is in Europe's interests. And it is in the interests of the wider world. But I must be clear. Britain wants to remain a good friend and neighbour to Europe. Yet I know there are some voices calling for a punitive deal that punishes Britain and discourages other countries from taking the same path.
>
> That would be an act of calamitous self-harm for the countries of Europe. And it would not be the act of a friend. Britain would not – indeed we could not – accept such an approach. And while I am confident that this scenario need never arise – while I am sure a positive agreement can be reached – I am equally clear that no deal for Britain is better than a bad deal for Britain.

There – she had said it. No deal is better than a bad deal. But did she mean it? Was she, indeed, capable of meaning it? For a large number of sound, sober Conservative MPs were convinced it would be madness to leave the EU without a deal. The term 'cliff edge' entered common use: it was what Britain would plunge over in the event of no deal. Dover and other ports would be brought to a standstill by queues of motionless lorries, unable to gain customs clearance and stretching all the way back to the M25 on the edge of London. Cargoes of fresh food would rot. Shortages of vital components would force manufacturers to shut down. Trade would wither, and foreign investment dry up.

May herself was such a prudent, law-abiding person that it was hard to see in her the political equivalent of Thelma and Louise, who at the end of the film drive their car off a cliff. That wasn't the sort of thing she did. She wasn't reckless enough, and in any case her party would not let her do it.

This was the missing bit in the Brexit coverage. Plenty of journalists could discourse on the single market or the customs union, and some even knew the difference between the two. But almost no one in the media understood the obligation which has lain on every Conservative leader since the creation of the party by Sir Robert Peel in the 1830s. Having created it, in 1846 he almost destroyed it, by defying his own back-benchers and repealing the Corn Laws. It took the Conservatives twenty-eight years to win another majority.

Every Conservative leader since Peel has known that his or her overriding duty is to keep the party together, and to do so regardless of his or her own convictions. May herself was trying to do this. She had been a Remainer, but now she had aligned herself with the stern, unbending Brexiteers in her party, and hoped everyone else would be dragged along in their wake.

At about the time of her Lancaster House speech, Johnson was at a conference in India, where he said of the French president, François Hollande: 'If Mr Hollande wants to administer punishment beatings to anybody who seeks to escape [the EU], in the manner of some World War Two movie, I don't think that is the way forward, and it's not in the interests of our friends and partners. It seems absolutely incredible to me that, in the 21st century, member states of the EU should be seriously contemplating the reintroduction of tariffs or whatever to administer punishment to the UK.'

There was not much difference between May and Johnson on the substance of Brexit (though he let it be known he was worried by her ambiguity about the customs union). But there was already a stylistic gulf. If the party one day decided it needed a driver reckless enough to put his foot down and head straight for the cliff edge, Johnson was, he reminded them, available.

On 29 March 2017, May invoked Article 50, a treaty provision, never before used, under which a state could leave the EU at the end of a two-year period. From then on, she was under increasingly acute time pressure to negotiate a withdrawal agreement, as Britain was scheduled to leave the EU at midnight in Brussels, 11 p.m. British time, on 29 March 2019.

CRUSH THE SABOTEURS

On 18 April 2017, May astonished the country by calling for a general election. She said Labour, the Liberal Democrats, the Scottish National Party and 'unelected members of the House of Lords' believed that 'because the Government's majority is so small . . . our resolve will weaken and . . . they can force us to change course'. This message was transmitted in headline form by the following day's *Daily Mail*: 'CRUSH THE SABOTEURS'.

The prime minister omitted the real reason she needed a bigger majority, which was in order to be able to defy those Conservative MPs who rejected whatever Brexit deal she brought back from Brussels. She needed to liberate herself from her own colleagues, not from the Opposition. But to put it that way might have sounded a bit unprincipled, as if all she cared about was entrenching her own power. She insisted instead that she was offering 'strong and stable leadership in the national interest'.

And while this was not the whole truth, it was not exactly insincere. The Conservative Party is an instrument for winning and retaining power by working out more quickly and surely than its rivals what the nation requires, and how to provide it. For many years it had been having the necessary but appallingly difficult argument about Europe. David Cameron tried to quell this row, telling Conservatives in 2006, at the first party conference since his election as leader, to stop 'banging on about Europe'. But by 2013, UKIP was banging on about Europe so successfully that Cameron decided he had to regain control of the subject by promising a referendum. Because he won the 2015 election, he had to keep his promise. Because he lost the referendum, he resigned, and May was now in charge of implementing the result.

Labour went along with her call for a general election, but the general assumption was that she was bound to win a resounding victory. After all, the Conservatives were twenty points ahead in the polls, and her opponent, Jeremy Corbyn, was widely regarded as a man unfit to govern. But however true that received opinion might be, it did not do justice to the Labour leader's gifts as a campaigner, which turned out to be much greater than May's. Corbyn enjoyed getting out of Westminster and meeting real people, and actually believed what he said to them in his speeches. May sounded stilted and dull, an out-of-touch goody-goody. Her constant repetition of the words 'strong and stable' provoked ridicule, as did her insistence — after being forced within a few days to abandon a manifesto proposal to fund social care through what the press labelled a 'dementia tax' — that 'nothing has changed', when anyone could see she had just performed a U-turn.

Since Corbyn was not going to become prime minister, there appeared to be no danger in voting for him, and registering a protest against an election which seemed to most voters to be superfluous, for had they not given their instructions in the referendum on EU membership held less than a year before, which pretty much the entire political class had promised to implement?

Johnson played scant part in the election. He was at one

point filmed, by the indefatigable Lottie Gammon, at a market at Thornbury, in Gloucestershire, holding a bowl of apples and asking in his best on-message manner, 'Who wants my fruit? Strong and stable.' Towards the end, when things did not appear to be going all that well, he was deployed as an anti-Labour weapon: 'The Corbyn negotiating team would arrive in Brussels like a family of herbivores at a watering hole of the lions, and they'd be eaten for breakfast.'

But this election campaign belonged to May, and on the night of 8 June 2017 the country learned that she had thrown away the slim majority won by her predecessor, David Cameron, only two years before. Corbyn increased Labour's share of the vote from 30.4 to 40 per cent, and gained thirty seats, while May, though she too increased the Conservative share of the vote from 36.9 to 42.4 per cent, ended up with thirteen fewer seats, and was only able to stay in power by cobbling up a deal with the ten Democratic Unionists from Northern Ireland, who gained a billion pounds to spend in the province. This was a humiliation. Far from strengthening her hand in the Brexit negotiations, she had weakened it, and the EU set out to drive a harder bargain.

After such a setback, there was clearly a strong case for replacing May. But who should the next leader be? The obvious candidate was Johnson. But Johnson himself knew that if he launched a leadership bid now, he would almost certainly fail. Too many of his colleagues did not trust him. They regarded him as a chancer, and looked around for a Stop Boris candidate. This was a tough gig, for all the other candidates had drawbacks too, chief among which was the lack of any proven ability to win elections.

And Brexit was plainly going to be an almost impossible project to see through to general satisfaction. The least bad course seemed to be to let May grapple with it and leave her to take the blame when it went wrong. She became, from June 2017, the Stop Boris candidate, a position she was to occupy for the next two years.

A PROVOCATION

On 16 September 2017 the *Daily Telegraph* published a long article by Johnson entitled 'My vision for a bold, thriving Britain enabled by Brexit'. This was a provocation, for it was based on a speech he had not been allowed by No. 10 to deliver. He tried, in an impudent manner, to cover himself against the charge of disloyalty by endorsing the hard Brexit the prime minister had set out nine months earlier in her Lancaster House speech. But no one was deceived, or even meant to be deceived: this was Johnson committing a calculated act of defiance, offering himself as the leader who would press forward with much greater determination.

He scoffed at difficult choices, declared that the Remainers 'number some of the people I love most in the world', and insisted that both Leavers and Remainers 'are coming together . . . and urging us to get on and do it': 'I believe we have an immense can-do spirit. I have seen it in action. But we also have a truly phenomenal ability to delay and to rack up cost. We have been able to blame bureaucracy and to blame Brussels, and my point is that after Brexit we will no longer be able to blame anyone but ourselves. Our destiny will be in our own hands, and that will be immensely healthy.'

Johnson repeated the claim painted on the Vote Leave bus, which had infuriated Remainers during the referendum campaign, and which many of them cited as a knock-down example of his mendacity:

And yes – once we have settled our accounts, we will take back control of roughly £350 million per week. It would be a fine thing, as many of us have pointed out, if a lot of that money went on the NHS, provided we use that cash injection to modernise and make the most of new technology.

The NHS is one of the great unifying institutions of our country. It is the top political priority of the British people and, under the leadership of Jeremy Hunt, it is indeed the top priority of the Conservative Party. Coming out of the EU will give us an opportunity to drive that message home.

Asked some days later for her response to this manifesto, May remarked that she was still in charge of Brexit policy, and added: 'Boris is Boris', a remark no more informative than her earlier 'Brexit means Brexit'. The prime minister did not feel strong enough to sack him. The home secretary, Amber Rudd, went on *The Andrew Marr Show* and said: 'I don't want him managing the Brexit process. What we've got is Theresa May managing that process. She's driving the car, to continue the allegory, and I'm going to make sure that, as far as I and the rest of the Cabinet are concerned, we help her to do that.'

A CLEAR MISUSE OF
OFFICIAL STATISTICS

On the day after the foreign secretary's manifesto appeared in the *Daily Telegraph*, the chair of the UK Statistics Authority wrote him a letter, quoted here in full:

Sir David Norgrove

Chair of the UK Statistics Authority

1 Drummond Gate

London

SW1V 2QQ

Rt Hon Boris Johnson MP
Foreign Secretary
Foreign and Commonwealth Office
King Charles Street
London
SW1A 2AH

17 September 2017

Dear Foreign Secretary,

I am surprised and disappointed that you have chosen to repeat the figure of £350 million per week, in connection with the amount that might be available for extra public spending when we leave the European Union.

This confuses gross and net contributions. It also assumes that payments currently made to the UK by the EU, including for example for the support of agriculture and scientific research, will not be paid by the UK government when we leave.

It is a clear misuse of official statistics.

Yours sincerely

Sir David Norgrove

A public rebuke by a senior official to a senior minister was unusual. It indicated not only the fury which Johnson aroused, but also the disrespect in which he was held. He on the same day sent a less terse but just as disrespectful reply. One of his essential qualities is impenitence, a refusal to bend the knee unless his very survival is at stake:

Dear Sir David,

I must say that I was surprised and disappointed by your letter of today, since it was based on what appeared to be a wilful distortion of the text of my article.

When we spoke you conceded that you were more concerned by the headline and the BBC coverage, though you accepted that I was not responsible for those. I suggest if the BBC coverage offends you that you write to the BBC.

You say that I claim that there would be £350 million that 'might be available for extra public spending' when we leave the EU.

This is a complete misrepresentation of what I said and I would like you to withdraw it. I in fact said: 'Once we have settled our accounts we will take back control of roughly £350m per week. It would be a fine thing, as many of us have pointed out, if a lot of that money went on the NHS.'

That is very different from claiming that there would be an extra £350m available for public spending and I am amazed that you should impute such a statement to me . . .

If you had any concerns about my article, it would of course have been open to you to address the points with me in private rather than in this way in a public letter. As it is, if you seriously disagree with any of the above, I look forward to hearing your reasoning.

Boris Johnson

Secretary of State for Foreign & Commonwealth Affairs

A PLEDGE TO THE READER

The reader will be reassured to learn that I am not going to attempt to recount every twist and turn of the Brexit negotiations, or indeed of the pandemic that followed. In the words of Max Beerbohm, 'To give an accurate and exhaustive account of that period would need a far less brilliant pen than mine.' My modest hope is to try to work out what kind of a person Johnson is, and what kind of a country would dream of making him its prime minister. (The word 'modest' is, by the way, written in jest.)

NAZANIN ZAGHARI-RATCLIFFE

On 1 November 2017 Johnson gave evidence to the Foreign Affairs select committee at the House of Commons. He was asked about the case of Nazanin Zaghari-Ratcliffe, a woman with dual British and Iranian citizenship who had been detained in Tehran since 3 April 2016, when she was about to board a plane home to Britain after visiting her parents with her small daughter. The foreign secretary said: 'When we look at what Nazanin Zaghari-Ratcliffe was doing, she was simply teaching people journalism, as I understand it, at the very limit.'

Johnson had blundered, for Zaghari-Ratcliffe had insisted as part of her defence that she was on holiday in Iran, and had never taught journalism there. Her employers in London, the Thomson Reuters Foundation, confirmed that she was not a journalist and had never trained journalists for them.

Johnson came under enormous and sustained criticism for this mistake, which was used as evidence against Zaghari-Ratcliffe when she returned to court in Tehran a few days later. Here, his critics said, was cast-iron evidence of his failure to master his brief.

Responsibility for Zaghari-Ratcliffe's detention rested with the Iranian authorities, and old Middle East hands said the real problem was Britain's refusal to repay £400 million which, in 1979, just before the fall of the Shah, had been paid by Iran for Chieftain tanks that had never been delivered. But many people thought Johnson had been culpably negligent, and the mistake was not forgotten, for the prisoner's husband, Richard Ratcliffe, continued for the next six years to wage a dignified and tenacious campaign in London for her release, which came on 16 March 2022, after the tank debt had at long last been settled.

In May 2022 Johnson met Zaghari-Ratcliffe for the first time. She later related, in an interview with Emma Barnett for *Woman's Hour* on Radio 4, that she had told him she 'lived under the shadow of his comment psychologically and emotionally for the next four and a half years'. The dignity and restraint with which she said this made it unanswerable.

As foreign secretary, Johnson's reputation was at a low ebb. In January 2018 he let it be known that at a forthcoming Cabinet meeting he was going to urge his colleagues to agree to extra health spending. He was rebuffed, and on 26 January 2018, Iain Dale, who knows the Conservative Party well, wrote in a piece for ConservativeHome:

> Boris Johnson must have a death wish. Any fool would have known that to brief in advance of a cabinet meeting that you thought the NHS should get an extra £100 million would blow up in your face . . .
>
> Many observers now doubt if there were a leadership election he'd make it to the final two. If the foreign secretary wishes to remain in government, he'd do very well to stick to his job and make a success of it, rather than try to trample on other people's areas of responsibility.

PRO BONO PUBLICO,
NO BLOODY PANICO

On 6 June 2018, Johnson addressed a private dinner at the Institute of Directors attended by about twenty members of Conservative Way Forward, a Thatcherite campaign group. The following day, BuzzFeed News published an account of what the foreign secretary had said, based on a recording obtained by its reporter, Alex Spence.

'I am increasingly admiring of Donald Trump, I have become more and more convinced there is method in his madness,' Johnson said, and went on: 'Trump to negotiate Brexit. What a fantastic idea [laughter]. How would he approach it? It's worth thinking about. How would Donald Trump have approached our Brexit negotiations? Actually it's bloody good . . . if I was still editor of *The Spectator* I would commission a cover story on exactly that theme. Imagine Trump doing Brexit. What would he do? He'd go in bloody hard. There'd be all sorts of break-downs, there'd be all sorts of chaos, everybody would think he'd gone mad. But actually you might get somewhere. It's a very, very good thought.'

He added that Brexit 'will happen', but 'the risk is that it will not be the one we want', for Britain could well end up 'in a sort of anteroom of the EU', still in the customs union and to a large extent in the single market, 'so not really having full freedom on our trade policy'. Johnson warned this outcome was being pushed by the Treasury, which is 'basically the heart of Remain'. To get the benefits of Brexit, he said, we must not give in to 'Project Fear', but must be willing to go through some dislocation: 'I think Theresa is going to go into a phase where we are much more combative with Brussels . . . You've got to face the fact there may now be a meltdown. Okay? I don't want anybody to panic during the meltdown. Pro bono publico, no bloody panico. It's going to be all right in the end.'

Johnson happens to share a birthday, 19 June, with Rear-Admiral Sir Morgan Morgan-Giles (1914–2013), who had a gallant and distinguished naval career before becoming, from 1964 to 1979, Conservative MP for Winchester. In 1972, when the Tories were in ferment over Britain's accession to the European Economic Community, as it was then known, the party leadership reckoned the 1922 Committee of backbenchers needed calming down, and that Morgan-Giles was the right man to steady the crew.

He prepared a judicious speech, acknowledging MPs' concerns while insisting they must remain loyal to their leader, Edward Heath. But when he rose to address the seething ranks, he found he had left his speech behind, so simply barked at them: 'Pro bono publico, no bloody panico!' This did the trick, and the expression remained in use among Tory MPs.*

It is characteristic of Johnson to use the phrase. He loves tradition, and especially tradition embellished with a touch of absurdity. *Pro bono publico* is a standard Latin tag, meaning 'for the public good'. Morgan-Giles felt inspired to echo this, in his bluff, good-humoured naval way, with the words 'no bloody panico'. That was Johnson's message too: he assured his listeners

---

* I am indebted to my friend the late Simon Hoggart, of the *Guardian*, for preserving this story.

that however bad things looked, there was no need to panic and it was all going to turn out fine. The officer's task is to put heart into the troops. Courage is communicated by courting danger and showing undaunted confidence, smiling and laughing rather than trembling and cowering. This is an aspect of leadership to which no purely managerial account of politics can do justice. Any prudent manager disapproves of taking what look like mad risks. And the prudent manager has a point.

FUCK BUSINESS

On 23 June 2018 the *Daily Telegraph* reported that at a Foreign Office reception at Lancaster House held the previous week to mark the Queen's birthday, Johnson had been asked about the fears of business leaders about Brexit and had replied: 'Fuck business.' According to two EU diplomats, he was in conversation with the Belgian ambassador to the EU, Rudolf Huygelen, at the time. A source close to Johnson explained he had been attacking lobbyists such as the EU-funded Confederation of British Industry.

Johnson in this period, the run-up to the Chequers summit at which Theresa May was going to try to persuade the Cabinet to back her Brexit plan, 'began to get more and more agitated', as one Eurosceptic Tory MP recalled afterwards. 'He was foreign secretary but he was coming up to people like me in the corridor and saying, "I don't know, I haven't seen, what's going on?"'

The prime minister had not told him what was going on, nor had she told David Davis, the Brexit secretary. Development of the government's Brexit policy was being conducted in deep secrecy inside No. 10.

RESIGNATION

On Friday 6 July 2018, the Cabinet met at Chequers and supported the prime minister's proposed negotiating position on Britain's future relationship with the European Union. Under this plan, soon afterwards published as a white paper, the UK and the EU would maintain a common rulebook for all goods, in order to enable frictionless trade. One of Johnson's advisers told me how disinclined he was to rebel at this point: 'Boris was very conscious of not being the Heseltine figure, was very careful – Chequers was about getting the best deal, not about getting rid of Theresa May.' In 1990 Heseltine had raised the standard of rebellion against Thatcher, mortally wounded her, but did not himself go on to wear the crown, which was won by the altogether less dashing figure of John Major. Johnson hung back, did not raise the standard of revolt, and even said at the dinner which concluded the proceedings that they now had a hymn sheet to sing from.

But at lunchtime that day, David Gauke, the justice secretary, had heard David Davis, the Brexit secretary, say to another Cabinet minister: 'If they think I'm just going to accept this and we're fine, you've got another thing coming.' And in the course of the day, Johnson had complained that May's proposals would leave Britain 'a vassal state', and had said that commending them was like 'polishing a turd'.

On leaving Chequers that night, Johnson rang one of his

advisers and expressed his unhappiness, which increased when he was sent the text of a comment piece endorsing the deal, written in Treasury officialese, to which he was asked to put his name, alongside that of Philip Hammond, the chancellor of the exchequer. Hammond was a Remainer who had never written an interesting article, while Johnson was a Leaver who had never written a dull one. To yoke them together in this way was an insult. Johnson's reply to the proposal was, his aides said, unprintable.

On Sunday evening Davis resigned. He invited Johnson to resign with him. This Johnson declined to do. But he did now have to make a choice on which his entire future might turn.

Davis explained in his resignation letter that he could not accept the 'common rulebook' proposed by May, which in his view would 'hand control of large swathes of our economy to the EU'. He said that in trying to sell her deal as Brexit secretary to the Commons, he would be 'a reluctant conscript', so she would be better off finding someone who believed in it. Steve Baker, for the last year undersecretary of state in the Brexit department, resigned at the same time, and at once re-joined the European Research Group, led by Jacob Rees-Mogg. Baker with enthusiasm took on the role of chief whip to the ERG, in charge of organising the Conservative parliamentary resistance to Chequers.

On Monday morning, Johnson conferred at his official residence in Carlton Gardens with his special advisers, David Frost, Ben Gascoigne and Lee Cain. They told him if he signed up to May's deal he would lose all credibility. The prime minister and the chief whip put pressure on him to give it a few more months. Lobby journalists waited outside the gates and the Sky News helicopter hovered overhead. Cheese baguettes and Coke were brought in for the foreign secretary and his advisers, who missed the lunch he was supposed to be hosting at the western Balkans summit, being held nearby. He spoke to the prime minister, and Downing Street announced he had resigned before he could announce it himself.

Some slightly odd pictures were taken of him sitting at his desk, looking uncomfortable as he signed his resignation letter. It was not usual for such an event to be photographed, and his critics took this as yet further proof that he was, in the words of David Lammy a Labour MP, a 'self-obsessed, vain egomaniac devoid of substance caring only about himself and advancing his career. Good riddance.' Time and again, we find any setback for Johnson interpreted as a final defeat. He has been found out, and will play no further part in politics. Sonia Purnell, one of his biographers, told the *New York Times* that Johnson had turned out to be 'totally vacuous'.

In his resignation letter Johnson wrote that the Brexit dream was dying, 'suffocated by needless self-doubt', and contended that by proposing to accept huge amounts of EU law, without any say in how it was made, 'we are truly headed for the status of a colony'. He went on:

> It is as though we are sending our vanguard into battle with the white flags fluttering above them. Indeed, I was concerned, looking at Friday's document, that there might be further concessions on immigration, or that we might end up effectively paying for access to the single market.
>
> On Friday I acknowledged that my side of the argument were too few to prevail, and congratulated you on at least reaching a cabinet decision on the way forward. As I said then, the government now has a song to sing. The trouble is that I have practised the words over the weekend and find that they stick in the throat.

This could have been the end of Johnson: resignation is often the prelude to irrelevance. But as soon as Johnson resigned, he shot to the top of the monthly ConHome survey of over 1,000 Conservative Party members saying who they wanted as the next leader, and stayed there. ConHome also published Cabinet rankings, giving net satisfaction ratings for ministers, and in these Theresa May sank to a barely credible minus 48 per cent, with other ministers all marked down too.

David Gauke, an astute and reputable Remainer who stuck with May, recognised that she had already lost the party membership: 'The response to Chequers . . . was a sort of roar of disapproval from the wider Conservative movement and a sense that, "No, we are not going to compromise on any of this and we're not going to make any trade-offs. If necessary, we will go no deal."'

Amid the turmoil, Johnson's opponents interpreted everything he did as motivated by self-interest. They assumed he was just scheming his way to the top. This was not exactly wrong, but it made them unable to perceive that to a considerable number of voters, Johnson's resignation was more principled than clinging to office would have been.

THE WILDERNESS MONTHS

According to one of Johnson's colleagues, in the months after his resignation, 'He was very depressed, constantly mourning the loss of his career.' How he had loved being foreign secretary. He went from being the chief of a great and glittering department to a grotty Commons office. Here he installed his bust of his number one hero, Pericles: to be exact, a plaster cast of a second-century Roman copy of the fifth-century BC bust of Pericles by Kresilas, purchased by Johnson in the early twenty-first century at the British Museum shop.

Johnson's parliamentary private secretary, Conor Burns, resigned on the same day as him, and offered to go on working for him in an informal capacity, preparing for the day when there would be a vacancy for a new leader. But this was quite a lonely time for Johnson. The conventional wisdom was that he was out of the picture.

A parliamentary researcher recalled seeing Johnson one day in Portcullis House, the part of the Palace of Westminster above Westminster Underground Station: 'I was walking through Portcullis House and he came down the stairs in the corner and walked over to the glass lift doors to look at himself and proceeded to untuck his shirt, loosen his tie and ruffle his hair. I swear that to complete the character he also grunted. He looked very smart and put together when he walked down the stairs and ever since I've been convinced that his bumbling posho personality is just a character.'

Johnson is an actor. By his costume, he indicates that he is not a stuffed shirt, a smug, conceited member of the Establishment; a conformist who wants to look like everyone else. So his hair is disordered, his shirt untucked, his tie not quite straight. His messy hair infuriates people who set high store by correct turnout. Alas for them, that is part of the point. Their irritation helps to show that he has not gone native, is not just another politician, still wants to subvert things.

There is something about Johnson as an actor which provokes disgust in some, delight in others. They could both be seeing part of him.

Of Johnson's special advisers, only Lee Cain, his press man, followed him into exile. They could sometimes be seen making their way through the Palace of Westminster, faintly reminiscent of Don Quixote and Sancho Panza.

One should not suppose Johnson had given up. Here is a glimpse of him at this time provided by Charles Moore, writing on 27 July 2019 in *The Spectator*: 'Over the years, I have often known Boris waver and hem and haw his way out of trouble, but I have come to understand that this is essentially tactical. It conceals utter determination. Shortly after he resigned in protest at Mrs May's Chequers plan last summer, I had lunch with him. Amid the usual merriment, abstracted pauses and moments of gloom, he suddenly looked at me and said: "I'm going to win, Charles." Because he spoke with perfect seriousness and at the low point of his public reputation, I noted this well.'

LETTER BOXES

Three days after he resigned, Johnson signed a new contract with the *Daily Telegraph* to write a weekly column, for which he was to be paid about £250,000 a year. The Advisory Committee on Business Activities (ACOBA) said this was 'unacceptable': according to the Ministerial Code, he should have consulted the committee first about any paid employment he took in the two years after leaving the government, and former ministers were also required to observe a three-month cooling-off period before they accepted any paid work. These rules existed, ACOBA pointed out, because of the danger that the conduct of a minister 'might be influenced by the hope or expectation of future employment', or indeed that the employer of an ex-minister might make 'improper use of official information'.

Johnson assured the committee he would not make use of any 'privileged information' which he had obtained while a minister. But the rebuke served to remind people, somewhat superfluously, that he had no respect for rules: a point known to anyone who took the slightest interest in his career long before he became prime minister.

On Monday 6 August, the most explosive of Johnson's early *Telegraph* columns appeared. He began, as he usually does, with a passage of autobiography. He had been in Copenhagen the other day for some international conference, got up early to go for a run, and was astonished to see Danes diving naked into the harbour for an early-morning swim. Denmark, he enthused, is a country which 'breathes the spirit of liberty', which is why he was a bit surprised to find that on 1 August the Danes had joined several other European countries – France, Germany, Austria, Belgium – in imposing a ban on the niqab and the burka, items of Muslim headgear which obscure the female face. He went on:

> If you tell me that the burka is oppressive, then I am with you. If you say that it is weird and bullying to expect women to cover their faces, then I totally agree – and I would add that I can find no scriptural authority for the practice in the Koran. I would go further and say that it is absolutely ridiculous that people should choose to go around looking like letter boxes; and I thoroughly dislike any attempt by any – invariably male – government to encourage such demonstrations of 'modesty', notably the extraordinary exhortations of President Ramzan Kadyrov of Chechnya, who has told the men of his country to splat their women with paintballs if they fail to cover their heads.
>
> If a constituent came to my MP's surgery with her face obscured, I should feel fully entitled – like Jack Straw – to ask her to remove it so that I could talk to her properly. If a female student turned up at school or at a university lecture looking like a bank robber then ditto: those in authority should be allowed to converse openly with those that they are being asked to instruct. As for individual businesses or branches of government – they should of course be able to enforce a dress code that enables their employees to interact with customers; and that means

human beings must be able to see each other's faces and read their expressions. It's how we work.

All that seems to me to be sensible. But such restrictions are not quite the same as telling a free-born adult woman what she may or may not wear, in a public place, when she is simply minding her own business. I am against a total ban because it is inevitably construed – rightly or wrongly – as being intended to make some point about Islam. If you go for a total ban, you play into the hands of those who want to politicise and dramatise the so-called clash of civilisations; and you fan the flames of grievance. You risk turning people into martyrs, and you risk a general crackdown on any public symbols of religious affiliation, and you may simply make the problem worse.

Johnson seems to have been taken aback by the volume of protest this produced. He was accused of stoking Islamophobia by likening Muslim women to 'letter boxes' and 'bank robbers'. Theresa May and Brandon Lewis, the Conservative Party chairman, called on him to apologise, which he declined to do. After receiving complaints about him, the party launched an investigation into his conduct. His defenders pointed out that he took, in his article, the view that the burka should not be banned. But to this day, the terms 'letter boxes' and 'bank robbers' are trotted out to prove, as far as his opponents are concerned, that he is a racist. I have quoted at length from the article so that you, the reader, can judge for yourself whether you think this true. In my opinion, while one could say he was tactless and tasteless, to convict him of racism on the basis of these two expressions is ridiculous.

MARINA WHEELER

On 6 September 2018, the news broke that Johnson and Marina Wheeler were getting divorced. They had married on 8 May 1993, a month before the birth of their first child. Wheeler was called to the Bar in 1997 and appointed Queen's Counsel in 2016. The divorce came as a great shock and sadness to their friends: 'They were lovely together,' as one of them put it. Many said that by her sound judgement Wheeler had for years acted as his 'intellectual underpinning', his anchor, and warned that without her he would be adrift. She had shown the greatness of heart, until their four children were grown up, to forgive his often flagrant infidelities. This time he wanted to keep the marriage going, but she said no.

Wheeler has been magnificently unforthcoming about the reasons for the breakdown. There were, however, two things in this period about which she did wish to talk. In May 2019 she was diagnosed with cervical cancer. After several operations, she recovered. She has since sought, by giving interviews and writing articles, to encourage other women to take the routine smear test which revealed her own cancer.

The second subject she wished to talk about was her book, *The Lost Homestead: My Mother, Partition and the Punjab*, published in November 2020. In it she tells the story of her mother, Dip (pronounced Deep), a Sikh who had never talked about her early life: 'Dip had her reasons. I just never really knew what they were.'

Wheeler discovers and describes the world of her mother as a small child, her father a Sikh doctor in the Punjab, living in a beautiful house surrounded by flowers, vines and orchards, and irrigated by canals. He had been awarded the Order of the British Empire for his service in dealing with a deadly outbreak of cholera during the Third Afghan War. He approved of the British, who to him were civilised people who knew how to run things efficiently, and who, indeed, had organised the building not only of the canals, which rendered arid land fertile, but of the women's hospital in the local town, which he helped found and run. But at least two of his children, Dip's older brother and sister, did not approve of the British, and wanted independence.

In 1947, amid terrible violence, independence came and Dip's family were forced to flee to Delhi. Their lost homestead was in the large part of the Punjab which is now in Pakistan. Her brother died at the age of twenty-one from TB: an even worse blow. Dip at the age of seventeen had to go through with an arranged marriage to a Sikh from a rich family with whom she had nothing in common. Of this failed marriage she had never spoken to her two daughters, Marina and Shirin, born to her second, much happier marriage to Charles Wheeler, celebrated BBC correspondent.

And now Marina refused, quite naturally, to talk about her own marriage. Asked on the *Today* programme about Johnson, she replied: 'I'm not wild about discussing my husband. As you know I've recently divorced him.' There is an undertone of humour, but also a reticence. Why should she invade her own and her children's privacy for the amusement of impertinent strangers? Perhaps one day one of the children will interview her and write a book as tactful, elegant and fair-minded as *The Lost Homestead* about what really happened.

While Johnson was foreign secretary, a friend with a deep knowledge of the Conservative Party warned her: 'Boris is going to be prime minister.'

Wheeler replied: 'Oh God, we've only moved in fairly recently.' She could not bear the idea of having to move again. Getting out of their house in Islington and into the foreign secretary's official residence had been quite traumatic enough. Wheeler has her own, high-level legal career, which was only, as she says elsewhere, possible because she had two full-time members of staff, Nicola, who for sixteen years looked after the children, and Luz, who for almost twenty years looked after the house.

When you are moving house, only you can decide what is to happen to your possessions – which clothes, books and pictures to keep, what to do with all the worthless but to you valuable objects you have accumulated. Johnson would be no help with this. He would be too busy, and as she said of him to the friend quoted above: 'You have to understand, he's not a feminist.'

Being married to the prime minister would entail an infinitely greater degree of scrutiny, many more photographs on leaving the house, impertinent comments not only about one's appearance but about one's influence, gross intrusions into one's private life.

'But surely it won't really happen,' Wheeler protested to her friend. What happened first, in July 2018, was Johnson's resignation as foreign secretary, after which, unobserved by the press, two furniture vans left Carlton Gardens. The break-up had already happened.

SUICIDE VEST

On 9 September 2018 the *Mail on Sunday* published a piece by Johnson in which he assailed with unusual vehemence Theresa May's approach to the Brexit negotiations, led on the EU side by Michel Barnier. The key concession had been made in December 2017, when the UK agreed with the EU that there would be no hard border on the island of Ireland. This meant the outer border of the EU's customs area would instead run down the Irish Sea, between Great Britain and Northern Ireland – unless, as May proposed, the whole of the UK remained in the EU customs area. Johnson courted the approval of Brexiteers who found such an outcome intolerable, of Unionists who would not stand for the idea of the UK divided by a border in the Irish Sea, and of anyone who thought May was a feeble negotiator:

> It is a humiliation. We look like a seven-stone weakling being comically bent out of shape by a 500lb gorilla. And the reason is simple: Northern Ireland, and the insanity of the so-called 'backstop'.
>
> We have opened ourselves to perpetual political blackmail. We have wrapped a suicide vest around the British constitution – and handed the detonator to Michel Barnier . . .
>
> We have been so mad as to agree, last December, that if we can't find ways of producing frictionless trade

between Northern Ireland and the Republic of Ireland, then Northern Ireland must remain in the customs union and the single market: in other words, part of the EU. And that would mean a border down the Irish Sea.

That outcome is completely unacceptable, as the PM has said, to the majority in Northern Ireland and to the UK Government; and yet that is the threat – to the integrity of the UK – that we have allowed our partners to wield. That is why Barnier seems so confident. That is why they are pushing us around. And we are now trying to sort it out, with a solution that is if anything even more pathetic.

We are now proposing our own version of the backstop: that if we can't find ways of solving the Irish border problem, then the whole of the UK must remain in the customs union and single market.

As with the burka article, Johnson's argument was ignored by his critics. What they found, or in some cases affected to find, intolerable were the two words 'suicide vest'. Alan Duncan, last encountered in the vignette entitled 'Duncan's Index', and still a Foreign Office minister, went for him on Twitter at midnight, having seen the first edition of the *Mail on Sunday*: 'For Boris to say that the PM's view is like that of a suicide bomber is too much. This marks one of the most disgusting moments in modern British politics. I'm sorry, but this is the political end of Boris Johnson. If it isn't now, I will make sure it is later.'

His outburst got a lot of coverage, but was not entirely sincere. Duncan confided to his diary that it was 'rather hyperbolic, but it's the only way to get noticed', and a couple of days later wrote a note to Johnson:

Dear Boris. It's not personal. Or at least it is not born of any animosity. It's just that if you are going to challenge the PM so threateningly I will in return support her vigorously and fight fire with fire. If she goes we all go. Noises off are constantly undermining our negotiating position. In essence I think that she is acting in the national interest and you are not. So it's out with the cannons. Country first . . . It's as simple as that. Yours ever, Alan.

Duncan is not the first person to announce, after pretending to be more scandalised than he really is, 'the political end of Boris Johnson'. Nor is he the first person to believe he can help fulfil the prophecy he has just made. Nor is he alone in enjoying making a splash. 'The number of times people have seen my tweet about Boris now stands at 2,012,408,' he recorded on 14 September, having noted the previous numbers too. Some weeks later, Johnson sent him this reply:

Dear Alan, On the contrary I fear it is the noises off, as you call them, that have been the only thing to stiffen the spine of our negotiations and postpone the day of abject capitulation! Boris.

CHARACTER ASSASSINATION

On the same day, 9 September 2018, the *Sunday Times* published 'a dossier on Boris Johnson's sex life', which had been drawn up by Theresa May's aides during the 2016 leadership race. Perhaps Johnson's suicide vest piece was supposed to distract attention from this, or indeed from reports about recent events in his private life. But the dossier proved a disappointment. There was nothing new in it about his sex life, or about anything else, for it consisted of material culled from Sonia Purnell's biography of him, published in 2011, and from my own life of Johnson, first published in 2006. A hostile quotation would often be followed by Johnson winning an election or taking some other step towards Downing Street. One could not help laughing at the inadequacy of the evidence gathered by the May campaign: inadequate, that is, if it was supposed to demonstrate, even to those who did not already believe this to be true, that Johnson was unfit for public office. After all, in 2016, even May, a public figure of unimpeachable respectability, did not suppose his record disqualified him from being made foreign secretary.

In their eagerness to drive him out of politics, Johnson's critics again and again talked up the case against him. This was always a temptation, for perhaps the moment of weakness had arrived when he could be finished off, if one denounced him at maximum volume. But some among the wider public often thought that what the critics chose to treat as a hanging offence

– for example the words 'letter box' or 'suicide vest' – did not sound quite so dreadful as all that. I am not discussing the merits of individual cases. My point is that, to some voters, these attacks often looked unfair, and may have encouraged some of them, in the privacy of the voting booth, to even things up by putting a cross next to Johnson's name. Although he had resigned from the Foreign Office, his end was not yet nigh.

CARRIE SYMONDS

Also on 9 September 2018 — a packed day even by Johnson's standards — the *Sun on Sunday* revealed that the new woman in his life was Carrie Symonds. She was born on 17 March 1988 and brought up by her mother, Josephine McAfee, in East Sheen, a suburb in south-west London. Her parents were not married to each other and she saw little of her father, Matthew Symonds, one of the founders of the *Independent* newspaper, who remained married to someone else. He had attempted to confer the post of chief features sub-editor on McAfee, without revealing to his colleagues that she was, to use his own rather old-fashioned term, his mistress. When Andreas Whittam Smith, the senior of the three founders, was told this, and further discovered that Symonds had taken McAfee to the SDP conference in Harrogate and charged the *Independent* an extra £10 for a double room, he was so indignant at the 'defrauding' of the company that he told the third of the founders, Stephen Glover: 'I think that I will have to ask him to leave. I do not see how I can work with him again.'

Glover put it to Whittam Smith that to sack and therefore ruin Symonds, who had done so much to get the newspaper up and running, 'for a little stupidity over a job' and a £10 expenses fiddle, would be quite wrong. Symonds stayed at the *Independent*, where I happened at the time of Carrie's birth to be working as a leader-writer. One may posit that she inherited some of his dynamism. He was a man of energy and enterprise, competitive, vulgar, keen on fast cars, aware that to others this enthusiasm might seem absurd, generally ready to be amused but quite willing to be offensive, indeed pretty good at being offensive, but also, beneath a sometimes crude and objectionable manner, a sensitive person who coped well with a severe stammer. Those who knew him better said his best qualities came from his mother, Anne Symonds. She worked for the BBC Overseas Service, and had not been married to Matthew's father, John Beavan, a successful newspaper man, among other posts political editor of the *Daily Mirror* and from 1970 Lord Ardwick, having been ennobled by Harold Wilson, Labour prime minister.

Carrie was educated at Godolphin and Latymer, an independent school in Hammersmith, and at Warwick University, where she read art history and theatre studies, for she had applied for one or two parts in films. She instead got a job working for her local MP, Zac Goldsmith, of whom she tweeted in 2016, when he had just lost his seat, that she owed him a lot, and but for him might never have worked for the Tories. She became a press officer at Conservative Campaign Headquarters, and then special adviser to John Whittingdale, who after the 2015 general election was appointed, much to his surprise, culture secretary. He told me: 'I didn't know Carrie [when she came to work for him]. I was told she was very good. She was fantastic: utterly loyal, very sound and great fun.'

She was also a Leaver, and this created an extra bond between her and her new boss, for in David Cameron's Cabinet the Leavers were in a small minority. Whittingdale was one of only six ministers – the others were Michael Gove, Iain Duncan Smith, Theresa Villiers, Chris Grayling and Priti Patel – who at the start of the EU referendum campaign, in the full glare of publicity, walked after a Cabinet meeting to the headquarters of Vote Leave. This stunt infuriated No. 10, which had not expected the Leavers to be so organised. On this and subsequent occasions, Symonds accompanied Whittingdale to Vote Leave. She was a fellow rebel.

In January 2020, Johnson, by then prime minister, came to Whittingdale's sixtieth birthday party at the Garrick Club, along with Carrie and their Jack Russell, Dilyn, the latter said to be the first dog ever admitted to the club, women having been allowed in as guests some years earlier. No occasion attended by Johnson is complete without a speech by him in which he flatters his hosts by attributing to them a major role in recent events. While under the spell of Johnson's oratory, it is possible to yield to the pleasant illusion that one was more important than one thought one was. He said Whittingdale had not only changed the course of British and European history, by being one of the senior ministers who broke with the government line, but had also 'changed my life in all sorts of ways'.

'John told me there was a seat going in Essex,' Johnson went on. Whittingdale assured him he would be 'an absolute shoo-in' as the next Conservative candidate for Rayleigh, instead of which, in the summer of 2000, he was 'roundly beaten by Mark Francois'. 'And you helped to bring me together with Carrie,' the prime minister continued, for at the headquarters of Vote Leave Johnson and Symonds began to get to know each other. Johnson was the star of the Leave campaign. The driver of the famous bus, bearing round the country the inflammatory £350 million figure, said having Johnson on board was like driving Beyoncé.

After working for Whittingdale, and for Sajid Javid, the communities secretary, while his special adviser was on maternity leave, in the autumn of 2017 Symonds applied for a job working for Johnson as one of his advisers at the Foreign Office.

She did not get it, indeed his staff were strongly against her getting it, but she offered instead to give him private advice on media strategy, and from this time became close to him. Meanwhile, she obtained the post of director of communications at Conservative Campaign Headquarters. Here she was soon on appallingly bad terms with some of her colleagues, and questions were raised about her expenses claims.

In January 2018 she learned that John Worboys, the taxicab rapist, was due for early release. She had been attacked by Worboys in 2007, when she was only nineteen years old. The Ministry of Justice said nothing could be done to challenge the Parole Board's verdict. Symonds was one of the women who launched a crowd-funded bid to overturn the decision, which they succeeded in doing. Her courage in doing this made it difficult to pursue her over the expenses claims. In August 2018 she resigned from CCHQ and went to work for Oceana, a global marine protection charity funded by Bloomberg.

Symonds' critics, who from the first were numerous, ignored the many affinities between her and Johnson. Before they met, each of them had joined and campaigned for the Conservative Party, a step neither of his previous wives would have contemplated. Symonds was adventurous, passionate, a risk-taker and rule-breaker, in some ways rackety and bohemian, vulnerable and fallible, but with a keen eye for the main chance, in love with the great game of politics, fascinated by political journalism, entranced by the question of who was going to get some plum job, ready to do everything she could to help either herself or one of her allies to get it. All this can be said of Johnson too.

She was, people pointed out, twenty-four years younger than him. In the eighteenth century Sir Robert Walpole, conventionally regarded as the first prime minister, had a mistress twenty-five years his junior, the witty and beautiful Molly Skerret. In the twentieth century, David Lloyd George, prime minister from 1916 to 1922, likewise had a mistress twenty-five years younger than him, Frances Stevenson, who had originally been his children's governess. In both cases, the mistress became after many years the second wife. These examples explode the assumption that in the pre-Johnson era, no trace of licentiousness had been found among the nation's leaders. Many people nevertheless thought the age gap between Johnson and Symonds unbecoming, and from the first, looked on her as a weakness rather than a strength.

At around this time, one of Johnson's advisers told him: 'If you're going to get rid of her, now's the time to do it.' Another said: 'You've had your fun, mate.' This second adviser, aptly described as 'very unmodern', was 'absolutely furious' that Johnson had allowed his marriage to collapse. Johnson stayed with Symonds. A friend of hers gave this explanation, one unlikely to occur to those who want always to find the most discreditable reason: 'They do genuinely love each other. In private, in that flat, they were genuinely in love, and very physically affectionate, and I think she adores him.'

SORRY, NO CHERRIES

Theresa May suffered one indignity after another. On 20 September 2018 the European Union humiliated her at a summit in Salzburg by rejecting the Chequers proposals, telling her she could not 'cherry pick' the bits of the single market that she liked. Donald Tusk, President of the European Council, added insult to injury by posting two pictures on Instagram of himself offering some cakes to May, with the captions 'A piece of cake perhaps?' followed by 'Sorry, no cherries.'

At Westminster, her proposed compromise was too European to satisfy her own Brexiteers, but not European enough to win the support of the many MPs who yearned to find some way to stay in the EU. These Remainers began to feel hopeful. They thought that if they blocked May's deal, they might be able to block Brexit altogether.

STARMER'S STANDING OVATION

On 25 September 2018, Sir Keir Starmer, the shadow Brexit secretary, won a standing ovation at the Labour conference by saying that 'nobody is ruling out Remain as an option' in a second referendum, which Labour would favour holding if Parliament rejected May's deal and the party could not force a general election. Demands for a second referendum, or 'People's Vote', were growing among Remainers, and this was a decisive concession to them.

Starmer was an inexperienced politician: he had reached the top as a human rights lawyer, and only entered the Commons in 2015, as MP for his home seat of Holborn and St Pancras. On one occasion I found myself having a drink with him and some other Labour people in a pub. Starmer asked me what Boris Johnson and Jacob Rees-Mogg were like – a reasonable enough question, for I knew them both. I hesitated, and turned the conversation into some other channel. Somehow it didn't seem quite the thing, in that friendly circle, to defend Johnson and Rees-Mogg. Sitting at my computer several years later, I think I should have said they were both formidable politicians, and that to beat them it was worse than useless to be drawn into disparaging their characters: one had to work out the appeal of their policies, and offer better ones.

By supporting a second referendum, in order to reverse the verdict of the first, Starmer supposed he was offering a better policy, but was naïve about the effect this might have on his party's electability. Brendan Chilton, general secretary of the pro-Brexit group Labour Leave, protested that Starmer's remarks were 'a betrayal' and 'a P45 to our MPs in the Midlands and Wales', which for many of those MPs turned out to be correct.

JOHNSON THE LIBERATOR

On the afternoon of Tuesday 2 October 2018 Johnson entered a hall in Birmingham filled with 1,400 people yearning to feel good about being Conservative. They had queued for hours to hear him address the ConHome rally. Since Sunday afternoon, when the annual party conference started, the mood among the Tory faithful had been tepid and uncertain.

'It's the hour of Boris,' my neighbour, Councillor Suky Samra from Walsall, said. 'I think he'll deliver today.'

On my other side was Councillor Rose Martin, likewise from Walsall, who said: 'If we don't take a clear direction on Brexit we will suffer in Walsall. David Cameron went off with his shopping trolley to Brussels. Came back with nothing. And we still haven't got anything in the trolley.'

Far below us, in the front row of the stalls, sat a number of MPs who had come to demonstrate their support, including Owen Paterson, Priti Patel, John Redwood, Steve Baker, Zac Goldsmith, Iain Duncan Smith and Conor Burns.

Before he could say a word, Johnson received a standing ovation, which he managed after a few moments to quell with downward motions of his hands. In the moment of silence that followed, someone shouted: 'Chuck Chequers!'

'It is great to be here in Birmingham where so many thoroughfares in the city are already named after our superb Conservative Mayor,' Johnson began, with reference to Andy

Street, mayor of the West Midlands. This joke dispelled any fears that the speaker might seek, in a misguided attempt to sound serious, to refrain from making people laugh. Not that his speech lacked a serious theme, which he soon enunciated:

> My friends, there is only one thing I really worry about in this critical autumn of 2018, and that is that after 200 years this oldest and most successful of all political parties should somehow lose confidence in its basic belief in freedom.
>
> And that after 1,000 years of independence this country might really lose confidence in its democratic institutions.
>
> And that we should be so demoralised and so exhausted as to submit those institutions – forever – to foreign rule.

The audience loved that. A great burst of applause greeted the word 'freedom'. No longer was the mood tepid and uncertain. Johnson had instilled the belief that a better Brexit was within reach, if only the prime minister, Theresa May, would stretch out her arms and grasp it.

He proceeded to flay the Labour Party: 'Surely to goodness we can take on this Tony Benn tribute act and wallop it.' The audience was being offered can-win conservatism, and it went down wonderfully well. He told a short story about his time on the *Wolverhampton Express & Star*, when he had to report on a couple with a small and sickly child who were in despair, and felt themselves to be 'prisoners of the system', because the council would not deal with the damp and mould in their council flat. Johnson presented himself as the liberator who would free the country from chains which May was too weak to throw off. He suggested she was guilty of a grave crime: 'It occurs to me that the authors of the Chequers proposal risk prosecution under the fourteenth-century Statute of Praemunire, which says that no foreign court or government shall have jurisdiction in this country.'

Another great cheer erupted, probably the first time for years that the Statute of Praemunire had been cheered at a Conservative conference. A semblance of loyalty to the prime minister was maintained, for Johnson said she could be the person who chucked Chequers and pursued a full, uninhibited Brexit.

There were more cheers when he denounced the idea of a second referendum, which would be a 'disaster for trust in politics'. This was a moment of catharsis for Conservative Leavers, Johnson enabling them to purge their feelings of despair.

MANACLES

On Saturday 20 October 2018, People's Vote, a group launched six months earlier at the Electric Ballroom in Camden Town, claimed that almost 700,000 people had attended its march in London in favour of a second referendum. The police later estimated the number at 250,000. On Sunday morning, Sir Keir Starmer, whose constituency seat of Holborn and St Pancras includes Camden Town, told Andrew Marr that Labour would table a second referendum amendment to May's deal, with the question to be: 'Do you want to leave on these terms or would you rather remain?'

On 14 November 2018, May reached agreement at Strasbourg with European leaders that the whole of the United Kingdom would stay in the customs union and just Northern Ireland would stay in the single market. Johnson at once said this was totally unacceptable, and Dominic Raab, who had succeeded David Davis as Brexit secretary, resigned along with two other ministers.

In a tumultuous Commons debate on 4 December 2018, May said: 'Do not let anyone here think there is a better deal to be won by shouting louder. Do not imagine that, if we vote this down, a different deal is going to miraculously appear. The alternative is uncertainty and risk – the risk that Brexit could be stopped; the risk we could crash out with no deal. And the only certainty would be uncertainty – bad for our economy and bad for our standing in the world. That is not in the national interest.'

Johnson spoke soon after her, and disagreed:

As has been said, after two years of negotiation, the deal has achieved an extraordinary thing: it has finally brought us together. Remainers and Leavers, myself and Tony Blair, we are united – indeed, the whole Johnson family is united – in the belief that the deal is a national humiliation that makes a mockery of Brexit. I am sorry to say this – these are hard truths – but there will be no proper free trade deals and we will not take back control of our laws. For the government to continue to suggest otherwise is to do violence to the natural meaning of words. We will give up £39 billion for nothing. We will not be taking back control of our borders. Not only have we yet to settle the terms on which EU migrants will in future come to this country, but we will be levying EU tariffs at UK ports and sending 80 per cent of the cash to Brussels. In short, we are going to be rule-takers. We are going to be a de facto colony. Out of sheer funk – I am sorry to have to say this to the House – we are ensuring that we will never, ever be able to take advantage of the freedoms we should have won by Brexit.

Under the terms of the backstop, we have to stay in the customs union, while Northern Ireland, and therefore the rest of the UK if we want to keep the Union together, will stay in regulatory alignment unless and until the EU decides to let us go. And why should they let us go?

And so on. Where is one to stop? Johnson went on to say: 'We on the UK side of the negotiation have been responsible for forging our own manacles, in the sense that it is almost as though we decided that we needed to stay in the customs union and in the single market in defiance of the wishes of the people.'

But I am in danger of breaking my pledge not to retell the whole sorry story of these negotiations. On 10 December 2018 May backed down from holding a Commons vote on her deal, for she knew she would be defeated. On Wednesday 12 December, Sir Graham Brady, chairman of the 1922 Committee, announced he had received letters from 15 per cent of Conservative MPs, enough to trigger a vote of confidence in her leadership. At PMQs, her husband, Philip May, watched her, most unusually, from the gallery, as if this might be her last appearance, or at least as if he was anxious to show his support. Immediately after PMQs the news broke that she had promised her MPs she would step down once she had ensured an orderly Brexit. That evening those MPs backed her by 200 to 117 votes. The Eurosceptics were ridiculed for having forced a contest they failed to win, but May herself looked even weaker. On the other hand, it was said that under the 1922 Committee's rules she could not be challenged for another year.

The Commons held 'meaningful votes' on her deal on 15 January 2019, when the government lost by a record 230 votes; on 12 March, when it lost by 149 votes; and on 29 March, when it lost by 58 votes. On this latter occasion, Johnson and Rees-Mogg voted for her deal, worried that otherwise Brexit might not happen, while the diehard 'Spartans' – the most unyielding Tory Eurosceptics – still voted against.

On 20 March, May annoyed MPs by delivering a short television address to the nation in which she blamed them for delaying Brexit. Earlier that day she had written to Tusk asking to delay Brexit from Friday 29 March, the deadline set two years earlier at the start of the negotiations, until 30 June.

Johnson wrote a piece for the *Telegraph* in which he ridiculed her failure to meet the original deadline: 'This was the Friday when Charles Moore's retainers were meant to be weaving through the moonlit lanes of Sussex, half blind with scrumpy, singing Brexit shanties at the top of their voices and beating the hedgerows with staves. This was meant to be the week of Brexit. And what has happened instead? In one of the most protoplasmic displays of invertebracy since the Precambrian epoch, this government has decided not to fulfil the mandate of the people.'

Collective Cabinet responsibility was breaking down. Ministers such as David Gauke and Amber Rudd who abstained rather than follow the government line were not sacked by May. The pressure on her seemed unbearable, speculation about who would replace her was rife, and yet she clung on.

On 1 April 2019, the Commons held indicative votes on eight possible ways forward, and could agree to none of these, though Kenneth Clarke's proposal that Britain stay in the customs union was only narrowly defeated, and would have passed if a few more diehard Remainers could have brought themselves to support it. Brexit was carried out in the name of parliamentary sovereignty, and had placed the Commons at the eye of the storm, with people tuning in to BBC Parliament from many parts of the globe to watch the debates and votes which would decide whether Brexit actually happened.

DINNER AT THE REES-MOGGS'

Soon after his resignation as foreign secretary, Johnson had lunch at Gournay Court, in Somerset, with Jacob Rees-Mogg, who lives there when he is in his constituency of North East Somerset, and whose family were away in Kent. Rees-Mogg told him he must go for the leadership, giving him two reasons: Johnson was the only person who could do Brexit, and the only one who could win an election.

Rees-Mogg's support was not decisive, but it was valuable. He was popular with Tory members, and helped persuade many of the European Research Group of Conservative MPs, of which he was elected chairman in January 2018, to support Johnson rather than Raab. The caricature view of Rees-Mogg as a frivolous figure was wrong: if one followed what he said on some topic, one generally found he had gone into it with greater care than his languid manner suggested, and had accumulated a store of knowledge and argument about the causes, such as Brexit, which mattered most to him. He might be wrong, but he was neither lazy nor dim, and it was lazy of the caricaturists to suppose that he was. Here was a man of moral and political seriousness choosing to back a candidate who was dismissed by many as immoral and flippant.

One of Johnson's gravest weaknesses as a candidate was that he did not know most of his fellow Conservative MPs. He was not a House of Commons man, in the sense of loving the place, its history, rules and personalities, and devoting generous amounts of time to it. As one of his advisers said: 'If you present him with a choice between sitting in his Commons office reading Shakespeare, and going to the Smoking Room to fraternise with people he doesn't really know, Shakespeare wins.' The same adviser remarked that, like Margaret Thatcher, Johnson was adored by the grassroots, but no more than tolerated by the parliamentary party. Here was a weakness which would at length prove fatal. During his spell as MP for Henley, from 2001 to 2008, Johnson had infuriated many of his fellow Tories by breezing into the Palace of Westminster – at top speed it took him eleven minutes to get there on his bicycle from his office at *The Spectator* – and attracting far more publicity than they did, while performing fewer of the unsung duties of a legislator.

Disraeli once remarked that parliamentary speaking, like playing the fiddle, requires practice. One is made to sit in the Chamber for hour after hour, waiting to be called, observing what works for other speakers, and at length discovering what works or doesn't work for oneself. Johnson excelled at addressing public meetings. He showed scant sign of acquiring the more conversational art of debating as a backbencher with fellow MPs, that odd mixture of respecting them as equals, while trying to prove one has the better arguments. They sensed that he did not regard most of them as his equals, and thought of them as minor figures. Here was an attitude that would contribute heavily to Johnson's downfall.

Rees-Mogg, elected in 2010 for North East Somerset, is without question a true parliamentarian. He became one of the few dozen MPs who keep the Chamber going by attending even the most recondite debates. If the whips needed someone to filibuster, Rees-Mogg could at no notice speak for any length of time on any subject. If the British constitution was in peril from some misconceived piece of legislation, he rebelled. Here was someone who not only showed he was a man of principle, but could defend those principles. When people questioned whether he, as a devout Roman Catholic whose views on such questions as abortion were faithful to Church doctrine but repugnant to many liberals, could ever be prime minister, he asked whether they thought a Muslim could ever be prime minister. He treated his opponents, even the Scottish Nationalists, with elaborate courtesy, and paid them the compliment of getting to know them and their arguments before explaining why he thought they were wrong. Like many people, they began by laughing at him, assuming from his Edwardian manner that he was an upper-class twit, and ended, once they got to know him, by respecting him, and even in some cases feeling fond of him.

Johnson came back into the Commons at the 2015 general election, sitting now as MP for Uxbridge and South Ruislip on the western edge of London. Until May 2016 he was seeing out his second term as mayor, and from July 2016 to July 2018 he was foreign secretary, neither of which roles was conducive to spending time in the Commons, even if his natural game had been sitting around getting to know obscure MPs while transacting obscure parliamentary business.

But in any election it is necessary to solicit the support of the electors, who in this case, until the final round, were Conservative MPs. Between Monday 21 January 2019 and Monday 4 March Jacob and Helena Rees-Mogg held a series of seven dinners in their house in Cowley Street, a few minutes' walk from the Commons, for Johnson to meet and talk to those MPs. In their dining room on the ground floor, Jacob sat at the far end of the table, in front of a portrait stretching almost from floor to ceiling of William Wentworth, 4th Earl Fitzwilliam, from whom Helena is descended.

Fitzwilliam inherited the great estates of his uncle the Marquess of Rockingham, prime minister in 1765–66 and 1782, employer of Edmund Burke and owner of the great house of Wentworth Woodhouse, where *Whistlejacket*, the astonishing picture by Stubbs of a horse rearing up on its hind legs against a plain background, used to hang. Today it is one of the most popular pictures in the National Gallery. One can make too much of these connections, but also too little. The eighteenth century was not absent as Johnson's campaign got under way. On the Rees-Moggs' stairs hangs a portrait of Alexander Pope, for whom his father, William Rees-Mogg, had a great admiration.

Johnson admires, as noted in my earlier volume, the altogether racier figure of John Wilkes, eighteenth-century libertine and fighter for liberty. This history matters. We are inspired by the idols of our youth. If we are lucky enough to have been introduced to them, the great figures of the past stay with us for the rest of our lives, and save us from the delusion that the world began yesterday and contemporary values are the only ones any decent person could ever have taken seriously.

At one end of the drawing room the volumes in a glass-fronted bookcase indicated some of the host's interests, though the books were arranged by one of his children: the works of Edmund Burke, Charles de Gaulle (in French), P. G. Wodehouse and *Wisden*. In the corner to the right of the bookcase are found a handkerchief which belonged to Charles I, and a portrait of Colonel Penruddock, who in 1655 led the Penruddock uprising against Oliver Cromwell, and after its failure was tried and beheaded at Exeter.

Helena Rees-Mogg sat at the near end of the dining table, with Johnson half-way down the left-hand side, and facing or next to him usually seven but sometimes nine other Conservative MPs, so the total number of people at dinner was either ten or twelve. During the first course, which might consist of smoked salmon and prawn mousse with milk toast, or crab croquettes in a scallop shell, the conversation was general. During the main course, likely to be veal escalopes with marsala sauce or Beef Wellington, Johnson would speak, and each of the guests would then put some policy proposal to him, to which he would respond, the idea being that he would demonstrate his interest in and grasp of policy, a side of him it would be easy to discount. Pretty much every MP has some policy idea which is not yet taken seriously, but to which he or she is passionately attached.

At the start of this series of dinners, Johnson abstained from alcohol, for he was being encouraged to smarten up his appearance before the leadership race proper got under way. For those who were not abstaining, Bollinger non-vintage champagne, or, sometimes, gin martinis were served before dinner in the drawing room, on the first floor, followed by white burgundy and claret with the meal.

Helena Rees-Mogg said of the dinners: 'I enjoyed them greatly. It was a privilege and fun to be able to help in some small way the encouraging of Boris Johnson as a leadership candidate and eventually as front-runner and winner.' Guests on a particular evening might consist of senior Brexiteers, semi-senior Brexiteers or young MPs. There were probably no Remainers.

The last point serves as a reminder that policy was of vital importance in this leadership election, and not just as something in which Johnson might take a polite interest. In Rees-Mogg, he had a supporter who had begun while still at Oxford to work out the case for leaving the European Union, collaborating with other undergraduates such as Daniel Hannan who later came to prominence as advocates of Brexit.

Johnson himself is often accused of having no principles; of being, indeed, entirely untrustworthy. To have the stern, unbending, monogamous Rees-Mogg among his supporters was a valuable corrective to the accusation that Johnson was a mere opportunist. Rees-Mogg had not jumped on board just because he spotted a passing bandwagon, or if he had, he was unusually far-sighted, for here is what he had to say of Johnson when I interviewed him in 2014 for ConHome:

> He's a very remarkable phenomenon. Incredibly capable, and very clever at actually getting across quite an important message, and making people like it. Which is very rare. I can't think of anybody else who does that. The other two very good politicians at the moment are Alex Salmond and Nigel Farage. But they get their message across in a very divisive way. You're either for them or against them.
>
> ConHome: So Boris is a possible leader when one is required?
>
> Rees-Mogg: Oh yes, very much so. But I'm sure the prime minister will go on [the interviewer's laughter here obscured a few words]. Quite seriously, I think the Tory Party makes a huge mistake in being so footloose and fancy-free about its leaders. I think we need to have leaders and stick to them. For all it's fun gossiping about who might be the next leader, we just need to be serious about it and say Cameron's our leader and there we go and we're backing him and let's get on with it.

During this interview with Rees-Mogg, I took the chance to ask him about a story which is too good to be lost to history.

Philip Dunne, MP for Ludlow, had some time earlier told me that his brother, Nicky, who now runs the Heywood Hill book-shop, had in 1997 acted as Rees-Mogg's agent in Fife Central, a safe Labour seat. Rees-Mogg was bound to lose, but did not fight as a mere paper candidate. He and Dunne worked hard to canvass the entire constituency, and Rees-Mogg insisted they hold a series of public meetings, which by 1997 was an old-fashioned idea. One evening they arrived at a church hall which was empty except for one woman with a small child on her lap. Dunne suggested they cancel the meeting. Rees-Mogg rejected this advice, and began to address the hall. After he had held forth for about half an hour, the woman put up her hand and asked: 'Is the mother and toddler group cancelled?'

When asked whether this happened, Rees-Mogg replied: 'Yes, that's absolutely true. But jokes are dangerous, because they get taken to be serious political points.'

NOBODY RUNS BORIS

'Nobody runs Boris,' a long-standing ally of his warned. Many people have tried to run him, and all have failed. He possesses an astonishing contacts book, but one he does not share. If you say to him in a would-be off-hand tone, 'I'm having lunch next week with Plantagenet Palliser,' he will not reply, 'Ah, Planty Pall and I have known each other since we were at Ashdown House. He's Wilf's godfather.'

The connections all run through Johnson's head, and are used by him to maintain direct contact with a vast range of people who can be brought into play as and when required. Hence his reluctance to surrender his mobile number, which, it emerged almost two years after he became prime minister, had been in the public domain since 2006. His phone was a defence against being taken over by an official machine that wanted to cut him off from rival sources of information.

It was also a way of keeping in touch with old friends, of whom he has a larger number than is generally realised. Several of them told me how touched they were to receive replies to their text messages even at times when Johnson was extraordinarily busy with other, weightier matters. He is loyal to his friends. 'There has never been a Falstaffian moment,' one of them said: the point at which Prince Hal, crowned King, tells Falstaff, 'I know thee not, old man.'

Johnson is so good at thanking people for their help that

each of them is inclined, quite understandably, to magnify his or her own influence over him. I have lost count of the number of people who have assured me that he or she was the person who persuaded Johnson to run against Ken Livingstone for mayor of London. The truth was that after consulting everyone who might help him to gauge his chances of success, he took the decision himself, having meanwhile attached to himself a lot of influential people who imagined they had taken the decision for him.

So too with the prime ministership. Johnson from his earliest years was seized with a yearning to attain the highest place in the state. In that sense his life is one long campaign, a perpetual attempt to get to and remain at the top. Such striving can make one deeply unpopular. From his schooldays he counteracted this by telling jokes. In the words of William Waldegrave, 'The British will let you get away with almost anything if you make them laugh.'

Johnson turned himself into the most entertaining conference speaker of his time. This is not something that can be done simply by waking up one day and deciding to be funny. The conference speech, whether serious or light in tone, is a difficult thing to bring off. Even if one possesses the necessary affinity with the audience, it takes prolonged practice and effort, which most politicians decline to put in, for they imagine they have more serious matters on which to spend their time. More fool them. In a democratic age, what could be more important than to know how to carry an audience with you, by showing that you are on their side, have a rapport with them, are, indeed, one of them, the division between ruler and ruled dissolving, or seeming to dissolve, in wave after wave of ecstatic applause?

I sense my puritan readers, if I have any, frowning as they read this. But it is true. The audience wants to be seduced. The more tedious the previous speakers have been, the greater its gratitude. Once a speaker is known to be good, there is, as Stephen Robinson, a former *Telegraph* colleague, said of Johnson, 'a presumption of hilarity'. People start laughing before any jokes have actually been told.

From 2005, when Cameron became Conservative leader and began a thoroughly professional programme of modernisation, which entailed playing down his own origins as a member of the ruling class and anything else which might be regarded as old-fashioned, Johnson started to profile himself as the anti-Cameron, the man not afraid to rejoice in old-fashioned education, and to pretend, for the amusement of his audience, to be Bertie Wooster. Wooster, like other politicians, would promise you a better tomorrow, but better still, he gave you a better today in Bournemouth, Brighton or Blackpool, or wherever the Tories were meeting that year. Woosterism was placed in the service of Boosterism, which meant boosting Boris.

The ConservativeHome website, founded in 2005 by Tim Montgomerie to campaign for the right of Conservative Party members to vote in that year's Tory leadership election, soon became critical of the victor, Cameron, angry with this cunning Old Etonian for opposing grammar schools and imposing an A-list of candidates on local parties. ConHome went into opposition. With financial support from its proprietor, Lord Ashcroft, it began each year to hold a rally at the party conference at which Johnson was the star attraction. He made Conservatives realise that flouting the party line, and doing so from a traditional perspective, could be tremendously enjoyable. Johnson was mobbed by his fans as he proceeded from the railway station to the conference centre. It could then take him half an hour to get from one side of the conference centre to the other. He was the closest thing the Conservatives had to a rock star.

Cameron and his team of fellow professionals held the coalition with the Liberal Democrats together for five whole years from 2010. He was expected, however, to lose in 2015. At the ConHome Christmas lunch, held in a private room at Boisdale Belgravia in January 2015 because it had not been possible to find a day in December when everyone was free, Paul Goodman, who had succeeded Montgomerie as editor and in due course recruited me as a regular contributor, conducted a sweepstake on how many seats the Conservatives would win in the general election to be held on 7 May 2015 – a date already known because of the Fixed-Term Parliaments Act. The smart money was on somewhere in the 270s or 280s, or – if the party did exceptionally well – the 290s. Because I thought Cameron was undervalued by the commentariat, and did not want to say the same as everyone else, but mainly because I had drunk several glasses of red wine of better quality than I was used to at home, I said 330 seats. My companions, most of whom were experts, wondered if I had gone mad. In the event, Cameron won 331 seats. This is the only time I have predicted a general election result with any accuracy.

In my inability to see into the future I am not alone: I do not know of a single pollster or pundit who managed to predict what would happen at all four of the contests in the period 2015–19: the general elections of 2015, 2017 and 2019, and the EU Referendum in 2016. One of the most striking aspects of those contests is that the experts, who presume to tell us what the people are thinking, turned out to be wrong. They did not know their own country.

A group started to meet to consider what Johnson should do in the event of a Cameron defeat at the general election in 2015. The main participants were Eddie Lister (chief of staff to Johnson at City Hall), Will Walden (Johnson's press man),

Ben Wallace (MP for Wyre and Preston North), Stefan Shakespeare (founder with Nadhim Zahawi of YouGov), Tim Montgomerie, Marina Wheeler and Johnson himself. Sometimes the meetings were held in Johnson's house in Islington, sometimes in Shakespeare's flat in the Barbican and sometimes in a private room at a restaurant.

Johnson generally arrived late, apologised profusely, for half an hour told everyone what he had been doing that day and then for an hour sought to inform himself about what had been going on in the parliamentary party and the press. Were Cameron and George Osborne really briefing against him? He could not believe it. Let alone that his friend Michael Gove had attacked him, though there was an attested case of Gove telling Rupert Murdoch, at a dinner in December 2013, that 'Boris is incapable of focusing on serious issues and has no gravitas'.

Not much was done in the way of planning. It seemed to the more serious people present that nothing useful had been achieved. But Johnson was all the while feeling his way towards decisions of his own about some extraordinarily difficult questions. A close colleague of his told me, 'He absorbs information in a totally different way to 99.9 per cent of people.' According to this colleague, Johnson 'can only articulate his ideas when writing', and 'his information is utterly untransferable to anyone else'.

Before writing comes talking. Both as journalist and as politician, Johnson talks to everyone, and is on receive as well as send. In the hope of learning something, he will talk, at least for a few moments, to any chance stranger, no matter how insignificant. In that respect, he is deeply egalitarian.

THE LONGEST PAUSE

On 18 February 2019, seven Labour MPs resigned from the party and said they would be sitting as The Independent Group, or TIG, swiftly dubbed the Tiggers. They were disgusted by Jeremy Corbyn's leadership, especially his inadequate response to anti-Semitism, and wished to adopt a wholeheartedly pro-European line. The next day they were joined by one more Labour MP, and the day after that by three Tories, Sarah Wollaston, Heidi Allen and Anna Soubry, so their total parliamentary strength stood at eleven. In the Commons they could be seen sitting behind the Scottish Nationalists, where in the early days they took selfies on their mobile phones. On 25 February, a cheery picture was taken of all eleven of them at dinner in Nando's.

In March they registered the new party as Change UK – The Independent Group, a slightly misleading choice of name, as they had no wish to change the constitutional position of the UK, and in fact proposed to keep it the same, i.e. inside the European Union.

In April they fielded a full slate of candidates for the European elections, including Rachel Johnson, sister of the prime minister, who was on its list in the South West. In 2011 she had joined the Conservative Party, only to find that to get on the candidates' list she would have to show she had devoted time to such humdrum duties as canvassing for her local MP. In 2017, she joined the Liberal Democrats, feeling that she really must do something to reverse the referendum result. Her husband, Ivo Dawnay, had already joined them.

In May 2019, Ross Hawkins, of the BBC, interviewed Rachel Johnson in Newquay, in Cornwall, for the *Today* programme, in her capacity as a Change UK candidate.

Johnson: 'We are the fresh alternative to the Lib Dems . . . that does things differently from the Lib Dems.'

Hawkins: 'Can you give me a single point about the Lib Dems that you disagree with? A single policy?'

Johnson responded to this question with a ten-second silence, towards the end of which Hawkins said, 'Long pause,' so listeners did not think the station had gone off air because of a nuclear attack.

It was the longest pause in recent broadcasting history. In the elections a fortnight later the Lib Dems got 19.6 per cent and Change UK only 3.3 per cent. Politics, it turned out, was a tricky business. Good centrist intentions were not enough. You also had to explain why you were not a Lib Dem.

FARAGE TRIUMPHANT

In the European elections on Thursday 23 May 2019, Nigel Farage triumphed at the head of another new outfit, the Brexit Party, which topped the poll with 30.5 per cent of the vote, while the Conservatives fell to fifth place, on 8.8 per cent, their worst ever result in a national contest. Theresa May admitted the game was up, and on Friday announced, her voice breaking, that she would be standing down as soon as her party could elect a new leader.

When I remarked to a senior member of the 1922 Committee of Conservative backbenchers that Johnson had been careful to avoid getting blood on his hands by assassinating May himself, and had left it to the '22 to wield the dagger, the senior member replied with a smile: 'Oh no, we thought it safer to leave it to Nigel Farage.'

Farage, born in 1964, the same year as Johnson, was a strikingly old-fashioned figure. He came before the public as a City gent in a pin-striped suit and covert coat, with an unconcealed love of golf, cricket, fishing and military history. At the end of a morning of hectic trading on the London Metal Exchange, he liked to go for a proper, old-fashioned lunch with any amount to drink. According to his biographer, Michael Crick: 'The favourite venue was the eighteenth-century Simpson's Tavern, in Ball Court, a narrow alleyway off Cornhill, which served traditional steaks and chops, and spotted dick for pudding, and which boasts of being "the oldest chophouse in London".'

Crick reminds us that the City in the 1980s was a mixture of public-school types such as Farage and barrow-boys from Essex. Farage himself has written: 'I liked the mix in the City – nobody cared how posh or how rough you were; you were rated on how much money you could make.'

High-energy, high-stakes risk-taking and a complete absence of cant: these were useful qualities if you wanted to go into politics, where many of the established figures suffered from low energy, risk aversion and an incurable addiction to cant, usually in order to conceal even from themselves their reluctance to get to grips with things.

Just as he had plunged straight into the City without first having his head filled with nonsense at a university, so Farage plunged straight into politics, and discovered what worked, and what didn't, by actually having a go, indeed by having many goes, during none of which did he gain election to the House of Commons, for he provoked enmity as well as adulation.

But he was elected in 1999 to the European Parliament, and it became increasingly difficult to work out how to deal with him and with the party he had helped to found and quite often led: the United Kingdom Independence Party, usually known as UKIP. The Conservatives had long assumed that in order to stay in touch with modern Britain, they must at all costs modernise themselves. The Cameroons, who from the election as party leader of David Cameron at the end of 2005 were running the show, reckoned this meant taking off their ties (especially old school ties), recruiting many more women and ethnic minorities, championing green issues and overseas aid, and generally showing themselves receptive to every progressive cause, notably same-sex marriage, while keeping as quiet as they could about the vexed issue of Europe. The way to modern Britain's heart was to demonstrate that they too were modern.

Farage confounded them by making an enormous noise about Europe, continuing to wear a tie, and swiftly becoming a dangerous rival. Here is what a *Daily Telegraph* columnist wrote about him just before UKIP did well in the local elections in 2014:

Take Nigel Farage, whom I met years ago and who has always struck me as a rather engaging geezer. He's anti-pomposity, he's anti-political correctness, he's anti-loony Brussels regulation. He's in favour of low tax, and sticking up for small business, and sticking up for Britain.

We Tories look at him – with his pint and cigar and sense of humour – and we instinctively recognise someone who is fundamentally indistinguishable from us. He's a blooming Conservative, for heaven's sake; and yet he's in our constituencies, wooing our audiences, nicking our votes, and threatening to put our councillors out of office. We feel the panic of a man confronted by his Doppelgänger . . .

Rather than bashing UKIP, I reckon Tories should be comforted by their rise – because the real story is surely that these voters are not turning to the one party that is meant to be providing the official opposition. The rise of UKIP confirms a) that a Tory approach is broadly popular and b) that in the middle of a parliament, after long years of recession, and with growth more or less flat, the Labour Party is going precisely nowhere.

Johnson, at this time mayor of London, implies in this column (for he was managing, characteristically, to perform both roles at once) that under a new leader, who will need to be a showman and a risk-taker as unabashedly old-fashioned in manner as Farage, the Conservatives can win back those UKIP voters.

There is something within most people that rejoices to see a famous old concern doing well. We are proud that Rolls-Royce engines continue to thrust many aircraft into the skies, Oxford and Cambridge are still world-famous universities, the City remains a great financial centre, Premier League teams draw fans from around the globe and the House of Commons shows how democratic accountability should be done.

We want to believe the resources of our tradition equal to any eventuality, which is one reason that Farage and Johnson became popular. Dulwich College, where P. G. Wodehouse and Raymond Chandler were educated, has more recently produced, in Farage, another entertainer. Eton College, where about two-fifths of Britain's prime ministers were educated, has recently produced, in Cameron and Johnson, two more prime ministers. Much of the commentariat supposes it is a grave disadvantage to have been to Eton. It actually remains an advantage, not only for its connections to the great world of power, but because it offers, to those who want it, an early training in politics, including the art of making oneself popular. And while the commentators cannot approve of anyone enjoying greater educational advantages than they did themselves, most voters couldn't care less about that, and would like to see a world-famous British institution continue to thrive.

Farage had set things up for Johnson. Eton was about to take over what Dulwich had started. An unfashionable note on which to conclude this vignette.

THE RISING STAR COMMUNITY

On Wednesday 5 June 2019, Times Red Box, the newspaper's breakfast time email, carried a comment piece by Rishi Sunak, Robert Jenrick and Oliver Dowden under the headline: 'The Tories are in deep peril. Only Boris Johnson can save us.'

Here was 'the Rising Star Community', as the manager of a rival team dubbed them, endorsing Johnson. The three authors, all junior ministers, smiled out from their joint byline picture. Before their piece appeared they had spent an hour questioning Johnson in Jenrick's house in Vincent Square, not far from the Houses of Parliament. Not long after Johnson's victory, all three were in the Cabinet.

Johnson is said, when shown the list of his first seventy parliamentary supporters, to have exclaimed: 'For fuck's sake go and find me some sensible people!' The sensible people were now coming on board. At the start of the Conservative leadership race of 2019, Johnson was unquestionably in the lead. But since no front runner had won this race since 1955, when Anthony Eden succeeded Churchill, victory was by no means certain, and might even be said to be unlikely.

THE STOP JOHNSON CANDIDATES

It was not yet clear who would emerge as the Stop Johnson candidate around whom his many critics could unite. Nominations for the leadership election opened on Monday 10 June 2019, and no fewer than nine other runners each managed to be nominated by at least eight MPs, the minimum requirement for entry to the race under the rules drawn up by the 1922 Committee. Three more would-be runners, Kit Malthouse, James Cleverly and Sam Gyimah, had earlier declared, but been unable to find eight supporters, and had already dropped out. Dozens more Conservative MPs had either been touted in the media as possible contenders, or had indicated at various points that they were thinking of standing. Just as every tennis player can fantasise about winning Wimbledon, so every MP can dream of being leader.

Who were these runners? Who did Johnson have to beat? I spent that week attending as many of the launches as possible, to write about them for ConHome, and to see the Tory tribe going about its most vital task, the selection of a new chief. Some of the events were held simultaneously, so it was impossible to go to them all. On entering the launch of Matt Hancock, then serving as health secretary, which was held early in the morning of Monday 10 June in a small room at the top of the South Bank Centre, we were handed Belgian waffles. There was more waffle to come, but made in England and less tasty.

'Let's move forward,' said the slogan on Hancock's little stage, the sort of sentiment which makes some of us want to stay where we are, or indeed to go backwards.

'Good morning,' Hancock said, in the manner of an eager young teacher dealing with a remedial class. 'You are the future of Britain.'

As we struggled to work out whether things were really that bad, Hancock gestured at the rain outside, through which could be discerned the London Eye and the Palace of Westminster.

'A metaphor,' he said. 'Dark clouds over Westminster.'

This too was somehow hard to accept, at least when stated by Hancock.

And sure enough, he at once descried a silver lining: 'I'm an optimist about the future . . . I believe the world is getting better . . . I love people.'

Not very Tory sentiments. We found ourselves listening to a Conservative Candide, according to whom everything is for the best in the best of all possible worlds, or would be if Hancock became prime minister.

'Everyone has something to give,' he declared. 'If you look deep inside anyone's heart . . . there's something of value.'

We remembered a line from a Jane Austen novel: 'Oh! he is black at heart.' But Hancock is no Austen. He promised to bring 'every ounce of energy and optimism' to the role of prime minister. Here at last was something to delight the Tory faithful. The man still thought in imperial units.

A journalist asked Hancock how he would beat Boris Johnson, and whether there were any skeletons in his cupboard. 'I don't think there's anything of great interest in my past,' Hancock said with entrancing candour. But he did not reveal how he was going to beat Johnson.

An agonising choice now imposed itself. Dominic Raab was

about to perform in the same building. If one went to hear him, one would keep dry. But Britain was not built by keeping dry. (This kind of rhetoric is infectious.) Off some of us went through the rain to Carlton House Terrace to hear Jeremy Hunt, Johnson's successor as foreign secretary, speak in the Royal Academy of Engineering. As we entered the building, Raab appeared on a television screen with subtitles which said, 'Bold and infused with some of that stubborn optimism.' More optimism! Hadn't Hancock already given us enough? And 'infused' made Raab sound like a trendy new gin which costs three times the price of an untrendy old gin.

'There'll be an announcement,' one of the MPs supporting Hunt said with a smile.

'What sort of an announcement?'

'A positive one,' he replied. 'You'll see.'

A kind Romanian woman was pouring cups of tea. She told me she was keeping out of the Tory leadership race. She was distressed to have queued for eight hours at a Romanian polling station in Harrow in order to cast her vote in the European elections, only for it to close an hour early, before she could do so.

Hunt's slogan was 'Unite to win'. We waited some time for him to join us. Outside, Big Ben could be seen, covered in scaffolding, through a gap in the trees in St James's Park; and nearer at hand, the glorious Corinthian capitals of the pillars on the outside of Carlton House Terrace, netted to stop birds roosting in them. But the interior of the building had been stripped of all mouldings, reduced to the impersonality of a business suite in a hotel on the edge of town.

Amber Rudd arrived. There was warm applause for her, and a susurration of camera shutters. She was at this point secretary of state for work and pensions. This felt like a serious campaign, run by serious people. The whole occasion was more weighty, more official than Hancock's half-hour had been. As Rudd said in her introductory remarks: 'This is a moment of profound seriousness.'

During the EU Referendum campaign she observed, famously, that Johnson was not the man you would want to drive you home at the end of the evening. From the start of her speech, we knew who would be driving her home – Jeremy Hunt: 'I know him to be a man of decency and integrity.'

Some of us wondered for a moment whether Rudd might be a better driver than either Johnson or Hunt. Penny Mordaunt was up next. She made the announcement: 'My name will be on Jeremy Hunt's nomination papers today.' There was a sense, as she spoke, of the Senior Service sticking together. Mordaunt was named after HMS *Penelope* while Hunt's father was an admiral.

On came Hunt. He observed the official decencies: 'Let me pay tribute to Theresa May.' What she has done in the Brexit negotiations is 'both significant and honourable'.

'A serious moment calls for a serious leader,' he went on. That is how he hoped to defeat Johnson: 'Choose me . . . for experience over rhetoric.'

The phalanx of Hunt supporters, themselves serious but not famous men, applauded in a disciplined and determined way. Here was the Establishment in all its stiff and decent glory. But how much of an impression would they make on the wider world?

Later the same day, Michael Gove, the environment secretary, staged the louchest launch of the campaign. Guests were given gold wristbands and ascended twenty-eight floors to the Skyloft at the top of Millbank Tower, where the crowd was stiffened by a contingent of volunteers from the more intellectual parts of Notting Hill. In a room with bare brick walls and fake wooden beams on a low ceiling, conversation was impeded by loud pop music, but an atmosphere of intense admiration for Gove prevailed. His backdrop was adorned with three words: 'Unite. Deliver. Lead.'

The candidate did not disappoint his fans, but the press did, by telling him, as Nick Watt of *Newsnight* put it, 'your campaign is in real trouble – you thought it was okay in a London dinner party to break the law by snorting cocaine'.

'That was bloody years ago,' a Gove partisan at the back of the room said in disgust, but Gove slipped into unctuous clergyman mode: 'You should reflect on your mistakes . . .'

Jason Groves, from the *Daily Mail*, suggested it was 'time to call it a day'.

'That's a totally shit question,' the angry man at the back exclaimed. 'Twat.'

Gove himself went on the attack: 'If I get through which I'm sure I will actually to the final two against Mr Johnson, this is what I will say to him: "Mr Johnson, whatever you do, don't pull out. I know you have before and I know you may not believe in your heart you can do it."'

Like some brilliant martial arts fighter, Gove sought to use his opponent's greater strength and weight to flip him over with a crash onto the floor. So Gove won top marks as a debater. The journalists who attended his launch generally came away saying it was the best yet. The media hoped to see, when the leadership election came to the final two, Gove and Johnson fighting it out in a repeat of the 'psychodrama' – irresistible term – of 2016, when Gove had betrayed Johnson. But Gove, who had announced on 26 May that he would be going for the leadership, and had established an early lead, had lost momentum after the revelation on 7 June, in a biography of him by Owen Bennett, that twenty years earlier he had taken cocaine.

Through the windows of the Skyloft a murky panorama of London could be viewed through the rain: Westminster Abbey, the Houses of Parliament, Lambeth Palace, and the Shard with its summit hidden in the cloud. Gove's prospects were murky too.

'Who would win in a fight – a lion or a bear?' The most enjoyable question on Tuesday was put by Oliver Milne of the *Daily Mirror* to Mark Harper, who was disappointed that his 'Ask Me Anything' policy had, after a good deal of toing and froing about Brexit, produced an exhausted silence.

'On the basis that the lion is the symbol of Britain,' Harper declared, 'I'm going to say the lion.' The title of 'least known Conservative leadership candidate in 2019' was hotly contested, but Harper, a former chief whip, mounted a strong claim.

Chris Heaton-Harris had earlier declared, at Andrea Leadsom's launch: 'We need a leader who is decisive and compassionate.' A reckless statement, alienating all those who wanted an indecisive and merciless leader. Rory Stewart gave the best speech so far at a leadership launch. He spoke in a circus tent between the London Eye and the railway running in to Charing Cross, the rumble of commuter trains helping his performance to sound connected to everyday life. Ken Clarke and Sir Nicholas Soames were among the ten or so Conservative MPs who had come along to support him. Gillian Keegan said a few words of introduction. Philip Lee and Guto Bebb were standing at the back.

A much larger number of the general public had come to hear him. The tent was full, the small, circular stage surrounded by an audience that was mixed by sex and age, though at a guess almost entirely university educated. I found myself sitting between a man on his way to a meeting with the Archbishop of Canterbury and a woman on maternity leave from a senior role in the City.

Stewart reminded me a bit of David Cameron, speaking without notes at his launch in 2005 and managing to convey a greater sense of possibility than David Davis had been able to achieve earlier the same morning. It is difficult to make compromise sound attractive. Stewart managed to do so. He said he wanted 'an energy of prudence – a very unfashionable word – I've come here because I believe in prudence.'

Whatever he set out to do in politics was infused with moral and spiritual purpose. He mentioned Gladstone with approval, and Thatcher too when asked about her. Like her, he respected tradition, and individual rights: 'I'm more of a Conservative than anybody else in the race.'

Here was a man who wanted to inspire us to do better. He spoke of 'the energy of shame' – the way we should feel that our prisons are 'not good enough', so we must do something about them. He referred to an 88-year-old woman who is looking after a 93-year-old man who is doubly incontinent, and said this is not good enough. That produced warm approval from his audience. And he said we need 'the energy of seriousness'. To him, the advocates of no deal were not serious. With the smile one might direct at a group of recalcitrant children who had to be helped to see the error of their ways, he said they were telling a 'fairy tale' and giving way to 'negativism'.

When asked what he thought about the latest attempt in the Commons to rule out either no deal or prorogation, he said he had not read the details, but supported the initiative: 'I am entirely against no deal and entirely against prorogation.'

He gave a charming account of his late, tartan-clad father, still angry, when they revisited Normandy on a D-Day anniversary, at the foolhardy tactics adopted by his commanding officer, which saw the whole company killed or wounded.

Stewart started by speaking from behind the kind of lectern

one might find at a party conference. But quite soon he said, 'I'm going to give up on the podium. I can't be bothered with the podium.' From then on he strolled about in front of the podium, or leant on it, almost ostentatiously relaxed. But not so relaxed he had forgotten the need to stop. He took some questions – half a dozen from the press, half a dozen from the audience – and then with commendable speed wound up.

This candidate entered Parliament in 2010. 'He's come out of his shell,' a journalist who had covered him over that time said after the meeting. The City woman on maternity leave said he would appeal to people who are fed up with the 'incredibly acrimonious' tone of the Brexit debate. At most events of this kind, the audience have been brought in merely to applaud. With Stewart, one felt a conversation was taking place, a relationship was being formed. He had become the early star of the leadership contest.

Somehow I had managed, while all this was going on, to miss Esther McVey's launch, which was disrupted by a man shouting, 'Excuse me, you are all fake news and these people are fake Conservatives.' This was unfair to McVey, who was running on a tough platform which included cutting overseas aid.

THE TORY TRIBE CHOOSES
A NEW CHIEF

The Johnson campaign held its launch a couple of days after the initial rush, on Wednesday 12 June 2019 in a large room at the Royal Academy of Engineering in Carlton House Terrace, expanded, it seemed, from the space used by the Hunt campaign by the removal of a partition wall. This was the best attended of the many launches that took place that week. I could only get a seat at the back of the room, where I found myself surrounded by dozens of MPs. The Johnson campaign was apparently so confident that it did not feel it had to put all its parliamentary supporters up at the front, where everyone would see them. I saw Carrie Symonds being ushered in through a side door by John Whittingdale. I also met a loyal friend of Johnson who was in tears, for she had only been told that morning about the launch, by those who were now running the show. She said they were shits.

It was hard not to cast one's mind back to Thursday 30 June 2016, when a smaller number of pro-Johnson MPs, sitting in a row at the front, turned out for the launch of his last leadership campaign, held in a room half the size of this one at St Ermin's Hotel. They only discovered at the end of his speech – an amazing *coup de théâtre* – that he had conducted a lightning retreat and was giving up, having two hours earlier been declared unfit for the prime ministership by his comrade in arms during the EU Referendum, Michael Gove.

In the summer of 2019 one could feel the Tory tribe rallying round Johnson, deciding by methods formally democratic, but really instinctive, that he was the chief they needed, the leader under whom they would prosper. Humphry Berkeley had said in 1963 that the old method of choosing a Conservative leader – the taking of soundings by senior figures – was 'more appropriate for the enstoolment of an African tribal chief', and later that year the 14th Earl of Home became the last Tory leader to be chosen by this method. Home himself recognised that although the 'magic circle' (as it was dismissively termed by one of its critics, Iain Macleod) worked well, it was open to the fatal charge of being an Establishment stitch-up, so would have to be replaced. He saw to it that Berkeley's suggested rule changes were adopted.* From 1965 onwards, when Edward Heath was selected as the Tory answer to Harold Wilson, the choice of leader was made by formal ballot of Conservative MPs. In 1998 the rules were changed, and the MPs' role has since been limited to the selection of the final two candidates, who are then put before the party membership.

All of which is significant, but is not the whole truth. The Tories are still a tribe, a highly sophisticated one, with a tremendous instinct for survival, and for eliminating anyone who endangers the tribe's survival. Their conduct cannot be understood just by looking at the rules. One might as well try to follow a game of cricket just by reference to the laws of cricket.

The first speaker at Johnson's launch was Geoffrey Cox. He was greeted with a wave of applause, many people supposing

---

* Interested readers are referred to chapter seven, 'The Importance of Mr Berkeley', in *A Conservative Coup: The Fall of Margaret Thatcher* by Alan Watkins.

– for those of us in the cheap seats at the back could not see what was happening – the candidate himself was coming on. 'I'm just the warm-up act,' Cox said, but it was a credit to the Johnson campaign to have obtained his services, for he enjoyed a reputation as the best warm-up act in the business. At the party conference in 2018, he came on before May, when the audience was promised a celebrity and feared being palmed off with some third-rate television performer, and gave a brilliant speech which included a tremendous passage from Milton's *Areopagitica*: 'Methinks I see in my mind a noble and puissant nation rousing herself like a strong man after sleep, and shaking her invincible locks. Methinks I see her as an eagle mewing her mighty youth, and kindling her undazzled eyes at the full midday beam.'

Cox at the Johnson launch felt no need to be tremendous. He said, 'a managerial and bureaucratic approach to politics will not suffice in our present situation', and received warm applause, but he knew people had come to hear Johnson, and soon made way. More applause, which the candidate had some difficulty in stilling, after which he said: 'Can you hear me?'

'Stop Brexit,' shouted a protester outside in the street. We could hear him too, but only faintly once someone shut the window.

'After three years and two missed deadlines we must leave the EU on 31st October,' Johnson said, without mentioning that he is a specialist in missed deadlines. His column never arrived at the *Daily Telegraph* at the stipulated time, for he knew the supposed deadline was not the real deadline.

He spoke for some time, daring if not to be dull, at least to be unexciting, for what front runner wants to be exciting? Johnson condemned Jeremy Corbyn and said the Tories' 'funda-mental moral purpose' was to bridge 'the opportunity gap between one part of the UK and the other', uniting the country as he had united London. He added that he stood for 'sensible moderate modern conservatism', with a prosperous free-market economy paying for first-class public services, and said he would take six questions from the press. The favoured organisations were the BBC, Sky News, ITV, the *Daily Mail*, the *Financial Times* and the *Guardian*. The most significant exchanges occurred when he came to the second question, posed by Beth Rigby of Sky News, who began: 'Mr Johnson, you brandish your Brexit credentials, but many of your colleagues worry about your character.'

Johnson [turning to one side in puzzlement and interrupting]: My parrot?

Rigby: Your character. Your former Foreign Office colleague Alistair Burt said your description of the PM's plans as a suicide vest wrapped around Britain was quote 'outrageous, inappropriate and hurtful'. He said this language had to stop. But it doesn't stop. You brought shame on your party when you described veiled Muslim women as letter boxes [cries and groans of protest from the audience] and bank robbers. People who have worked closely with you do not think you're fit to be prime minister.

Johnson: Well, Beth, I'm delighted that many of my former colleagues seem to dissent from that view [applause]. But nonetheless I want to make a general point, you've asked a fair question, Beth, and a good question, and I want to make a general point about the way I do things and the language I use.

Because of course occasionally plaster comes off the ceiling as a result of a phrase I may have used, or as a result of the way that phrase has been wrenched out of context and interpreted by those who wish for reasons of their own to caricature my views.

But I think it is vital that we as politicians remember that one of the reasons why the public feels alienated now from us all as politicians, is because too often they feel we are muffling and veiling our language [applause], if I might put it that way, not speaking as we find, covering everything up in bureaucratic platitudes, when what they want to hear is what we genuinely think.

And if sometimes in the course of trying to put across what I genuinely think I use phrases and language that have caused offence, of course I'm sorry for the offence that I have caused, but I will continue to speak as directly as I can, because that I think is what the British public want to hear [applause].

The striking thing here was the frequency and sincerity with which the audience applauded him. The Tory tribe, or the considerable part of it represented at this launch, groaned at Rigby when she told him he brought shame on his party, and instead hailed him as a leader who would bring freedom from the reign of virtue which people like her wished to enforce. The harder the time he was given by censorious journalists, the better he did. He profiled himself as the man with the courage to tell truth to the media Establishment.

Johnson had worked out how to handle the feral beasts of the British press. But although this was a successful launch, the feral beasts' appetite is unbounded, and one could not help thinking they would one day find some way to rend him limb from limb.

SAJID JAVID

'Brexit & Beyond' – the slogan adorning the lectern of Sajid Javid, the home secretary – sounded like the title of the chapter towards the end of the guidebook where you are told about the bits of the country you do not need to see if you are in a rush. It also recalled Buzz Lightyear's catchphrase in *Toy Story*, 'To infinity and beyond!'

Javid held the final launch, on Wednesday 12 June 2019, after Johnson had already launched. He was delayed for several hours by his duties in the Commons, so his friendly campaign staff urged us to have a drink. Ruth Davidson, the leader of the Scottish Conservatives, who was to introduce him, bounced about telling jokes. The view from the Skyloft was as wonderful as ever, and thanks to the absence of disco music, the atmosphere was less louche than when Michael Gove had held his launch there, a long time ago as it now seemed, though it was only on Monday.

Here were Javid himself, Tim Montgomerie, founder of ConHome, David Burrowes, MP for Enfield Southgate from 2005 to 2017, and Robert Halfon, chair of the Javid campaign and MP for Harlow since 2010. They had been friends and fellow Conservatives since the four of them met in the late 1980s at Exeter University, where they renamed part of the Student Union building 'Norman Tebbit Corridor'. One looked in vain for that kind of progressive measure in Javid's leadership programme.

Davidson introduced him with a short and charming speech: 'Now this is a phrase I've not used very often, but he's the man for me.' Javid came on with a broad smile. He described how, when he looked for a job in banking, the 'old school bankers with their old school ties' had no time for him. He was very down on old school ties. Johnson the Old Etonian would not do. Javid was pitching as the cheeky outsider, the non-traditional Tory, Westminster's version of Davidson.

Yet Javid and Davidson were in many ways highly traditional figures; an affirmation of the Conservative tradition; living proof of the adaptability of this form of politics. Davidson was from a working-class background, in her mid-twenties came out as a lesbian, and when she stood for the leadership of the Scottish Tories said that 'in terms of embarrassing personal details that I want to get out of the way and address first of all, the rumours are true, yes, I did used to work for the BBC.' She was also an enthusiastic member of the Territorial Army: an unimpeachably traditional activity. Javid was the son of a bus driver from Pakistan who had arrived in Rochdale, in Lancashire, with one pound in his pocket, worked immensely hard, admired Margaret Thatcher and in due course set up his own business. His five sons have all done well: Sajid, whom we had come to hear, had the ability and drive to make a fortune in banking, and now held, at the Home Office, one of the great offices of state.

His actual script was uninspiring. He allowed himself to say 'our best days do lie ahead of us'.

Nick Watt, of *Newsnight*, asked if Javid was worried about the introduction by Johnson of 'Trumpian tactics' in the UK.

Javid replied: 'I think that was a warm-up act for me.' But he had already said he was concerned about divisive politics.

'I would like to be able to write a story about this leadership election which is not about Boris Johnson,' one of the reporters covering Javid's launch said as we marched back along Millbank to the Palace of Westminster. That was virtually impossible. The press criticised Johnson, but could not ignore him. He dominated the coverage.

ALDOUS MACREADY

Aldous Macready, the recently elected Conservative MP for Crumbleton, a northern post-industrial seat, surveyed the leadership contenders with rapt interest. He could not pretend to himself that all was going well for him at Westminster. The expenditure of time, energy and money required to wrest Crumbleton from Labour hands had been colossal, stretching his slender resources to the limit, and his majority was now such as to oblige him to lavish even more time on his constituents than his undoubted public spiritedness would have inclined him to do. The fly-tipping problem in Balaclava Road, which at the time of writing has still not been satisfactorily resolved, had impelled Macready to try to shame the local, still Labour council into action by hiring a van into which he and his key, often sole ally in Canalside Ward, the indefatigable Councillor Mohammed Afzal, were one Sunday morning to be found loading a derelict fridge. They were rewarded with a small, badly reproduced picture at the bottom of page eight of the *Crumbleton Times*, which despite its proud history as a journal of record was reluctant to accept that Labour's long-standing dominance of the town's politics might be drawing to a close.

Macready had renounced, as he promised he would if elected, his career as a local solicitor, which was just starting to flourish. The lovely and sparky Pru Nicolson, to whom he had hoped to get married, broke off their relationship, saying she was not cut out to be a trailing spouse. He arrived alone at Westminster, where no one had any idea who he was.

Nor did Macready have any idea how to draw attention to himself. The gift for publicity is like sex appeal: some people have it, and get themselves talked about, while others, painfully aware that they do not have it, shrink back into themselves, and become less appealing than they might otherwise have been. Macready encountered various well-known figures at Westminster, none of whom seemed to remember, the next time he met them, who he was, and two of whom, hearing only the word 'Aldous', seemed to have got him muddled up with Peter Aldous, the MP for Waveney.

He steeled himself to make his maiden speech, in which he sang the glories of Crumbleton, birthplace in 1753 of a revolutionary piece of textile machinery, and paid generous tribute to his Labour predecessor, the insufferable Jimmy Macdonald. No one took any notice of this speech, though the editor of the *Crumbleton Times* did invite him to take over Jimmy Mac's 'Letter from Westminster', for many years the dullest feature in the paper. Macready laboured mightily over his early columns, and found it was harder than he expected to be both loyal and interesting. Others who had arrived at the same time as him, or after him, took their first steps on the ladder of promotion, and he did not. He had become, with terrible swiftness, one of the hundreds of disappointed men (they are still mostly men) who infest the Palace of Westminster.

With the onset of the leadership election, all this changed. Suddenly he was sought after, his talents were recognised, his prospects were bright. Emissaries from all the candidates wanted to get to know him, to learn what he wanted, even to hear his thoughts on the regeneration of Crumbleton. It was like being at a race meeting where everyone was urging you to back their own horse. For the first time since he arrived at Westminster he felt powerful. He had a vote in the leadership election.

Macready had got into the habit of taking a solitary lunch in the Terrace Cafeteria, where he had become, as most patrons of that establishment do, firm friends with Betty and Rita, two warm-hearted members of staff who took him under their wing. Betty usually saw him first, and would call out, 'Rita, look who's here, it's Aldous', and with them he felt appreciated.

On the day he met Boris Johnson, he had sat down to eat some jerk chicken with rice, with several dollops of sauce poured over the whole thing for him by Betty, in the dark, warm, panelled dining room of the cafeteria, a womb where he could hide from a world which had no use for him, and was reading a pamphlet about urban regeneration so he did not look too alone, and suddenly Johnson was there. He had entered from the side door which led to the Commons barber and the offices of various senior MPs, and was in a tearing hurry, followed by a single, almost bald camp follower, but stopped by his table and said 'Aldous!'

Macready raised his head with a start. 'Boris!' he replied.

'Good to see you!' Boris said. 'I was saying only this morning that what we need is Crumbleton conservatism, Crumbleton is how the cookie crumbles, crumbs it's got to be Crumbleton, you know the kind of thing. Can't stop now. Late for lunch. Got to give a speech. Can I pick your brains some time about Crumbleton conservatism?'

'Yes of course,' Macready said, and with that, Johnson was gone, waving appreciatively to Betty and Rita as he went.

With his sensitivity to atmosphere, Johnson had detected, after his resignation as foreign secretary, what it was like to be a lost soul in the House of Commons. He saw that Macready was a lost soul, and within twenty seconds had started to seduce him.

Macready returned to his jerk chicken. Already he felt inclined to support Johnson in the leadership race, and after anxious discussion with the emissaries of the various campaigns, and much solitary cogitation, that is what he ended up doing. He received no reward from Johnson, who did, however, remember his name, and expressed astonishment that Macready was not yet a junior minister.

Macready laboured under an obscure sense of dissatisfaction with Johnson, for having led him on, and with himself, for allowing this to happen. He felt that to recover his self-respect, it might one day be necessary to show Johnson who was actually in charge.

THE COMMITTEE CORRIDOR

How perky most MPs looked on the morning of Thursday 13 June 2019, the day of the first ballot, as they walked down the Committee Corridor on their way to vote. This magnificent passage runs almost the whole length of the Palace of Westminster, behind the lofty committee rooms with their grand pictures and high windows looking out over the River Thames. The corridor, too, has a high wooden ceiling, and benches down each side, with panelling above which are hung portraits of former prime ministers. It was here on the evening of 20 November 1990, amid almost unbearable excitement, that hundreds of people jammed themselves round the door of Committee Room 12, in which Tory MPs had gathered to hear the result of Michael Heseltine's challenge to Margaret Thatcher. She got 204 votes to his 152, which was not quite the 15 per cent margin of victory she needed under the then rules, and that was the end of her prime ministership.

In mid-June 2019 teams of campaigners were encamped on the benches near the doors in and out of Committee Room 14, where the voting was taking place. Journalists loitered, chatting to each other and to the MPs, and a roaring trade was being done in rumour, gossip and expectation management, everyone posing the great, fascinating, soon to be decided question: 'Who's In? Who's Out?'

The less you knew about the answer to that question, the

keener you were to loiter in the corridor talking to the journalists. The Johnson campaign was not much in evidence. Gavin
Williamson, who had done so much to help Theresa May when
she won in 2016, was known to be working for it. When asked
by a less experienced MP who he was going to back this time,
he had simply replied: 'The winner.' And Grant Shapps had
already made a spookily accurate spreadsheet for the Johnson
campaign, showing how every one of the 313 Tory MPs could
be expected to vote. A more highly informed source said the
wonderful spreadsheet had actually been created by Horton
Shapps, his teenage son. Anyhow, everyone knew Williamson
and Shapps were desperate to return to the Cabinet, and were
confident that Johnson would be able to gratify their wish.
James Wharton, an amiable and still youngish ex-MP who had
lost Stockton South in 2017, was also one of the people running
the campaign, and was said by other members of the Johnson
team to be doing excellent work.

It was all very jolly, this suspension of the usual routine, the
knowledge that the cards were even now being reshuffled and
one might end up on the winning side. Suddenly the prime
minister came in view. Theresa May wore a yellow top, a long
black coat and a frozen smile. Looking to neither left nor right,
she marched swiftly up the corridor followed by a handful of
aides.

'How did you vote?' a reporter had the temerity to ask her
as she emerged from Committee Room 14 after casting her
ballot.

'That's none of your business,' she replied. Her manner was
that of one suffering from a nightmare from which she cannot
wake up. It had presumably occurred to her that one day her
portrait would hang somewhere in the Palace of Westminster.
The Committee Corridor was hung with twenty-four of her

predecessors, with a few empty spaces where a picture had temporarily been removed for some reason. Starting at the Commons end of the building, these reminders of prime ministerial mortality were, going backwards in time, Churchill, Chamberlain, MacDonald, Baldwin, Bonar Law, Lloyd George, Asquith, Balfour, Rosebery, Gladstone, Aberdeen, Russell, Peel, Grey, Wellington, Canning, Grenville, Pitt the Younger, Shelburne, North, Newcastle, Pelham, Spencer Compton and Walpole.

'I'm incredibly depressed by the whole situation,' a Tory peer informed me as I reached Walpole at the far end of the corridor. But I had the impression that the noble lord quite enjoyed being gloomy.

Back outside the voting, Rory Stewart strode up and down, self-collected but tense, the Orde Wingate of the campaign, a regular soldier dropped in deep behind enemy lines, pursuing a more daring and original strategy than anyone else. His campaign to save the Tory Party from a Johnson leadership hung in the balance. Was his bandwagon about to roll? A handful of converts in the last hour and he would go through as the most inspiring alternative to his fellow Eton and Balliol man.

As the chancellor of the exchequer emerged from the committee room, a reporter inquired: 'Mr Hammond, who did you vote for?'

'I'm not telling you,' he replied in a grumpy tone, and strode off.

Two imposing, tail-coated attendants emerged at noon from the committee room and with solemn majesty carried the black ballot boxes next door, where the counting was to take place. At one o'clock, Cheryl Gillan of the 1922 Committee read out the results. Johnson had gained more votes, 114, than the next three candidates combined: Hunt 43, Gove 37 and Raab 27, with Javid just behind on 23. Stewart, with 19, had gained the handful of converts he needed to stay in the race. Hancock, with 20 votes, decided to withdraw, and Leadsom, 11, Harper, 10, and McVey, 9, were eliminated because they had failed to meet the 5 per cent threshold.

Hancock went to see Johnson, pledged allegiance to him, and asked to be made chancellor of the exchequer. After Hancock left the room, Johnson turned to an aide and made the sign of the wanker.

The next round of voting did not take place until Tuesday 18 June, for most MPs are not around at Westminster on Friday, and many are also not around on Monday. Johnson, hands in pockets, leaning forward, communicated confidence as he strode away down the Committee Corridor after casting his vote. 'See you there,' he said, for he is a master of the boldly meaningless but vaguely welcoming phrase. He looked forward to seeing us 'there', wherever 'there' might be. Perhaps he meant Downing Street.

Jeremy Hunt emerged from Committee Room 14. 'Some gossip for you,' he said to the waiting press. 'I'm the 242nd person to vote.' This sounded better than it reads. It was amusingly unfunny.

And here was the prime minister, in a lime-green coat and a cream dress, moving so fast in her tight little entourage that there was no hope of engaging her in conversation. Her face was set in a horrible smile. The careers of British prime ministers die in public.

Members of the campaign teams for the different candidates sat on the benches either side of the entrance to Committee Room 14, making a note of the MPs who had voted. Gillian Keegan, the MP for Chichester, who had given the speech introducing Rory Stewart at his campaign launch, looked extremely cheerful. When told this, she said she always looks extremely cheerful. But perhaps she had reason to be. One of Johnson's most ebullient supporters said: 'I totally underestimated the Stewart bandwagon! I think he's going to go through!' Here was Shoshana Clark, Stewart's wife, communicating calm assurance as she strolled up and down the corridor. And here was Stewart himself, the insurgent leader, feeling his band of irregulars growing to a point where it could annoy or even confound his rivals.

'Mr Gove, how are you feeling?' someone said as he arrived, rather red in the face, to vote.

'Very well, thank you,' he said with his customary politeness.

Dominic Raab somehow got in and out of the Gladstone Room without anyone spotting him. He was not raising his profile, and was heading for elimination, for he would get only thirty votes, just below the 10 per cent threshold which had now to be met to carry on. Most of his supporters, including Nadhim Zahawi, then switched to Johnson, even though Zahawi had originally warned a friend, while explaining the case for backing Raab: 'Have you seen Boris up close and how it works? I think it could go really wrong. We can't risk someone who could go spectacularly well but it could go spectacularly badly.'

We racegoers in the corridor were determined Stewart should go through to the next round. It was the sporting instinct: the insistence on creating an exciting contest, and the knowledge that only Stewart had the mettle to provide it. He proceeded to jump to thirty-seven votes, a gain of eighteen, more even than Johnson, who had fourteen more. The race was on.

As the prime minister made her escape after casting her vote on Wednesday morning in the third round of the leadership contest, her demeanour that of one who has suffered a ghastly personal tragedy and wants to be left to grieve in peace, a schoolboy leapt up from one of the benches along the wall of the Committee Corridor and took two or three jerky steps towards her. She realised he wanted to speak to her, stopped, turned, gave a smile of grave politeness, and shook him by the hand.

The schoolboy returned to his seat and said: 'I'm so happy I got to do that. Just the prime minister, the current prime minister!' He did not want his name to appear in print, but there could be no doubt he was delighted to have met Theresa May.

This touching scene formed an exception to the general mood. The Committee Corridor was more often rent by eruptions of hectic gaiety. It was like a cocktail party without the cocktails.

'He's going to be the director of communications,' a veteran Tory MP said, pointing at a journalist who was supposed to be close to Boris Johnson.

'Oh fuck off,' the journalist replied.

'He's got the language already,' the MP said.

Boris Johnson arrived to vote with just one MP, Conor Burns, in attendance, hovering like a solicitous butler a yard behind his master.

Jeremy Hunt claimed everything is going 'extremely well'. He added that he is 'always an optimist' – an unConservative disposition. 'Have you got the votes?' someone asked. 'I think so,' Hunt replied.

Sajid Javid seemed perky. 'You were very good,' a passing MP told him.

James Cleverly, a Johnson supporter, made an announcement to a part of the corridor that was at that moment almost deserted: 'This is the most unpredictable electorate in the world. We hope to continue to make progress.'

But where was Stewart? During the previous two rounds, he had been there in the thick of the fighting, saving the souls of Tory MPs by looking them in the eye.

On Tuesday night, during a television debate between all five remaining candidates, he had even taken off his tie – was this a late, desperate bid for the support of David Cameron? And then in front of millions or at least thousands of viewers he hung his head in despair – the emotion this sort of television programme induces in most of us, but not the way to hearten his rebel band. Stewart made a principled last-ditch stand against cakeism by setting his face against tax cuts. He would not peddle the glib insincerities this ghastly format required. He told me while I was writing this book that he 'fluffed' the debate, which was the first time he had appeared together with Johnson, and 'couldn't land a blow on him', while 'the others on the stage understandably were determined to knock me out'.

On Wednesday, his supporters turned up late. Sir Nicholas Soames, a fellow of infinite jest, was despondent. Stewart himself looked grim. Only his wife, Shoshana Clark, and the MP who spoke at his launch, Gillian Keegan, continued to smile. When the result came through, he had lost ten votes, and found himself knocked out of the contest. It was like one of those Jacobite rebellions which start so promisingly, only to fizzle out. Conventional forces had butchered the Highlanders. What a horrible way to go. Hanoverian blood flows in Johnson's veins, but did he have to be quite so brutal?

Stewart himself took refuge beyond the seas at Harvard University, and lived to fight another day. He will be back later in this book.

Johnson's vote had risen to 143. The choice for the Stop Johnson candidate now lay between three candidates who together had also mustered exactly 143 votes: Hunt 54, Gove 51 and Javid 38.

On the morning of Thursday 20 June, the arrival of the Javid campaign in the Committee Corridor created a momentary stir. They were led by Robert Halfon, riding on a Roller Scoot which for this purpose became a Roman chariot rather than a mobility scooter. Knowing they now had no hope of victory, they paused for a team photo. Simon Hoare, sitting just outside Committee Room 14 with a Javid badge, shouted 'Hang on! Hang on! I've missed every single photo!' and ran down the corridor in order to join the group, which included the candidate himself, Victoria Atkins and Chris Philp.

All morning the Javid and Hunt campaigns traded jokes across the corridor, Hoare quoting the late Bob Monkhouse's line: 'When I said I was going to become a comedian, they all laughed. Well, they're not laughing now, are they?'

It would be wrong, however, to suggest the contest was fought in a spirit of unwearying amity. It also prompted colleagues to say disobliging things about each other.

'I'm one of Jeremy's greatest fans,' an MP remarked. 'I'd say there are only three things wrong with him. One is that he's the Establishment candidate, the second is that he's Theresa May in trousers, and the third is that he still looks like the head boy at Charterhouse.'

The journalists in the corridor were determined to discover what 'black arts' were being employed to fix the race for second place. The politicians tended to suggest with an innocent air that no conspiracies were afoot. Sir Alan Duncan brought a historical perspective to this question. He remarked that this was his seventh leadership contest, and recalled that in the first two – the fall of Margaret Thatcher in 1990 and the challenge to John Major in 1995 – Tristan Garel-Jones referred to MPs who fell away from the cause of those leaders as 'the fuckpig scumbags', colloquially known as 'the FSBs'.

When the result of the fourth ballot was announced, we discovered that Gove, with 61 votes, was now two ahead of Jeremy Hunt on 59. Javid had fallen back to only 34, so was eliminated, while Johnson had risen to 157. The race for second place was neck and neck, and a final round of voting was held between 3.30 and 5.30 that afternoon in order to decide the matter.

Johnson's total rose by only three votes, to 160, but Hunt shot up to 77, two ahead of Gove on 75. Could it be that the Johnson campaign had lent Hunt the votes needed to beat the more dangerous Gove? It seemed likely.

We faced a final between Johnson and Hunt, who would appear in front of Conservative Party members at a total of sixteen hustings round the country. 'It's going to be a long month,' one of my colleagues in the Commons press gallery remarked.

RED WINE SPILLAGE

On the evening of Friday 21 June 2019, the *Guardian* published the following report:

> Police were called to the home of Boris Johnson and his partner, Carrie Symonds, in the early hours of Friday morning after neighbours heard a loud altercation involving screaming, shouting and banging. The argument could be heard outside the property where the potential future prime minister is living with Symonds, a former Conservative party head of press.
>
> A neighbour told the *Guardian* they heard a woman screaming followed by 'slamming and banging'. At one point Symonds could be heard telling Johnson to 'get off me' and 'get out of my flat'. The neighbour said that after becoming concerned they knocked on the door but received no response. 'I [was] hoping that someone would answer the door and say "We're okay". I knocked three times and no one came to the door.'
>
> The neighbour decided to call 999. Two police cars and a van arrived within minutes, shortly after midnight, but left after receiving reassurances from both the individuals in the flat that they were safe.
>
> When contacted by the *Guardian* on Friday, police initially said they had no record of a domestic incident at the address.

But when given the case number and reference number, as well as identification markings of the vehicles that were called out, police issued a statement saying: 'At 00:24hrs on Friday, 21 June, police responded to a call from a local resident in [south London]. The caller was concerned for the welfare of a female neighbour. Police attended and spoke to all occupants of the address, who were all safe and well. There were no offences or concerns apparent to the officers and there was no cause for police action.'

Johnson and Symonds have increasingly appeared together at public events in recent weeks. The former mayor of London topped Thursday's ballot of Conservative MPs in the party leadership contest and is now the favourite against Jeremy Hunt to be the next prime minister.

The neighbour said they recorded the altercation from inside their flat out of concern for Symonds. On the recording, heard by the *Guardian*, Johnson can be heard refusing to leave the flat and telling Symonds to 'get off my fucking laptop' before there is a loud crashing noise.

Symonds is heard saying Johnson had ruined a sofa with red wine: 'You just don't care for anything because you're spoilt. You have no care for money or anything.'

The neighbour said: 'There was a smashing sound of what sounded like plates. There was a couple of very loud screams that I'm certain were Carrie and she was shouting to "get out" a lot. She was saying "get out of my flat" and he was saying no. And then there was silence after the screaming. My partner, who was in bed half asleep, had heard a loud bang and the house shook.'

How bad was this incident? Had Johnson's leadership campaign just been derailed? Even if, as the police said, the occupants of the flat were 'safe and well', the thought of having Johnson to stay for more than a day or two in a flat one wanted to keep clean and tidy was horrendous. No one takes less trouble to leave things clean and tidy, for as Lynn Barber, who has interviewed him more than once, later observed: 'He operates best in the context of muddle. When reporters heard that he'd had a great row with his girlfriend Carrie and hared round to his house, they never discovered the cause of it; but they came back with a photograph of the filthy interior of his car – illegally parked and densely strewn with newspapers, clothes, coffee cups and food debris – which shocked many readers far more than any row with his girlfriend.'

A friend of Symonds recalled that after the *Guardian* piece she was driven out of her flat in Camberwell, which was besieged by the press pack: 'It was like fox-hunting – the press were after them – they were being hunted down.' She hid in dwellings lent by various well-wishers, including a huge, barely furnished flat near Portland Place. Fantastical stories circulated about what had happened that night in Camberwell, but neither Symonds nor Johnson had any interest in dwelling on the matter. Johnson went the following day to Birmingham, for the first hustings in the Tory leadership campaign.

THE BIRMINGHAM HUSTINGS

The queue for the first hustings of the Tory leadership campaign, held on Saturday 22 June at the International Convention Centre in Birmingham, was so long there was a danger of not getting in. Iain Dale, a broadcaster who knows the Tory Party inside out, interviewed first Johnson and then Hunt in front of an audience of over 1,000 Conservative Party members:

Dale: Now you know as well as I do that there is one subject on everybody's lips today and they want to know why the police were called to your house in the early hours of Friday morning [friendly laughter from the audience, who perhaps had not expected Dale to come so directly to the subject which was indeed being talked about by everyone].

Johnson [smiles a genial smile, pauses a moment, replies in a robust tone]: Thank you, Iain . . . I think what people have come here today, seductive interviewer though you are, I think people have, I don't think they want to hear about that kind of thing ["that kind of thing" said at top speed, as if hurrying past a dangerous point; some of the audience clap and cheer], unless I'm wrong, I think, forgive me, I think what they want to hear are what my plans are for our country and our party [further applause]. I know you're going to have to come back and I salute your indefatigability as a journalist, but I'm under the sad obligation of wanting to get my message across to our party.

Dale: Well you've just taken up a minute with that answer which has told us absolutely nothing [some applause for Dale too]. If the police are called to your home it makes it everyone's business. You are running for the office of not just of leader of the Conservative Party but prime minister. So therefore a lot of people who admire your politics do call into question your character, and I think it is incumbent on you to answer that question.

Johnson: That's okay [jabs out his hand at Dale in a manner which suggests it's not okay], that's a fair point, and people are entitled to ask about me and my determination and my character and what I want to do for the country. And let me just tell you that when I make a promise in politics about what I'm going to do I keep that promise, and I deliver . . .

Dale: With respect you're completely avoiding my question.

Johnson [indignantly]: Well I've told you I was going to tell the good folk who have come here, you asked about my character, actually, I'm not avoiding your question, you asked a very direct question about my character, and what I'm telling you, what I'm telling you . . .

Dale [breaking in]: All right. Let me put it another way. Does a person's private life have any bearing on their ability to do the job as prime minister?

Johnson: When you look at my determination to deliver for the people who vote for me, when I say I will do x I generally speaking deliver x . . . [applause].

Dale: Just answer. It is a very simple question. I shall ask Jeremy Hunt the same question as well. Does a person's private life . . . [interrupted by quite vociferous boos from the audience].

Johnson: No, no, don't boo the great man.

Dale: When he answers this question I will move on [angry shouts]. Does a person's private life have any bearing on their ability to discharge the office of prime minister [further cries of protest]?

Johnson: Look I've tried to give the answer quite exhaustively.

Dale: So just be clear you're not going to make any comment at all on what happened last night.

Johnson: I think that's pretty obvious from the foregoing [laughter].

I have quoted this exchange at length because it shows Dale — a former Conservative parliamentary candidate who served as David Davis's chief of staff during the latter's unsuccessful leadership campaign in 2005 — giving Johnson a pretty hard time, and Johnson showing an implacable determination not to answer questions about his private life, and whether it has any bearing on his ability to do the job of prime minister. Readers will take different views about whether Johnson's answers were reputable or disreputable. What mattered in Birmingham was that the Tory tribe sided with Johnson, and began to boo Dale. The question of character had been raised, just as it had been raised at the launch in London by Beth Rigby of Sky News. Anyone in the slightest bit interested in the man who was about to become prime minister knew he had separated from his second wife, was living with a woman twenty-four years younger than himself, had just had a late-night row with her which led to the police being called, and refused to answer questions about his private life.

A senior member of Hunt's team who was in Birmingham, speaking to me some time later, said of Johnson: 'He handled it really badly.' But a senior member of Johnson's team who was also there, and who spoke to me later, said of Birmingham:

'I was standing at the back. I saw a lot of the front row was full of Jeremy Hunt supporters – Alan Duncan was hissing and spitting at Boris – and the lovely Philip Dunne. I said to Boris's organising team, you need to sort out the front row. So I sat between Philip and Alan. Iain Dale had to ask about the wine-spilling. Boris said, "Oh I don't think people want to know about that." He sort of got away with it. He was the show. When Jeremy came on for his turn there was a feeling of anti-climax. The caravan had moved on. The audience had seen what they came for.'

'He was the show.' The curious truth, infuriating for his critics, was that he was able to turn his late-night row with his girlfriend to his advantage. Johnson was box office in a way that Hunt was not; he connected with the public in a way that Hunt could not; he was questioned about his private life in a way Hunt never would be. The most scandalous thing anyone knew about Hunt was that a radio presenter had once by accident called him Cunt. Hunt was reputable, so not open to attack from moralists in the way that Johnson was.

But this meant Hunt got no chance to show steadiness under fire, of the kind demonstrated in Birmingham by Johnson. And it meant that Hunt was not now in danger of having the worst possible construction put on his behaviour. Johnson was exposed to that danger, and this was not the least of the reasons why he appealed to the Tory tribe. It too felt that quite often the worst possible construction was put on its behaviour, with any amiable and admirable characteristics it might possess simply ignored.

The Conservatives were in power at Westminster, but were less embedded than they used to be in the life of the nation. Their membership in the 1950s had been about three million. In that post-war era of growing prosperity one might feel prompted to join the party because one was frightened of socialism, but one could also regard it as a natural, sociable activity which appealed to people from all backgrounds and did not mark one out as a zealot or even as someone much interested in politics. The Young Conservatives, who in the 1950s had a huge membership, were known as a marriage bureau. To join the Conservatives at this time was no odder than joining the local bowls club, running a stall at the village fete or collecting on behalf of some organisation to which nobody could object, the Royal National Lifeboat Institution, say, or the Royal Society for the Prevention of Cruelty to Animals.

By 2019 Conservative Party membership had fallen to only 160,000. There were areas of the country which within living memory had boasted thriving Conservative associations, where by now the party was pretty much extinct. Conservative clubs, sometimes called constitutional clubs, where one could pop in for a cheap pint of beer, were dying out too. It was the same story in education. Many fewer school and university teachers were Conservative, or even conservative.

The members who were going to decide this election often found themselves derided as old, white and unrepresentative of modern Britain. The Conservatives were accused of scheming to sell the National Health Service to rapacious American capitalists: after all, the only people the party cared about were the super-rich who contributed nothing to the common good and kept their ill-gotten gains in the Cayman Islands. This was the tone of quite a bit of the coverage, often written by journalists who had never met, let alone spent any time with, ordinary Conservative members who were doing their best to keep things going at local level.

Johnson cheered them up, he had a humanity and generosity about him which are not often found in politics, and they were not inclined to consider him as evil as his detractors said he was. He went on after the hustings to Sutton Coldfield, to a meeting of 400 Conservatives in the garden of Tessa Miller, a well-known local activist. He arrived looking exhausted, but when he went into the crowd it revived him, and he gave a speech that they much enjoyed.

THE TORY SENSE OF HUMOUR

On 24 June 2019 Max Hastings warned *Guardian* readers that the Conservative Party 'is about to foist a tasteless joke upon the British people – who will not find it funny for long'. It was Hastings who in 1988, as editor of the *Daily Telegraph*, had rescued Johnson, just dismissed by *The Times* for making up a quote. And it was also Hastings who in 1989 gave him his big break by sending him to Brussels, where Johnson distinguished himself, or as his critics said disgraced himself, by ridiculing the European Union's plans to take more power at the expense of the nation states, powers which extended, according to him, to standardising the rules governing the shape and size of bananas and condoms.

A subject that had previously been reported in a responsible but dull way became in Johnson's hands highly, even irresponsibly, amusing. In that sense, Hastings' judgement in sending him to Brussels had been vindicated. For although as an editor Hastings showed little interest in or capacity for abstract thought, he had the much more valuable characteristic of seeing and appreciating the often disruptive genius of the various contributors whom he recruited to the *Telegraph*. Johnson's office in Brussels was soon adorned with herograms from his editor, who held out against suggestions from grand Tory Europhiles that Johnson should be sacked.

But in 2012, when Johnson was riding high as mayor of

London, Hastings wrote: 'If the day ever comes that Boris Johnson becomes tenant of Downing Street, I shall be among those packing my bags for a new life in Buenos Aires or such-like, because it means that Britain has abandoned its last pretensions to be a serious country.'

When Johnson entered Downing Street, Hastings continued to live near Hungerford. It seemed that, like many journalists, he sometimes exaggerated. It was even possible to see his fulminations against his former protégé as compliments, for they sprang from the realisation that the rise of Johnson might prove unstoppable. Nobody denounces a nonentity.

And Hastings had put his finger on another point. He called Johnson 'a tasteless joke'. He and others did not find Johnson funny, or had ceased to find him funny once entry into No. 10 was on the cards. They wanted a serious person at the top, in order to show, as Hastings put it, that we are 'a serious country'.

No venture is more hopeless than to try to persuade people who do not find a joke amusing that it was in fact funny. Either one laughs out loud the first time, or one never laughs. My intention here is to point out a distinguishing feature of Tories such as Johnson, which is that they are not taken seriously. They are regarded as frivolous, and generally speaking this is correct. They are frivolous, though a better term would be impudent. There is within them a vein of anarchy. They yearn to annoy the prigs. They can't bear the kind of solemn, self-important, self-satisfied person who looks down on the rest of us, and tells us to pipe down and do as we are told by an Establishment that congratulates itself on being wiser, worthier and better educated. The British idea of freedom includes the right to be as rude as we like about those who are running the show.

This is why Johnson on his way up became so hard to stop. He communicated an unholy joy in teasing the prigs, who if they were unwise, which they generally were, responded by becoming more priggish: 'You can't say that!'

Could you say it? The question could, at the time, be seen if one wished as one of taste rather than morals. What Johnson said was often in dubious taste. It wasn't difficult for his opponents to condemn him on grounds of tastelessness. That was how he turned up the volume and got people talking about him. In both journalism and politics he went several notches beyond where a careful young careerist who was anxious not to upset people would have gone. Johnson enjoyed causing offence, though of course it is difficult, in advance, to calibrate the strength of the explosion one will set off, or the precise course of the succeeding row. He had the advantage of surprise, because he was the one planting and detonating the bomb. But this also meant, quite often, that he was the one most in danger of being blown up. No matter: he enjoyed the danger. Thoroughly irresponsible, the prigs declare, and one may feel a twinge of sympathy with them. But what a vivid spectacle the explosions provided. While the going was good, he carried all before him. Fatal difficulties only arose when he had to decide what to do with his victories.

Johnson, born in 1964, is in some ways a product of the revolution which was already taking place in that period, believing as he does in sexual liberation and the freedom to say what one likes, no matter how rude. He is a satirist, alert to the gap between what people say and what they do. The higher someone's protestations of virtue, the greater the like-lihood that they are a humbug. He revels in rudeness, and admires that quality in Samuel Johnson (no relation):

When a young man lamented that he had lost his Greek, Johnson replied, 'I believe it happened at the same time, sir, that I lost all my large estates in Yorkshire.' And when a magistrate was droning on about how he had sent four convicts to a penal colony in Australia, Johnson said he wished he could be the fifth. He was, in other words, not only funny but also rude, and that helps to explain his popularity then and since.

In a nation addicted to evasion and embarrassment, we treasure people who are rude, because we assume (rather primitively) that they are more likely to tell the truth. Johnson was once disparaging the works of Laurence Sterne when a Miss Monckton said that well, actually, she thought they were really rather good.

'That is because, dearest, you're a dunce,' he said.

People are 'blockheads' or 'dogs', and when he was asked who was the greater poet, Derrick or Smart, he said, 'Sir, there is no settling the point of precedency between a louse and a flea.' For all their famous hypocrisy, the British also love a person who seems honest about his pleasures, however vulgar. Johnson once said, 'If I had no duties and no reference to futurity, I would spend my life driving briskly in a post-chaise with a pretty woman', and there he articulates the eternal dream of the British male. Is that not the manifesto of Jeremy Clarkson, and all the millions who follow him?

Is that not the manifesto of Boris Johnson? Though in *Johnson's Life of London*, the book this is taken from, he also wrote paeans of praise to John Wilkes and Keith Richards, both of whom went a bit further than driving briskly in a post-chaise.

Those who never laugh at Johnson's jokes will never understand him, and will congratulate themselves on not understanding him. The incomprehension of his enemies made the whole thing funnier, but woe betide him if his friends ever decided he had gone beyond a joke.

CELIA MONTAGUE

Asked on 25 June 2019 by a television interviewer what he did to relax, Johnson said he liked painting old wine boxes so they looked like buses. People laughed, and discussed whether this could be true. As so often, he had turned something important into a joke. He began by saying 'I like to paint', before veering into an account of using his paintbrush to make wooden crates which had held two bottles of wine look like double-deckers complete with passengers.

Celia Montague painted the portrait of Johnson on the back cover of this book. In it he looks more earnest than he does in almost all the photographs that have been taken of him. While he was still mayor of London, she met him at a book launch and asked whether she could paint his portrait. He asked in a tone of horror if he would have to buy the portrait. As soon as she had reassured him that he would not have to part with any money, he gave his consent.

Montague arrived at City Hall for the first of the two sittings which had been agreed, and waited in his outer office, 'listening involuntarily to some very intense, high-energy exchanges' between members of his staff. To calm her nerves, and save time when she actually got in to see him, she put up her easel and mixed some paints.

At long last she was admitted. He was signing a pile of title pages for his Churchill book. She was appalled by the light in his office, and wondered where she should get him to sit. Spirited conversation took place on various extraneous topics. He enthused about the paints she had already mixed, and in order to buy herself more time to think how to go about the picture, she found herself asking, 'Do you want to have a go?'

He jumped at it, and began to paint a self-portrait. While he worked with furious concentration, entirely focused on his work, she took photographs of him. In her opinion, his self-portrait, 'though obviously satirical, shows an amazing familiarity with the details of his facial features'. She wondered 'how many of us could produce an account of our own face like that, without reference at least to a glance in the mirror?' When he had finished, he declared he would paint her, and produced a creditable likeness, though she claims he shaved thirty years off her age.

During her study of him, she observed that he has 'two charming physical characteristics'. One is his voice, 'a lovely warm chest voice with a great bubble of laughter and enjoyment in it'. The other is 'a quirk of the mouth that makes him look both shy and mischievous at the same time'. In the middle of his upper lip, he has 'a little protrusion, a very slight point — like the beak of a baby bird, which pushes down over his bottom lip when he's feeling uncertain or playing for time'.

He sat a second time for her, at her studio in Oxford, and was going to give further sittings, but then the EU Referendum intervened. She concluded she would have to paint him from the photographs she had taken of him while he himself was at work. This she never normally does, and she found it agony, with his nose a particular difficulty.

But by deciding to do the picture from photographs taken when, being lost in his work, he was not playing up to the camera or to an audience, she has caught him with quite a different expression from the one he wears when he is trying to amuse, seduce and distract. She has caught him being serious.

At the end of 2016, Montague asked the Master of Balliol, Sir Drummond Bone, whether the college might be interested in acquiring her portrait of Johnson. Sir Drummond replied that 'whilst in normal times we might well be interested in a painting of Boris, Brexit has meant that these are not normal times, and such an acquisition would at the moment be extremely controversial, to put it mildly.' In plain language, if Balliol bought the portrait it would be torn to pieces by the current generation of students.

A DOUBLE GAME

Four weeks before he became prime minister, Boris Johnson was given a list of eighteen people from whom to choose a chief of staff. The length of the list suggested it had proved impossible to draw up a short list of two or three genuinely impressive candidates, and the net had therefore been cast wide, and caught quite a few individuals who would be totally out of their depth trying to run Downing Street. Johnson offered the post to Eddie Lister, who had been his chief of staff at City Hall, but then thought better of it, and withdrew the offer.

Brexit was the great and urgent task that awaited the new prime minister. If, after years of insisting that given sufficient determination, leaving the European Union would not be at all difficult, Johnson then failed to do it, he would within months find himself a lame duck.

While May was prime minister, Johnson had remained in touch with Dominic Cummings, who in 2016 steered the Vote Leave campaign to victory. There is an affinity between the two men. Like Johnson, Cummings is audacious, a risk-taker, sees quickly to the heart of a problem and relishes bold action to solve it, especially if while doing so he can confront and confound the stupid, timid, complacent, indecisive, self-interested Establishment. The two men were to fall out after the general election of December 2019 because at that point Johnson became the Establishment, and Cummings started to attack him.

But in the summer of 2019 the great obstacle to getting Brexit done was still the House of Commons. Cummings understood this perfectly. Here for him was the Establishment in all its perfidy. The media, too, with its determination to see things in SW1 terms (the postal district of London containing Whitehall and Parliament), was contemptible. Cummings later wrote: 'If you want to study effective action in politics there is no better case study than Bismarck. He was playing a completely different game to everybody else . . .'

Cummings admits 'it would have been better for the world' if Bismarck had been assassinated when an attempt was made in Unter den Linden in 1866. But really his admiration for Bismarck knows no bounds, and he quotes some brilliant remarks by Bismarck which plainly describe Cummings' own outlook:

> Politics is gambling for high stakes with other people's money . . . Politics is a job that can be compared with navigation in uncharted waters. One has no idea how the weather or the currents will be or what storms one is in for. In politics, there is the added fact that one is largely dependent on the decisions of others, decisions on which one was counting and which then do not materialise; one's actions are never completely one's own. And if the friends on whose support one is relying change their minds, which is something one cannot vouch for, the whole plan miscarries . . . One's enemies one can count on – but one's friends!

Bismarck was not a parliamentarian. Nor was Cummings. The latter's greatest success had been anti-parliamentary: masterminding Leave's victory in the referendum campaign.

He could not bear the buttering up of one's intellectual inferiors which a parliamentary career requires. Cummings has appalling manners. His demeanour is often that of a grumpy teenager who does not see why he should be polite to the grown-ups. He despised many Tory MPs, including many senior and distinguished Eurosceptics, and told them so during the referendum campaign.

Here was another affinity between Cummings and Johnson. For Johnson too, though fond of some Tory MPs, had a low opinion of many others. He did not say so, of course: that has never been his way, and in any case, he needed the support of those MPs both to become and to remain leader. The nearer Johnson got to the top, the less inclined he was to disparage his fellow MPs. He needed to charm them, and on the not sufficiently frequent occasions when he put his mind to it, he was very good at it. Johnson in the tea room was excellent. He was good too at the despatch box, remembering who they were and what each of them cared about, for his memory is astounding.

Devout Eurosceptics did not know quite what to make of him. They knew he was not really one of them, but they also knew he was probably their best hope of getting Brexit done. A senior Tory Eurosceptic said of Johnson's campaign for the leadership (the references are to Grant Shapps, Gavin Williamson, Lynton Crosby and Iain Duncan Smith):

I kept saying something's going on – who's running this campaign? – it's not Shapps or Williamson – there's another mind at work. It became clear it was Lynton.

But there was still something funny going on, and Iain was talking a lot to Lynton. And Lynton was being held at arm's length. So at one point Iain becomes chairman of the campaign. Iain still couldn't quite get to grips with what was quite happening. There was still something going on.

I kept saying, 'Where is Dominic Cummings? What's he up to?' And then suddenly Dominic Cummings emerges from the shadows. You'll find a tweet from Steve Baker pleading with Boris not to have Dominic in the government. A lot of us warned in private this was completely disastrous, and would end in tears, and so it has proved. But it was obvious that Boris had been suborned by Dominic. As soon as Dominic appeared, Lynton said, 'Right, I'm having nothing to do with it.'

It was clear in advance that the employment of Cummings would cause a lot of grief with the parliamentary party, added to which, Cummings had an unfortunate tendency to fall out with his employers and denounce them in a no-holds-barred sort of way. After a brief spell in 2002 as director of strategy during Duncan Smith's leadership of the Conservative Party, Cummings declared in a piece for the *Daily Telegraph* on 26 October 2003: 'Mr Duncan Smith is incompetent, would be a worse prime minister than Tony Blair, and must be replaced.'

Duncan Smith's position had by then become untenable, and a few days later his own MPs declared by 90 votes to 75 that they had lost confidence in him. On 5 November 2003, Nicholas Garland, the *Daily Telegraph*'s political cartoonist, wrote in his diary:

On the day after Iain Duncan Smith was at long last pole axed, Boris wrote a piece in the *DT* saying that he had voted against IDS, but with a heavy heart, conscious of the Leader's tremendous achievement, and feeling some shame at his own treachery.

I spoke to Boris the next day: 'Boris, how could you write all that garbage . . .?'

'I know, I know,' Boris interrupted in an anguished voice.

'I mean, really, what a load of . . .'

'I know, don't go on, when I saw it this morning,' his voice rose, 'I nearly vomited!'

He began spluttering with laughter.

'God he is so awful. It's such a relief when he's gone. He's a liar too, a frightful little crook.' Boris had told him to do a John Major, that is, put himself up for a vote of confidence, which he'd lose, but that was better than wriggling around waiting to be knifed. IDS told him that was exactly what he wanted to do, but the new rules meant he was not allowed to.

'I went and checked the rules,' said Boris indignantly. 'The man was lying. The rules were quite clear. That option was open to him.'

He said that conversations with IDS were pointless because you could never pay attention to what he was saying. His grammar and vocabulary were so weak that in your head you were correcting what he was saying the whole time, making it impossible to attend to the matter under discussion.

Boris was very funny as usual, but I did wonder why on earth he'd written all that crap. There is something odd about Boris. The buffoon act is so brilliant that you can come to think that behind it is a peculiar character who doesn't really feel anything much about anything.

On 25 June 2019, Johnson's campaign put out a statement which said: 'Boris Johnson has appointed Iain Duncan Smith MP as the campaign chairman for the membership stage of his leadership campaign. He will be working closely with James Wharton and Mark Fullbrook.'

This was evidently an attempt to restore confidence after the red wine incident, which had burst upon an astonished world only a few days earlier. Wharton, a former MP, and Fullbrook, one of Lynton Crosby's partners, were said to have done a good job running the campaign. Duncan Smith had not been appointed to run anything, but to reassure his Eurosceptic friends on the Tory backbenches. Duncan Smith was not content with this somewhat limited role and tried to get involved, as Peter Cardwell relates in his memoir, *The Secret Life of Special Advisers*:

Just days before Boris was announced as the new leader of the Conservative Party, IDS attempted to ring him several times to suggest they have a strategy discussion at the campaign's headquarters at the home of Andrew Griffith, a Sky executive who later worked in Downing Street and became an MP in December 2019.

Boris ignored both calls and texts until finally IDS texted to say he was on his way round. With IDS en route, Boris quickly ordered his entire team to race up the stairs to the first floor of the house and, well, hide from their alleged chairman as he rapped on the door of the building, demanding to be let in.

It was a farcical scene, orchestrated by the man who would be prime minister of the United Kingdom just hours later. Eventually, IDS gave up knocking on the door and ringing the bell, and the Johnson team gingerly made their way downstairs again to their makeshift offices to resume their work.

It should be borne in mind that Johnson was extremely busy in the weeks before he became leader. This was the first time party members had chosen a prime minister, as opposed to a leader who might become prime minister, and they were given numerous opportunities to inspect the final two candidates. The Birmingham hustings on 22 June were followed by appearances by Johnson and Hunt in Bournemouth, Exeter, Carlisle, Manchester, Belfast, York, Darlington, Perth, Nottingham, Cardiff, Maidstone, Cheltenham, Wyboston, Colchester and, on 17 July, in London: a gruelling schedule, entailing much travelling and many speeches.

At the same time Johnson had to be ready to start forming a government the moment he became PM. His team were working in an at that time largely empty house in Great College Street, which had belonged to a Tory MP, Adam Afriye, and had now been acquired by Andrew Griffith. It was just round the corner from Westminster Green, where the media camped for months on end, with the Houses of Parliament as a backdrop, while covering the excitements of this period.

Civil servants appeared at the house in Great College Street, wishing to know who in the event of a Johnson victory would require passes for No. 10, contracts of employment et cetera. 'The Fisher Price Make Your Own Cabinet Kit,' as one of Johnson's advisers dubbed it, was brought in: a huge, magnetic white board along with magnetic labels bearing the names of all the people for whom places must or at least might be found. A new prime minister has more freedom to appoint the Cabinet he or she wants than is likely to recur. But it is a far from unfettered freedom, for it is by handing out jobs that loyalty is rewarded and different factions within the party are conciliated: two aspects of government which idealists tend to overlook.

'There was no evidence whatever of the presence of Dominic Cummings,' one of Johnson's advisers recalls. 'Nobody knew that he was involved.'

If one wanted, one could convict Johnson of playing a double game. He announced the appointment of Duncan Smith but hid upstairs in order to avoid talking to him, while keeping secret the identity of the man who would be his chief adviser.

CUMMINGS COMES ON BOARD

On Sunday 21 July 2019, when Cummings had just flown back from holiday, Johnson cycled to see him in Islington. Cummings has since published an account of their conversation, with what he says are 'not exact quotes but close':

Johnson: If we don't find a way through the impasse, I'll be the shortest run PM ever . . . The Tory Party is pretty hopeless. The leadership campaign was a shambles. If I go into No. 10 like that I'm dead. The Vote Leave team knows how to win under extreme pressure and I'm under extreme pressure. I need you to assemble your old team and somehow find a way through . . . I know they hate you, all I care about is winning.

Cummings: There may not be a way through without an election but any which way it will be an extreme situation, lots of SW1 has gone mad . . . They're trying to overthrow the biggest democratic vote ever, we're entitled to use extreme measures to stop them . . . I'll only do it if it's crystal clear all spads report to me. Vote Leave worked because I actually ran it.

'Politics is gambling for high stakes with other people's money,' as Bismarck put it. Johnson had hired the only man he knew who could find a way through the difficulties that had defeated May.

JOSTLING INSTINCTS

On 23 July 2019 members of the Conservative Party met at the Queen Elizabeth II Conference Centre, the concrete pile across the road from Westminster Abbey, to hear the result of the leadership election. Johnson had received 92,153 votes to Hunt's 46,656: a decisive victory. In his acceptance speech, which lasted just over six minutes, he thanked everyone, including his opponent, and told the assembled throng: 'I know there will be people around the place who will question the wisdom of your decision [laughter], and there may even be some people here who still wonder quite what they have done.'

After this admission, perhaps meant to reassure anyone who might worry that he was succumbing to hubris, he went on:

And I would just point out to you that of course nobody, no one party, no one person, has a monopoly of wisdom, but if you look at the history of the last 200 years of this party's existence you will see that it is we Conservatives who have had the best insights, I think, into human nature, and the best insights into how to manage the jostling sets of instincts in the human heart, and time and again it is to us that the people of this country have turned to get that balance right, between the instinct to own your own house, your own home, to earn and spend your own money, to look after your own family, good instincts [clenches his fists, as if showing his readiness to fight for these things], proper instincts, noble instincts [pause], and the equally noble instinct to share and to give everyone a fair chance in life and to build a great society, and on the whole in the last 200 years it is we Conservatives who have understood best how to encourage those instincts to work together in harmony to promote the good of the whole country.

And today at this pivotal moment in our history we again have to reconcile two sets of instincts, two noble sets of instincts, between the deep desire for friendship and free trade and mutual support and security and defence between Britain and our European partners, and the simultaneous desire, equally deep and heartfelt, for democratic self-government in this country.

And of course there are some people who say that they're irreconcilable and it just can't be done. And indeed I read in my *Financial Times* this morning, devoted reader that I am, seriously [moderate laughter], it's a great British brand, I read in my *Financial Times* this morning that no incoming leader has ever faced such a daunting set of circumstances. Well I look at you this morning and I ask myself, do you look daunted? Do you feel daunted?'

The camera panned to the audience, which sat in polite silence, unresponsive to his appeal. 'I don't think you look remotely daunted to me,' Johnson went on, but only got them to applaud when he said their mission was to defeat Jeremy Corbyn. All that stuff about jostling instincts had not connected either with the Conservatives, or with the pundits who declared in solemn tones that they were disappointed with his acceptance speech.

But for Johnson himself, jostling matters, and one may guess that his ear catches the martial derivation of the term, for to jostle used to mean to joust, and a joust was when two knights rode towards each other at a tournament and each tried with his lance to unseat the other. Jostling was a rougher activity than one might think. In 1536 Henry VIII suffered a serious accident while jousting, knocked out for two hours and his legs left with splinters from a shattered lance which turned to ulcers. Some historians date the deterioration in his character from this time.

When Johnson appeared on *Start the Week* on Radio 4 on 14 November 2011 in order to talk about his London book, he asserted that 'greatness is produced by the spark of competition and London is the arena where talents come together and jostle, and it's because of that jostling that you get Shakespeare – if Shakespeare hadn't had to compete with Dekker and Kidd and Marlowe he wouldn't necessarily have put so many bums on seats.'

Johnson had jousted against nine other Conservatives and unseated them all. He was a rougher and tougher competitor than those who wrote him off as a buffoon had been prepared to admit.

THE TOP OF THE GREASY POLE

On Wednesday 24 July 2019, Johnson went to see the Queen, accepted her request to form a government, and on returning to Downing Street made a statement in which he insisted 'the doubters, the doomsters, the gloomsters, they are going to get it wrong again, the people who bet against Britain are going to lose their shirts, because we are going to restore trust in our democracy'.

Johnson proceeded to make at least a dozen promises. Britain would be coming out of the European Union on 31 October, 'no ifs or buts'. There would be another 20,000 police officers, twenty new hospital upgrades and 'we will fix the crisis in social care once and for all with a clear plan we have prepared'. In education, 'we are going to level up per pupil funding'. New roads and railways would unite the country, 'answering at last the plea of the forgotten people and the left behind towns by physically and literally renewing the ties that bind us together'. Freeports, satellites, extra incentives to invest, a bioscience sector liberated from anti-genetic modification rules, measures to protect the welfare of animals, free trade deals: here was a great display of energy, but couched in cautious, pragmatic language. The new prime minister was setting out what sounded like, and indeed was, an election manifesto which would appeal to Labour voters.

The struggle to get Brexit through the Commons, a task

which had defeated Theresa May, would be a severe test. Johnson appointed a Cabinet which consisted almost entirely of those who had declared their support for him, albeit in some cases only recently, after their own leadership bids had failed. Sajid Javid became chancellor of the exchequer, Priti Patel home secretary, Dominic Raab foreign secretary. Jeremy Hunt, who had been foreign secretary, was offered defence, but turned it down, so Johnson gave it to Ben Wallace, one of his longest and most faithful supporters. Matt Hancock stayed at health, Liz Truss went to trade, Steve Barclay remained Brexit secretary, Gavin Williamson was rewarded with education, Grant Shapps went to transport, Jacob Rees-Mogg was made Leader of the House, and so on down the pecking order, with other Johnson loyalists tucked into less conspicuous posts which were still worth having. Most of the senior figures in May's team were consigned to the backbenches, though Amber Rudd, an old friend of Johnson, remained at work and pensions.

MISSION STATEMENT

On Thursday 25 July 2019, Johnson delivered his first Commons statement as prime minister, 'on the mission of this new Conservative government'. He sounded more comfortable as captain of the team than he had in any of his previous parliamentary roles, telling the House:

> Our mission is to deliver Brexit on 31st October, for the purpose of uniting and re-energising our great United Kingdom and making this country the greatest place on earth. And when I say the greatest place on earth . . . I'm conscious some may accuse me of hyperbole. But it's useful to consider the trajectory on which we could now be embarked. By 2050 it is more than possible that the United Kingdom will be the greatest and most prosperous economy in Europe, at the centre of a new network of trade deals . . . with the road and rail investments . . . the investment in broadband . . . our country will boast the most formidable transport and technological connectivity on the planet . . . unleashing the productive power . . . of every corner of England, Scotland, Wales and Northern Ireland . . . no town is left behind ever again . . . net zero . . . freeports . . . bioscience . . . blight-resistant crops . . . satellites . . . there is far too much negativity about our great country.

Johnson added that 'in the ninety-eight days that remain to us we must turbo-charge our preparations to make sure there is as little disruption as possible to our national life', should it prove necessary to leave the European Union without first concluding a deal. 'I have today instructed the chancellor of the duchy of Lancaster to make these preparations his top priority.' That was now Michael Gove.

Trap after trap was laid for his opponents: they were not as brave, enterprising and democratic as he was. 'Since I was a child I remember respectable authorities asserting that our time as a nation was past, that we should be content with mediocrity and managed decline.' One notes that 'respectable' is used by Johnson as a dismissive term. He pointed at the Labour benches and said, 'there are the sceptics and doubters'. According to the new prime minister, 'there is every chance that in 2050, when I fully intend to be around, though not necessarily in this job, we will be able to look back on this extraordinary period as the beginning of a new golden age for our United Kingdom.'

It fell to Jeremy Corbyn, as Leader of the Opposition, to reply to Johnson. 'No one underestimates this country,' he said, 'but the country is deeply worried that the new prime minister over-estimates himself.' On Europe, Corbyn demanded: 'If the prime minister continues recklessly to pursue No Deal, does he accept he would be expressly flouting the will of this Parliament?' Even more strikingly, Corbyn called on Johnson to 'go back to the people' and hold another referendum, in which, if the deal 'fails to protect jobs . . . Labour will in these circumstances campaign to Remain'. Corbyn claimed 'we have a hard-right Cabinet staking everything on tax cuts for the few and a reckless race to the bottom Brexit'. He certainly wished this were so.

Johnson retorted:

A most extraordinary thing has just happened today . . . . Did anyone notice the terrible metamorphosis that has taken place like the final scene of *Invasion of the Body Snatchers*? At last this long-standing Eurosceptic . . . has been captured, he has been jugulated, he has been repro-grammed by his honourable friends, he has been turned now in to a Remainer [cheers] . . . Of all the flipflops he has performed in his tergiversating career that is the one for which I think he will pay the highest price. It is this party, the government, that is now on the side of democ-racy in this country. It is this party that is on the side of the people who voted so overwhelmingly in 2016. This Parliament promised time and time and time again to deliver the people's mandate. And the reality now is that we are the party of the people. We are the party of the many and they are the party of the few.

Johnson sought, from the start of his prime ministership, to turn the tables on his parliamentary opponents. He would turn weakness into strength. With the people at his back, he would rout the Remain majority arrayed against him. He was the incumbent, and he would set the agenda.

He proceeded to take a total of 129 questions. Ian Blackford, for the Scottish Nationalists, welcomed him as 'the last prime minister of the United Kingdom': a prospect which seemed far from remote. 'Do the honourable thing,' Blackford went on. 'Call a general election. Let the people of Scotland have their say.' In the short term, Blackford might, paradoxically, be an ally: Johnson wanted to call an election.

Sir Oliver Letwin, one of the most thoughtful and eloquent of the Conservatives who were determined to prevent a No Deal Brexit, told the new prime minister: 'I personally will certainly vote for any arrangement he makes for an orderly exit from the EU.'

This was not as helpful as it sounded, for Johnson was threatening a disorderly exit.

LIES

But could one believe a word the new prime minister said? An accomplished parliamentarian put that question during those first exchanges on 25 July 2019, referring to the seven principles on public life drawn up in the 1990s by a committee chaired by Lord Nolan:

Angela Eagle (Labour, Wallasey): 'The sixth principle of public life reads:

"Honesty.

"Holders of public office should be truthful."

'Can the Prime Minister stand at the despatch box and tell us whether, in his public life so far, he has maintained that principle?'

The other six Nolan principles, drawn up in the 1990s when John Major's government was under heavy fire for 'Tory sleaze', are Selflessness, Integrity, Objectivity, Accountability, Openness and Leadership. But while Johnson's most severe critics would say he failed to uphold any of these, Honesty was the one they reckoned it was easiest to prove he had flouted.

Whole books could be written about the lies of which he stood accused. Indeed at least one book has been written on this topic, *The Assault on Truth: Boris Johnson, Donald Trump and the Emergence of a New Moral Barbarism* by Peter Oborne, published in 2021, in which the author declared: 'Standards of truth telling, I will prove, collapsed at the precise moment

Boris Johnson and his associates entered Downing Street in the early afternoon of 24 July 2019.'

Oborne worked for Johnson from 2001 to 2005 as political editor of *The Spectator*, and in 2005 published a book called *The Rise of Political Lying*, in which he declared: 'Britain now lives in a post-truth political environment.' In this earlier period, Oborne was a fierce critic of Tony Blair, prime minister from 1997 to 2007, and of Blair's press man from 1994 to 2003, Alastair Campbell.

Oborne now contended that under Johnson, things had got much, much worse. He recalled the justification used by Blair's New Labour apparatchiks for departing from the truth: 'They felt (with good reason) that a venal Tory-supporting press had distorted, misrepresented and often lied about Labour policy. So Blair and his advisers felt there was no way that Labour could win power, let alone retain it, if it relied on telling the truth.'

According to Oborne, 'Blair paved the way for Boris Johnson', who 'has never needed a noble justification for lying', but 'lies habitually, with impunity and without conscience'.

Many people agree with Oborne, which is why I have quoted him. Dominic Cummings wrote of Johnson in a blog published on 5 July 2021: 'He rewrites reality in his mind afresh according to the moment's demands. He lies – so blatantly, so naturally, so regularly – that there is no real distinction possible with him, as there is with normal people, between truth and lies. He always tells people what they want to hear and he never means it. He always says "I can't remember" when they remind him and is rarely "lying".'

Rory Stewart put the case most eloquently, writing of Johnson in a piece on 6 November 2020 in the *Times Literary Supplement*: 'He is the most accomplished liar in public life – perhaps the best liar ever to serve as prime minister . . . He has mastered the use of error, omission, exaggeration, diminution, equivocation and flat denial. He has perfected casuistry, circumlocution, false equivalence and false analogy. He is equally adept at the ironic jest, the fib and the grand lie; the weasel word and the half-truth; the hyperbolic lie, the obvious lie, and the bullshit lie – which may inadvertently be true.'

Wonderful stuff. What a loss Stewart is to the Conservative Party. But what, the reader may ask, is my own opinion? Do I too think, in Oborne's words, that Johnson 'lies habitually, with impunity and without conscience'?

This is in some ways an easy question to answer. Yes, Johnson tells lies. He lied in 1988 when he was sacked by *The Times*, and he lied in 2004 when he was sacked by Michael Howard. In a tight spot, he wonders whether he can get away with some lie, and he considers himself under no obligation to tell the truth about his private life. By the time that he fell, in July 2022, his ministerial colleagues had lost patience with him because the Downing Street line which they were sent out to defend so often turned out to be untrue.

And yet I think that to condemn him as a liar, and leave it at that, is a temptation which should be resisted. My objection is not that this is wrong, but that it is used as a knock-down argument by people whose real objection to Johnson lies elsewhere. One can simplify things by shouting 'Liar', but it is more often the case that he engages in exaggeration or wishful thinking. He has not the slightest concern for facts. He looks on people and events with the eye of a caricaturist, who tells the truth by exaggerating it. He is a storyteller, a dramatist, a collector and projector of images. John Bercow, who as Speaker of the House of Commons during Johnson's early months as prime minister saw a good deal of him, declined on *Broadcasting House* on 2 May 2021 to call him a liar, but said he has 'an insouciant and flippant disregard for the accuracy of what he says'.

One of the great drawbacks of calling Johnson (or anyone else) a liar is that you cannot then debate against him. Hence the rule in the Commons that you cannot call your opponent a liar. The old-fashioned term 'honourable', by which our legislators are still addressed, turns out to be practical. It means that MPs have to try to argue with each other, not merely chuck mud or ascend into the higher cant.

None of this exonerates Johnson. As Bercow said, 'an unwillingness to correct falsehood is ultimately corrosive of public trust in politics'. A flippant disregard for accuracy is not the same as lying, but Johnson has often been convicted of both. This whole subject is more complicated than the hanging judges arrayed against him are willing to admit.

In their anger, some at least of those judges reach a perfectionist position. Johnson is perfectly bad and they themselves are perfectly good. They would no doubt reject, with all due modesty, the second part of that sentence. But they are in danger of implying, or of being taken to imply, that if only we had perfectly honest politicians, all would be well. The man in the pub who says of politicians, 'They're all liars', and who expects nothing better, at least avoids that error. For the trouble with perfect honesty as the answer to all discontents is that it is easy to posit situations in which it is the duty of a politician not to be honest.

William Waldegrave, who served as a Tory minister from 1981 to 1997, when he lost his seat, got into dreadful trouble when he was imprudent enough to say this. His account of the agony through which he passed can be found in his memoir, *A Different Kind of Weather*. Here is one passage, when he is asked in 1994, while appearing before a parliamentary committee, whether ministers should always tell the truth:

'Of course,' I replied without hesitation. But the week before, my old CPRS colleague Robin Butler, by now cabinet secretary and head of the civil service, had written to the Scott inquiry to defend his predecessor Sir Robert Armstrong's view that sometimes it was not advisable to tell the *whole* truth. Robin had been part of the Treasury team that had organised the devaluation of the pound when James Callaghan was chancellor. Could a chancellor, presiding over a fixed exchange rate, but planning to devalue, say what he planned to do if asked a direct question? Of course not, argued Robin: the devaluation would have occurred there and then if he had said so. I repeated this argument, naming Callaghan.

It did not occur to me that I was criticising Callaghan by saying this. Nor, as far as I am aware, did the select committee think there was anything amiss. But a clever, if erratic, young journalist on the *Evening Standard*, Peter Oborne, spotted a story. 'Minister says it is right to lie,' screamed the headline. Then, in one of those temporary spasms of madness that afflict the press sometimes, the heavens fell in.

Oborne has since written that 'I felt a bit guilty about this', for it was 'agonised honesty and not cynical depravity' that had led Waldegrave to say that 'ministers were sometimes (in very rare and constrained circumstances) entitled to lie'.

Suppose you are sent to negotiate some international treaty on behalf of your country. Should you, when asked, give away your entire negotiating position, and admit all the concessions you are willing to make? Of course not, for it is your duty to arrive at the best settlement you can reach. But given that you are duty bound to do the best you can for your country, are you allowed, to some extent, to bluff? Can you pretend, at the outset, to be more intransigent than you really are, in order to extract some concessions from the other side, and have room for making some concessions of your own?

Ah, it may be objected, you are talking about international diplomacy, and of course in this fallen world a certain amount of deception is to be expected when dealing with other countries. But even here, the question is not straightforward. No less an authority than Talleyrand sought, at the end of his long and remarkable career, to correct the widespread prejudice against diplomacy, as being a science of deceit and duplicity: 'If good faith is necessary anywhere it is above all in political transactions, for it is that which makes them firm and lasting. People have made the mistake of confusing reserve with deceit. Good faith never authorises deceit but it admits of reserve; and reserve has this peculiarity that it increases confidence.'

What we generally mean, when we insist on honesty, is that in a democracy, politicians should tell the truth to their own voters. Here there is no excuse for lies.

Very well. But what about a party leader who conceives it his or her duty to keep the party together? Is he or she allowed to be totally candid about his or her own views? Such a belief would be utterly naïve. Collective responsibility, which is required to keep not only a government together but also any opposition which aspires to offer an alternative government, demands that the individuals involved to some extent suppress their personal opinions.

This can be covered by Talleyrand's allowance of 'reserve' – something, incidentally, which Johnson practises on an ample scale. But at what point does reserving one's personal opinion shade into lying? Perhaps never. A coating of tactful hypocrisy may suffice. You do not have to announce, when standing for election, that you have found your manifesto full of bogus promises and your party leader a twerp. But there may come a point, if you go in for that sort of thing, when you start to sound hypocritical, and the public is not keen on hypocrisy.

Winston Churchill remarks, in his essay about Lord Rosebery, on 'the compromises, the accommodations, the inevitable acquiescence in inferior solutions' which get forced on the practical politician. Of course one struggles against these compromises, one strives to get one's own way. By 1904 Churchill had reached the point of leaving the Conservative Party and joining the Liberal Party for twenty years, after which he became once more a Conservative. In his own words, he ratted and reratted. Odd behaviour for one who was later to become, thanks to his leadership in 1940, the great Conservative hero.

Churchill recounts how he and Rosebery – who had already served, briefly and unhappily, as Liberal prime minister – hoped in the early years of the twentieth century to change the whole basis of politics: 'He was out of sympathy with the Liberals: I was soon quarrelling with the Tories. We could both toy with the dream of some new system and grouping of men and ideas, in which one could be an Imperialist without swallowing Protection, and a social reformer without Little Englandism or class bitterness. We had certainly that solid basis of agreement and harmony of outlook upon middle courses, which is shared by many sensible people and was in those days abhorrent to party machines. Need one add that the party machines always prove the stronger?'

Those words were written in the 1930s, when Churchill's greatest days were still ahead of him, and the Conservative Party machine was against him. For a long time he was out of it. Only disaster brought him back into it, and even then he had quite often to go along with policies, such as the alliance with Soviet Russia, against which he would once have fought tooth and nail.

Here is how Johnson answered Eagle's point regarding the sixth principle of public office, honesty: 'I think that if the hon. Lady looks at what I have promised the British public and promised the electorate in my political career, and looks at what I have delivered time and time again, she will see that when I have said I would deliver X, I have delivered X plus twenty, whether it was cutting crime in London, investing in transport or building more homes – more by the way than the Labour mayor ever did. I am very proud of my record and stand and fight on my record.'

Those who wrote Johnson off as an inveterate liar set a low bar for him to clear. He could without much difficulty demonstrate that on quite a few occasions he had kept his promises. How unscrupulous of him, it may be said, to lead the British public astray by actually doing what he said he would do.

But he has not actually answered Eagle's question, which was whether in his public life he had been truthful. He contends instead that he has delivered. This evasion worked well enough as long as he did deliver, or in the case of Brexit could assure his supporters he was just about to deliver. But by the summer of 2022, the delays in delivering economic results looked as if they were bound to be considerable, and the question of trust became more pressing than ever. Did his supporters any longer believe him when he assured them they were marching to the promised land? On a host of non-economic issues, where he had offered explanations which turned out to be false, many Conservatives no longer trusted him. The question of credibility became for him a matter of life and death, and none of the arguments made here, about the complicated nature of politics as actually practised and the inadequacy of the word 'liar' as a description, would be able to save him.

NORTH LONDON REMARKS

'It looks like we're going to crash out. Do you think we should get some bags of rice?' This remark was heard by the author in north London on 8 August 2019. Already there were fears that Johnson was going to do what he threatened to do, and leave the EU without a deal, whereupon trade would grind to a halt and there would be nothing to buy in the shops.

'I think getting nice bread might be the difficult thing,' was heard on 11 November 2019. People in north London, and in many other parts of the country, were still worried.

They were supposed to feel worried. For as one of Johnson's advisers later put it to me, 'We knew the EU had to believe we would walk away without a deal, so we knew we had to implement a bit of a madman strategy.'

The early months of Johnson's premiership were a period of tremendous strain. Admittedly the last two years of Theresa May's premiership had been a period of tremendous strain too. But in Johnson's case the strain was intentional. He and Dominic Cummings reckoned that only by intensifying the crisis could they solve it. In August 2019 a friend of mine visited Cummings in Downing Street and was told by him that the government's opponents would take it to court, after which Boris would gain an election, appeal to the voters, and 'smash' those opponents.

Perhaps the most north London remark I have ever heard, or at least made a note of, was: 'Philippe Sands is against it.' This was said in April 2018, after the United States, France and Britain bombed targets in Syria.

SEX

'I would go to bed with him tomorrow. I lie. I'd go to bed with him today. And so would my daughter.' The speaker, a lady of a certain age but unimpaired vigour, had discovered I was at work on a life of Johnson, and was imparting her feelings about him. We were at dinner in one of the English counties, and a number of hunting people were ranged round the table, for the house where I was staying took me as close as I generally get to the world of Surtees, chronicler of the zestful, disreputable, whole-hearted world in which, as Mr Jorrocks puts it, ''Unting is all that's worth living for – all time is lost wot is not spent in 'unting – it is like the hair we breathe – if we have it not we die – it's the sport of kings, the image of war without its guilt, and only five-and-twenty per cent of its danger.' Mr Jorrocks later adds that 'there was no young man wot would not rather have a himputation on his morality than on his 'ossmanship.'

I glanced across the table at a gentleman who was out of earshot, and asked: 'What would your husband say?'

'He'd laugh!' my neighbour replied. 'When my beautiful daughter lived in London, she used to pursue Johnson on his bike. I think he's got the female vote.'

Hunted through the streets of London by a lovely young woman! No man likes to acknowledge that some other man is more attractive to women. They do not, one assures oneself, go for Johnson's looks. What they love is the zestful, disreputable, whole-hearted way in which he pursues them. There is something flattering about such neck-or-nothing keenness. These remarks do not, evidently, apply to all women. Some are disgusted by him.

And some change their minds about him.

Consider the case of Sasha Swire, married to a Tory MP, Hugo Swire, who was a friend and supporter of David Cameron and served in his government. Her father, Sir John Nott, had likewise been a Tory MP and minister. She knew that world well, but was herself quite often treated, as someone who did not have a career of her own and worked as her husband's parliamentary researcher, with insulting condescension. In 2020 she published *Diary of an MP's Wife*, covering the period 2010–19. Here she describes three days spent as guests of David and Samantha Cameron at Polzeath, in Cornwall, in August 2011: 'Conversation is basic and non-political. D talks a lot about sex, as does H – they are typical of a certain type of Englishman who no longer knows how to flirt because they have become terrified of causing offence. What they do instead is become lewd and chauvinistic with each other, which is the safe zone, instead of with us. In fact, if a woman actually came on to them I think their eyes would pop out of their heads, blood would rush to their faces (in DC's case) and they would run for the nearest shelter – probably under their wives' skirts.'

Cameron declared, as part of his political persona, his support for marriage. We find him here as the Englishman who would be terrified of having an affair. Johnson does not feel that terror, but does not at first appear to advantage in Swire's diary. In September 2012, soon after he has shone while welcoming the world to the London Olympics, she writes of him:

Unfortunately, the Olympics have given him a platform to parade his populist touch without having to worry about anything as trivial as collective responsibility for government policy. The idea of His Blondness with a finger on the nuclear button scares the shit out of me; it also scares the shit out of me that people don't see him as the calculating machine he really is. This is a man who has no obvious political identity or any proven ability to grasp difficult questions and decisions, there is always someone behind the scenes doing it for him, as with all of his election campaigns. He has never shown any loyalty to his party or to his government, only ever to himself. He is also driven by jealousy of Dave.

In March 2016, as the EU Referendum campaign gets under way, Hugo reports back from a dinner in Mayfair that Cameron 'is very fired up about Boris and determined to finish him off'. In October 2017, she writes that Johnson's star is sinking: 'The past few weeks have highlighted how he is clearly not a leader-in-waiting.' In March 2019, she observes that the Johnson leadership campaign is 'always shambolic', an assumption which will prove unsound. She also quotes Rory Stewart going 'completely insane' and telling some MPs, 'It's going to be Boris against me, and I'm going to take Boris down.' In July 2019, by which time Johnson is on course for victory, she says 'the odds that he will be the shortest-serving PM are pretty high'.

But on 20 August 2019, when Carrie Symonds is away on holiday in Greece, Sacha goes to a 'small and select' dinner at No. 10, and sits on the PM's right:

Boris is about the best placement you can get. Cheeky. Flippant. Enthusiastic. Bombastic. Ebullient. Energetic. We have a good laugh.

I kick it off: 'You can't serve this food, it's disgusting. You'll never convert a Remainer with this slop.'

'Cripes, it's not that bad, is it?'

'Goat's cheese and figs? The goat's cheese is three Dairylea triangles crushed together. It's inedible.'

'Here, Sasha.' He makes me a sandwich: a lump of butter, followed by a piece of rocket, a fig, because he thinks a piece of bread might improve it.

I accept. He stuffs in more mouthfuls and knocks back the cheapo plonk at an alarming rate. I look at his rotund build, thick, creased neck, pale, sweaty face, and characteristic dishevelled appearance; he looks back, as if he is working out if I'm shaggable or past my sell-by date . . .

I don't know what will happen to him, because events make politicians, but I have changed my view of him. Yes, he is an alley cat, but he has a greatness of soul, a generosity of spirit, a desire to believe the best in people, a lack of pettiness and envy which is pretty uncommon in politics, and best of all a wonderful comic vision of the human condition.

Johnson has seduced her, though she also thinks he 'is desperately lonely and unhappy on the inside'. That is part of the seduction, the making of a connection with a sympathetic woman: he does not hide his vulnerability, need and desire. Men feel so competitive with him, and so irritated by his success, that they deny or discount this aspect of his political appeal. Bloodless theorists are incapable of describing it, for it does not fit with their theories. Here is a snatch of dialogue between Johnson and Swire:

'You're related to Joe Strummer, aren't you?' he says with his mouth full.

'No, that's Hugo. His stepsister Lucinda was married to him—'

'Marvellous man, Joe Strummer, marvellous, I loved him.'

'In fact,' I say, 'Hugo has two claims to fame, that one, and the other is that he stepped out with Jerry Hall.'

Boris's jaw drops onto the table.

'Hugo . . .and Jerry Hall? Never!'

He proceeds to shout down the table: 'Hugo, did you shag Jerry Hall?' Everyone turns to Hugo, who is rapidly reddening. 'I can confirm there was a brief romance,' says H. The other wives look appalled by this unexpected turn in the conversation . . .

When did a PM last shout down the table, 'Hugo, did you shag Jerry Hall?' It is an eighteenth-century question, and Johnson is in many ways an eighteenth-century figure, at ease with sex and money and rudeness.

OVER-PROMOTED BATH TOY

On 28 August 2019, Jacob Rees-Mogg, the Leader of the House of Commons, flew with two other Cabinet ministers from London to Aberdeen. They made their way to Balmoral, where the Queen was spending the summer, and asked her to approve an order in council proroguing Parliament from some time in the week beginning 9 September until 14 October. The monarch is obliged to follow the advice of her ministers, so did so. The government contended that the previous parliamentary session, which began after the 2017 general election, had lasted longer than any since the Long Parliament of 1640–60, the period of the English Civil War and its aftermath.

But the prorogation which Johnson and his colleagues had obtained was at least five times longer than was normal, and provoked a furious outcry. John Bercow, the Commons speaker, who was on holiday, issued a statement denouncing it as 'a constitutional outrage'. Appeals were made to the courts in Scotland, Northern Ireland and England to declare the prorogation illegal, and Remainers condemned Johnson for engaging in an undemocratic manoeuvre, in order to cut parliamentary scrutiny and reduce their chances of blocking a No Deal Brexit on 31 October.

Johnson annoyed them further by recording a short video in which, speaking in an energetic tone intended to suggest forward movement, he claimed that a new Queen's Speech, to be delivered on 14 October, was needed so the government could lay out its plans to invest in the NHS, deal with violent crime and cut the cost of living. A barely suppressed smile played about his lips as he issued these provocations, which he posted on Twitter. The point of prorogation was so to infuriate the Remainers that they overplayed their hand.

The following day, the actor Hugh Grant replied to Johnson's tweet with a tweet of his own which said: 'You will not fuck with my children's future. You will not destroy the freedoms my grandfather fought two world wars to defend. Fuck off you over-promoted bath toy. Britain is revolted by you and your little gang of masturbatory prefects.'

Some said the atmosphere was as bad as it had been at any time since the Civil War. This was an exaggeration: ferocious constitutional battles have broken out at quite frequent intervals since then. But with Brexit still not done, and the country split down the middle about whether it ought to be done, there was undoubtedly a crisis.

LABOUR PAINS

One might have expected that with the government under heavy fire, the Opposition would be cock-a-hoop. But this was not so, for the Leader of the Opposition, Jeremy Corbyn, faced grave difficulties of his own. He remained in office because a majority of Labour activists supported him, but his own MPs, who knew him best, continued to consider him unfit to be prime minister.

And Brexit posed an appalling problem for the Labour leader. The activists were for the most part devout Remainers, while a considerable number of traditional Labour voters were devout Leavers. How could he hold this coalition together? Any Labour leader would have found this a tricky conundrum, but Corbyn added several problems of his own. He had been observed, early in his leadership, to be reluctant to sing 'God Save The Queen'. He had no enthusiasm for the monarchy or the armed forces, was an alleged sympathiser with various terrorist movements, and again and again denied that Labour had a problem with anti-Semitism, even though many MPs and members said there undoubtedly was such a problem.

Meanwhile, Johnson went round in broad daylight stealing Labour's clothes. The legislation to create the NHS had been put through Parliament after the Second World War by Nye Bevan, the great Labour firebrand, and the Tories had voted against the way he decided to organise the hospitals. This meant they could ever afterwards be accused of not believing in the NHS, even though much of it had been planned during the war by a long forgotten Conservative politician, Henry Willink. Johnson set out to efface this anti-Tory view. During the referendum, his bus had said that Brexit would mean more could be spent on the NHS, and no hospital was now safe from a prime ministerial visit. His propagandists recorded innumerable videos of him talking to doctors, nurses and patients. Corbyn could not strike that note of uplift, and if he recorded any videos of himself visiting hospitals, they went unnoticed.

Labour canvassers had already found in recent years that things were harder for them on the doorstep. In 2015 they lost all but one of their forty-one Scottish seats. In England and Wales, the 'my father would turn in his grave if I voted Tory' vote was also shrinking. A Labour activist in London told me that when he went canvassing in seats on the Thames estuary which the party had quite often won in the past, and which it certainly needed to win again in the future if it was to form a government, he found when he knocked on the doors of voters who had previously declared their support for Labour, 'these people wouldn't even talk to you'.

In his view, 'a lot of these people think they have failed'. They reckoned they had not done well in life, and this meant their reaction to Labour campaigners was to say, or at least to think: 'Don't keep telling me things are crap, I have failed. I see my own failure reflected back at me.' They remembered their hopes and aspirations in earlier decades, the 1950s, 1960s and 1970s, and they said: 'You failed in giving me that vision. I should have stuck with the glow of the Queen, the Empire.' Labour posters in the 1945 general election, the party's first and most celebrated landslide victory, had 'oozed optimism', this canvasser pointed out. Under Corbyn, the party was unable after his honeymoon period to convey the slightest sense of optimism.

'How do you win the right to be heard?' the canvasser asked. 'Boris Johnson does it by being entertaining and positive.' Corbyn could not match this entertainment value and positivity. His supporters were locked in a bitter fight with the Blairites for control of the party, conducted at local level, ward by ward, constituency by constituency, consuming vast amounts of time and energy and poisoning the atmosphere. Alastair Campbell, once Tony Blair's press man, wrote a piece in the *New European* of 30 July 2019 entitled: 'Why I no longer want to be re-admitted to Labour', in which he referred to 'Johnson unspeakably now prime minister and changing the dynamic of the political debate'. The term 'unspeakably' conveys the inability even of a man with the acute news sense of a former tabloid journalist to make sense of the Johnson story. Labour under Corbyn could not offer even the appearance of being united against Johnson. Remainers loved to point out, with justice, how great the new prime minister's difficulties were, perhaps so great he was doomed to fail. But the difficulties facing the Opposition were in many ways just as intractable.

After hearing Johnson's promises on 24 July 2019, his first day in office, a Labour activist said to me: 'Labour should have done this. He's taken empty political space.' But few commen-tators of a left-wing persuasion were prepared to write anything along those lines, for they had already told their readers that Johnson was a disgrace to public life. And how could such a despicable person ever do something good?

BATTLE IS JOINED

MPs returned to Westminster on Tuesday 3 September 2019 from their six-and-a-half-week summer recess and plunged into battle. Those Conservatives who wished at all costs to stop Johnson driving the nation off the edge of a cliff, which in their view was what a No Deal Brexit would amount to, had no time to lose, as the following week the Commons was going to be prorogued, i.e. shut down, for over a month.

The Tory rebels knew the drill, as they had already performed this manoeuvre while Theresa May was prime minister. In co-operation with senior Labour backbenchers including Hilary Benn and Yvette Cooper, and with the help of the speaker, John Bercow, who bent the rules of procedure in their favour, they once more set out to seize control of the Commons order paper – its agenda, showing what business was about to come before it – and pass a bill which would prevent a No Deal Brexit.

Sir Oliver Letwin (Conservative, West Dorset) rose on 3 September to explain what he and fellow rebels sought to achieve. Letwin had worked in the 1980s for Sir Keith Joseph and Margaret Thatcher. He entered the Commons in 1997, and from 2005 to 2016 was David Cameron's right-hand man, an intellectual trouble-shooter sent in to sort out intractable problems. He had a quite remarkable gift for getting on with people in other parties and making common cause with them, which was one reason why the coalition formed in 2010 between the Conservatives and the Liberal Democrats had lasted for five whole years. Although many people questioned his judgement, nobody doubted his generosity and integrity. Letwin told the House:

> Instead of constituting a threat to the EU that will force them to capitulate and remove the backstop, the government's intention or willingness to lead the country into a no-deal exit is a threat to our country. The prime minister is much in the position of someone standing on one side of a canyon shouting to people on the other side of the canyon that if they do not do as he wishes, he will throw himself into the abyss. That is not a credible negotiating strategy, and it is also not a responsible strategy, given that the rest of us are to be dragged over the edge with the prime minister.

Letwin, speaking from high to the Speaker's right, was surrounded by a group of supporters including Sir Nicholas Soames, Dominic Grieve, Philip Hammond, Justine Greening, Alistair Burt and Sir Peter Bottomley. Jeremy Corbyn, the Labour leader, was up next, and was so dull and diffuse that Letwin and his friends started to look a bit embarrassed at receiving support from so inept an ally.

Jacob Rees-Mogg, the Leader of the House, rose and declared that 'what is proposed today is constitutionally irregular'. He accused Letwin of 'stunning arrogance' for supposing it was all right to subvert the Commons' proper role in scrutinising legislation, and the government's role in initiating it, in order to defy the will of the people as expressed in the referendum. And he said that if MPs had lost faith in the government, the proper course was to bring in a motion of no confidence, which if passed could make Corbyn prime minister.

But, he went on, the government's critics won't do that: 'They are afraid, they are white with fear because they do not want the Right Honourable Gentleman to be in Downing Street.' So they have instead, Rees-Mogg went on, engaged in 'legislative legerdemain' – pronounced 'legerdemane' rather than in the French manner – in order 'to create a marionette government' and impose 'possibly indefinite vassalage' upon this country.

When the vote was taken at 10 p.m. that evening, twenty-one Conservatives rebelled, and the government lost by 328 votes to 301. If all twenty-one had instead voted with the government, it would have won by 322 to 307.

'It's not a good start, Boris,' someone shouted from the Labour benches.

Johnson rose and said the people must now decide in a general election who should go to represent Britain in Brussels at the European Council on 17 October. If the people chose Corbyn, 'he will go to Brussels and beg for an extension'. On the other hand, the prime minister declared, 'If I go to Brussels I will go for a deal and I believe I will get a deal.'

Corbyn retorted that keen though he was on an election, he wanted to get the bill to avert a No Deal Brexit through Parliament first. Michael Gove, sitting next to Johnson, became extremely animated, gesticulated wildly at Corbyn, and was rebuked by the Speaker: 'Yes, we know the theatrics he perfected at the Oxford Union.' In these days there were also plenty of theatrics outside among the demonstrators in Parliament Square. The strain and excitement of these proceedings was tremendous. Each side was deeply convinced of the justice of its cause and thought it could win.

JOHNSON'S PURGE

After the vote, the Conservative whip was withdrawn from the twenty-one rebels. They were:

Anne Milton
Caroline Nokes
Antoinette Sandbach
Rory Stewart
Sir Nicholas Soames
Ed Vaizey
Stephen Hammond
Richard Harrington
Margot James
Sir Oliver Letwin
Guto Bebb
Richard Benyon
Greg Clark
Alistair Burt
Steve Brine
Ken Clarke
Justine Greening
David Gauke
Dominic Grieve
Sam Gyimah
Philip Hammond

They included, in Ken Clarke and Philip Hammond, two former chancellors of the exchequer, and a considerable number of other former ministers, notably Grieve, Gauke, Letwin and Clark. In other words, they were not some fringe bunch of cranks, but until recently pillars of the Conservative governments in which they served. To many people it seemed the cranks were now running the show.

MARGOT'S EXPERIENCE

'I find Boris one of the most difficult characters to evaluate and reach a conclusion about,' Margot James said. 'My reading of him has been characterised throughout by that old saying, "The triumph of hope over experience."'

Margot (it would feel absurd to call her James, so she will be Margot here) thought this was by Oscar Wilde, which it could be. But it is actually from Boswell's *Life of Johnson*: 'A gentleman who had been very unhappy in marriage, married immediately after his wife died. Johnson said, it was the triumph of hope over experience.'

We met for breakfast at The Electric Diner in Portobello Road in July 2021 so Margot could recount what it was like being one of the twenty-one Tory rebels. She was not one of the most famous figures in the rebellion, but pretty much everyone who knows her likes and esteems her. She is an elegant and friendly woman who communicates honesty of intention rather than any desire to strike low blows. In 2010 she was elected MP for Stourbridge, in 2018 she was made minister of state for digital and the creative industries by Theresa May, and on 18 July 2019 (a week before Johnson became prime minister) she resigned from that post so she could vote against the government and in favour of a motion designed to forestall the prorogation of Parliament.

'I think the reason I'm always hopeful about Boris, but thus far usually disappointed,' Margot said, 'is because I really thought a lot of him as mayor of London. I thought he was a very good mayor. But he didn't make much impact in Parliament when he was re-elected in 2015. It's not that I expected him to come around and get to know people who'd been elected in 2010, but I would have expected more involvement in the Chamber.'

She went on:

When he was made foreign secretary I thought that was a really brilliant move on the part of Theresa May, and I thought the man will rise to the occasion. He will morph into someone who takes the job seriously, reads enough of the briefing papers to be across it. But he didn't, and I think that trait was captured in that select committee hearing when he let Nazanin Zaghari-Ratcliffe down, and that was I think unforgivable.

And I think there's a place for that in politics [getting by without reading the papers first], sometimes you have to adopt those tactics to survive, but I think he's done it all too often as prime minister, and that's why I don't think he's really suited to being prime minister.

What, I asked, was it like losing the whip? 'The most painful thing was the difficulties I had explaining myself to my Conservative Association in Stourbridge,' Margot replied.

There were some people I was close to, not all of whom were ardent Brexiteers, but most of whom were, and they took my vote against the possible prorogation of Parliament as a disloyalty to the cause they passionately believed in.

To me it wasn't that at all, but it was to them. And I had some conversations before the vote, the day of the vote, and that was far and away the hardest aspect of it. And it plunged me into a late state of indecision. I felt I was letting down people who'd worked for my elections, supported me throughout, and whom I would count either as close friends or certainly people I respected.

But you see, I was a keen student at university of Machiavelli, and is it better for the Prince to be loved or feared? And at that point Boris had made his decision, certainly egged on by Cummings, that if you have to choose, it is better to be feared.

The thing that shocked me most in that whole episode is a small thing. We all went in to see the prime minister on the morning of the vote – anyone who could be there, out of the group of twenty-one – and during the discussion, sitting round the Cabinet table, there were about fifteen of the twenty-one, those of us who could make it. Boris sits where the prime minister always sits, Amber Rudd was on his left-hand side looking more and more uncomfortable as the meeting went on, she resigned I think the next day [actually two days after the rebellion].

Several colleagues raised the issue that it was all very well to think that getting Brexit done – not that we'd alighted on that slogan at that point – would be achievable with the support of seats we could win at the general election in the north. And Anne Milton made the point that it's all very well winning seats up north, but if it involved losing seats like Guildford [her own seat] it wasn't a very clever strategy.

And Boris just turned to her, waved his hand and said,

'Well we might,' as if to say, 'Collateral damage, collateral damage, move on, move on,' and she was absolutely, I mean we were all shocked at that. He was very dismissive.

Many people will see in Johnson's reply a portent of his downfall. If he was going to be so inconsiderate, so lacking in empathy towards his own MPs, no wonder they decided, less than three years later, to defenestrate him. But at this point he was working to a shorter timescale. His overwhelming need was to communicate firmness of purpose. His mentality was that of a rugby player driving for the line, heedless of any injuries he might inflict on those who stood in his way. If he had paused to comfort Milton for the possible loss of Guildford, word might have gone round that he was weakening. With the benefit of hindsight, we can see that the prospects of the Conservatives holding Guildford were by no means as poor as Johnson suggested. Milton's majority over the Liberal Democrats in 2017 was 17,040. In December 2019, Milton stood in Guildford as an Independent and got 4,356 votes, while her successor as the Conservative candidate, Angela Richardson, received 26,317 votes and held the seat with a majority over the Lib Dems of 3,337.

During the meeting in the Cabinet room, Greg Clark, himself a former Cabinet minister, put a few questions to Johnson, who suggested he speak to Cummings. Clark duly put in a call, but had hardly begun to speak when, in Margot's account of this celebrated incident, 'Cummings went into a whole tirade – "You fucking Remainers, when will you get the lesson?" – swearing and bellowing at him down the phone.' So Cummings too was doing his bit to communicate firmness of purpose.

Mark Spencer, as chief whip responsible for disciplining Conservative MPs, tried a different approach with Margot:

What happened was I was in the tearoom, and Mark Spencer, who's a lovely man, came in and sat by me, and he spoke very quietly. He didn't really try to persuade me, but he very kindly wanted to make sure that I really, really did understand the consequences if I did, that losing the whip might mean I wouldn't be able to stand as a Conservative candidate at the next general election.

He was very, very nice. Nothing could have persuaded me at that point. It was about eight or nine o'clock. I'd got through the wobble following my conversations with some of my association members. The group was very mutually supportive. We would meet pretty much every day in one of our offices. One gained a lot of support from that.

'Which other rebels,' I asked, 'did you have most to do with?'

Margot: 'Amber Rudd, Nicholas Soames I was close to – wonderful man, so uplifting. Anne Milton's a great friend of mine. Steve Brine. Greg Clark, who I worked for at BEIS [the Business department, pronounced "Bays"] and had huge regard for and still do. Caroline Nokes.'

Margot agreed with Clark and others that she would only oppose prorogation, and leaving without a deal. On other measures, she supported the government, which meant there could be a way back:

When we got the whip back, this was another side of the prime minister I liked, at this point the meeting was in his Commons office, about eight or ten of us round the table, we'd all been summoned there by the chief whip half an hour before, and the PM talked to us as if he was just a headmaster talking to a group of students who'd had a reprieve about something very common or garden, and he went into some of the negotiations, and said, 'I don't like what you did, you definitely made it more difficult for us, we felt you pulled the rug from under us, but we got there in the end, so I've appreciated the support you gave since.'

So he was just very kind of free with his discussion, his language – it was quite refreshing. Svengali [i.e. Cummings] was in the corner. Ever present. Always in the corner. I think it's easier to blame Cummings for the whole thing than to blame the PM. But I know that's not right, because ultimately the prime minister employed him, which I thought was a very, very bad decision. It created a poisonous atmosphere in No. 10. Ministers were treated with contempt.

Margot was one of the ten rebels to whom, at the end of October, the whip was restored. With some others, notably Grieve and Gauke, the wounds were too deep, the antipathy between them and Johnson too bitter, for reconciliation to be possible. They missed no opportunity to declare that he was a terrible person, and when the election came some of them stood again in their old seats against the Conservative Party. None of them succeeded in getting elected: a proof, if one were needed, of the near necessity, if one wants to get elected, to belong to one of the established parties. Six of those who made their peace with the party stood down at the subsequent general election, but four stood again, and were re-elected. Five more of the rebels, it may be noted, have entered that retirement home for former MPs, the House of Lords, and one of those, Lord Benyon, is at the time of writing a minister.

Why did Margot not stand again for Stourbridge? 'I think I would have had to get the PM to ring my association chairman, and I think he would have done that,' she said. But she felt she would then be 'in hock, a supplicant forever afterwards to the man [Johnson] who saved my skin and worse to the cadre of Brexiteers who ran my association.'

She explained that many of the Conservatives in Stourbridge who had selected her as their candidate at the end of 2006 had passed on by 2018–19, 'and we'd had an influx of Brexit people from UKIP as well'. When chosen in 2006 she was not asked a single question about Europe, but by the end 'that was all they cared about'. She wondered now if she had gone for the right seat in the first place: if she had been the MP for West Worcestershire, or for Newbury or Aylesbury, she thought she would probably have survived.

Before she got the whip back, Johnson came round the Commons tearoom, where there happened to be a vacant seat next to her, as someone else had just left:

He disregarded the rest of the table and he said, 'Ah Margot!' You know the rest. Came round. Sat. Engaged me in a one-to-one. This openness again. This openness was so refreshing in a prime minister. There he was saying, 'I wasn't at my best at the despatch box the other night.' This was when he'd been rude to a Labour MP, very dismissive about very legitimate concerns. He said: 'I wasn't at my best, I'd been at the UN till three in the morning and then I had a flight back, and it wasn't me at my best.'

And then he talked about some of the negotiations and he thanked me for my support over these difficult votes.

I couldn't help the fact that I was really bucked up by this encounter. I couldn't help it.

But there is a darker side to him, which we haven't really dwelt on. This ability to move on and leave a trail of disappointment and commitments that have never been followed through. He just moved on and left this trail in his wake. I think in politics it is better to proceed with more of a plan so that you minimise disaster for others.

I'm afraid I think the PM errs on the side of the cavalier. I don't approve of that. I think that's true in his personal life as it is in his political life. I think that trail probably accounts for what you read about the state of No. 10, which is a good deal of chaos.

AFTER THE REBELLION

Ruth Davidson, who had often expressed reservations about Johnson and a few days earlier had resigned the leadership of the Scottish Conservatives, tweeted after the purge: 'How, in the name of all that is good and holy, is there no longer room in the Conservative Party for @NSoames? #anofficerandagentleman'

The removal of the whip from Sir Nicholas Soames was particularly painful for Johnson. As early as 2001, when he was seeking selection as the candidate for Henley, he related how his friend Soames 'had given me a piece of advice, bawled at me down a mobile phone as though to some idiotic junior officer lost on manoeuvres'. The advice was not to tell jokes, and seems to have been helpful, for Johnson got the seat. And then in 2014 he had brought out, with the blessing of the family, *The Churchill Factor: How One Man Made History*, an account of Soames's grandfather, Winston Churchill.

On the day after the purge, Johnson told some of his closest advisers that he thought maybe the whip should be restored to Soames, and to one other of the rebels. The adviser went on: 'We had to shout at him – it would destroy the whole effect – we just had to refuse, basically.'

Johnson can be astonishingly tender-hearted. He wants to help, or at least to comfort, friends who are in trouble. This is usually discounted as evidence of his need to be loved, and no doubt that is a factor. (Which of us, by the way, does not need to be loved?) But he is not, by instinct, a hanger and flogger, determined to punish anyone who has crossed him. Where some would be vindictive, he is often (though not always) magnanimous.

There was plainly now, as would so often be the case during Johnson's premiership, a need to mend fences with his own party. On the evening of 4 September 2019, Damian Green, MP for Ashford and formerly Theresa May's right-hand man, published a letter to Johnson on behalf of the One Nation Caucus: 'We are now calling upon the Prime Minister to reinstate the party whip to these colleagues and demonstrate to us he is intent on leading a party open to the full range of Conservative views.'

Tim Montgomerie went on *The World at One*, on BBC Radio 4, to talk about the purge. He recalls the presenter, Sarah Montague, who was operating from a temporary studio erected on Westminster Green, saying to him before he went on air: 'This is nuts, isn't it. Absolute nuts.'

That was the received view in metropolitan circles. Montgomerie, by contrast, was all in favour of the purge. He had far greater knowledge of and sympathy with Conservative activists than is generally found among national commentators, and at the start of April 2019 had written a Thunderer piece for *The Times* in which he supported the motion of no confidence in their MP just passed by members of Dominic Grieve's local association in Beaconsfield. According to Montgomerie, the activists were quite right, for Grieve, a distinguished parliamentarian, had committed 'political fraud' by promising to uphold the EU Referendum result, but then seeking to overturn it.

Senior Tory Leavers rallied round Grieve, and said it was outrageous to seek to deselect him. Johnson did a sympathetic tweet: 'Sad to hear about Dominic Grieve. We disagree about

EU but he is a good man and a true Conservative #grievefor-beaconsfield.' But Montgomerie recalled getting a call from Cummings, who said: 'You are completely right and all these people defending him are completely wrong.' Now that, six months later, the twenty-one had been sacked, Montgomerie thought: 'It was sad, it was heart-rending, because people like Ken Clarke, these were great Conservatives. David Gauke, lovely man, but he was wrong on all of this. The family was splitting up, but it needed to be done.'

On the day after the rebellion, the Commons rushed through Hilary Benn's bill preventing a No Deal Brexit. Johnson then tried and failed to force a general election: the motion to hold one was supported by only 298 MPs, far short of the two-thirds majority required.

WHAT'S THE STORY?

The logic of what Johnson had done was impeccable. He did not have a majority in the House of Commons, so intended to provoke the other parties into agreeing to hold an election, which he was confident he could win. But there was no point in winning an election if he then found his majority was wiped out by a group of Conservative MPs who had resolved, on the vital question of Brexit, to vote against him. Hence the purge.

And there was a second, equally cogent reason for being so ruthless. He needed to frame the election as a struggle between himself, determined to get Brexit done, and the House of Commons, which was doing all it could to thwart him. The louder the cries of anguish from his opponents, the more they showed how serious he was. They had become, as it were, his allies, though most of them were too angry with him to see this.

He was deliberately forcing things to a crisis. By insisting he would not seek another extension beyond 31 October 2019, and that if necessary he would leave the EU without a deal, he forced, or at least encouraged, his Remain opponents to tie his hands, as they did with the Benn Act passed on 4 September, and in many cases to admit that by means of a second referendum, they wished not merely to soften Brexit, but to stop it altogether. He incited at least some of them to become more extreme, more hysterical, less easy for normal, reasonably calm people to support.

But there could be no guarantee, amid the noise and smoke of battle, that this strategy was going to work. Like many people, I watched these events with deep perturbation. Was the Tory Party destroying itself? To expel twenty-one MPs in one fell swoop seemed terrible. I admired the rebels' moral courage. In the referendum, I had voted Remain, but I thought both sides had good arguments, and unlike many Remainers, I was not distraught when Leave won. My indecision will attract the scorn of partisans on both sides, but was heartfelt. The slower pace at which a book is written allows time for second thoughts, but I am unfitted for a leading role in either politics or journalism, for it usually takes me several days to perceive when things have changed, let alone to work out whether the change is for the better.

The best politicians, advisers, editors and reporters know in an instant when the story has changed. Johnson's swiftness in that respect is exemplary, and as prime minister he set out to be the one who was doing the changing, or if that was not possible, the one who expressed in the most felicitous way the public reaction to some new development. A successful leader says what millions of unknown people already think. Hence the paradox that the leader of a free country possesses little freedom of speech. Johnson, though he made headlines by striving to expand by a small amount the bounds of acceptable language, was almost as much of a prisoner as everyone else. Here is what an earlier writer said about freedom of speech, or the lack of it, in the ruling class:

The House of Lords is the richest and most powerful collection of persons in Europe, yet they not only could not prevent, but were themselves compelled to pass, the Reform Bill. The daily actions of every peer and peeress are daily falling more and more under the yoke of *bourgeois* opinion, they feel every day a stronger necessity of showing an immaculate front to the world. When they do venture to disregard common opinion, it is in a body, and when supported by one another; whereas formerly every nobleman acted on his own notions, and dared be as eccentric as he pleased. No rank in society is now exempt from the fear of being peculiar, the unwillingness to be, or to be thought, in any respect original.

That was John Stuart Mill in 1840, reviewing *Democracy in America* by Alexis de Tocqueville, and giving as an example the behaviour in 1832 of the House of Lords, when it yielded to pressure to pass the Reform Bill.

The process of placing their lordships 'under the yoke of *bourgeois* opinion' had by the time of Johnson's prime minister-ship come to include 'Valuing Everyone training', which according to the official explanation helped 'ensure that everyone working at Parliament is able to recognise bullying, harassment and sexual misconduct'. Nobody would wish to palliate or deny the seriousness of those matters. But in the summer of 2021 I met a peer who had just been on this course, and at the end he asked the instructor whether it was still all right to be rude to Old Etonians. 'Oh yes,' she replied without a moment's thought.

DANGER GOOD FOR LIBERTY

People were often rude about Johnson. They said he was the worst prime minister ever. This has been said about most prime ministers, for their principal function is to take the blame when things go wrong, and people tend to assume that what is going wrong now is worse than what went wrong before. '*O tempora, O mores!*' – 'O what times, O what customs!' – as Cicero put it a bit over 2,000 years ago.

Johnson took these insults with a good humour which for a time added to his popularity. Initiation through hardship is an ancient tradition. The newcomer is subjected to cruel and unusual punishments and, provided he accepts these without complaint, is welcomed into the school or regiment. This is as true of the new officer as of the humblest recruit, and applies to politics as much as to other walks of life. Each new prime minister faces often unexpected trials which will show whether he or she is up to it. Perhaps in the honeymoon period those trials can be sailed through without apparent difficulty. But the trials recur at quite frequent intervals, and at the end, the PM fails some test and is thrown out.

We do not like any prime minister to be firmly in the saddle for more than a short period of time. Since the start of the twentieth century, only three prime ministers – Salisbury, Baldwin and Wilson – have left office at a time of their own choosing, and all three probably reckoned, correctly, that their health could not much longer sustain the burden of leadership. We wish our rulers to be precarious, so that any time we want to throw them out, we can. When Johnson looked, and indeed was, in danger, he was providing us (by 'us' I mean the British people) with something we wanted. We loved the high-wire act with no safety net, for it showed that Johnson was, in the end, our servant, not our master. He served at our pleasure, and on incurring our displeasure, out he went. Such insecurity of tenure is good for liberty. This point escapes technocrats who think success in government means drawing up a blueprint, to be implemented by efficient ministers and civil servants, backed by a solid parliamentary majority, so everything goes smoothly through.

All great reforms are preceded and accompanied by years of turmoil, during which those with a vested interest in the status quo resist some fundamental change which will mean they lose out. Usually the whole subject has been argued about for a long time before anything much happens. Slave owners did not want to lose their slaves, but Parliament at length decided first the slave trade, and then slavery itself, must go, and worked out a compensation scheme for slave owners. The United States stumbled into a civil war in which slavery was one of the principal issues at stake. I do not want to over-simplify this history, but merely to point out that abolition was an extraordinarily difficult and complicated business to see through, and even when, from a legislative point of view, it was complete, it wasn't over in the real world, where grievous injustices still existed. The Royal Navy needed a long time to eradicate the Atlantic slave trade, and political and military intervention would be required over an even longer period if former slaves in the American South were to enjoy civil rights.

Brexit was often written about, by experts, as if it was a purely technical problem, to which it should be possible to devise a purely technical solution. This was to ignore the deep emotions that were stirred on both sides. Devout Remainers feared their whole world was being stolen from them. They felt they had become, or had always been, European. How often one heard them lament that their children would not be able, once Brexit happened, to live and work in Brussels or Berlin. A crime, a theft, a violation was being committed against them. Their emotional outbursts against Johnson were sometimes, no doubt, confected, but were also expressive of a real attachment, a real devotion to a certain idea of Europe.

On the other side too, deep attachments to the nation and its symbols were at root emotional, however reasonable one might seek to show these loyalties to be. I am conscious (or sometimes unconscious) of rationalising preferences which are felt, and command my devotion, because of who I am. The word 'identity' is often bandied about, but is too feeble a term to express such rooted affection, such love of the familiar, the disposition to enjoy and tend what we are fortunate enough to have inherited, rather than to hanker after speculative improvements which might prove illusory. The reader is referred to Michael Oakeshott, and especially to *Rationalism in Politics*, in which he remarks that to the rationalist, 'not to have a doctrine appears frivolous, even disreputable.' Johnson had no doctrine, so was dismissed by his opponents as frivolous and disreputable.

YOUNGER BROTHER

On Thursday 5 September 2019, Jo Johnson, younger brother of the prime minister, issued a statement on Twitter: 'It's been an honour to represent Orpington for 9 years & to serve as a minister under three PMs. In recent weeks I've been torn between family loyalty and the national interest – it's an unresolvable tension & time for others to take on my roles as MP & Minister. #overandout'

This admission that family loyalty and the national interest could not be reconciled was a heavy blow, and the prime minister looked discombobulated as he arrived an hour late for a visit to a police training academy in Wakefield. Remainers were excited by this development, and in many ways they were right to be. Here was a sober, sombre, reliable member of the Johnson family saying he could no longer support the PM. Perhaps the whole rickety edifice was falling apart.

HERCULES AND ATHENA

On 9 September 2019 Johnson went to Dublin for talks with Leo Varadkar, the Irish prime minister. They gave a joint press conference at which Varadkar observed that 'if there is a deal, and I think it's possible', Johnson would then have to negotiate free trade agreements with the EU and the US, which 'is going to be a Herculean task for you, but we do want to be your friend and your ally, your Athena in doing so'.

Johnson laughed as Varadkar said this. The goddess Athena helped Hercules to perform at least three of his twelve labours, but also knocked him out after he had gone mad and murdered his wife and children.

SUPREME COURT

On 24 September 2019 the Supreme Court ruled that the decision taken at the end of August to prorogue Parliament was unlawful. This meant, Lady Hale, the president of the court, and her ten colleagues unanimously agreed, that the decision was null and of no effect. Gina Miller, the businesswoman who had brought the case, said the ruling confirmed that 'we are a nation governed by the rule of law, laws that everyone, even the prime minister, is not above'. John Bercow, the Speaker of the House of Commons, instructed the authorities to prepare for the resumption of business the following day.

Remainers celebrated this rebuff to the prime minister. It was widely felt that he had suffered a severe defeat, and it was certainly true that the government had lost the case.

THE DEAD PARLIAMENT

The highlight of the first day back at the Commons, 25 September 2019, was Geoffrey Cox's performance, when asked, as attorney general, about the advice he had given the government on the legality of prorogation. It was worth returning to Westminster to watch how he dealt with this. He began with a joke about the recent proceedings in the Supreme Court: 'I took a close interest in the case.' That was followed by prolonged laughter. He added that 'if every time I lost a case I was called upon to resign, I would probably never have had a practice,' and continued with an unreserved admission of defeat: 'In legal terms the matter is settled.' As far as telling the House what his advice had been, he observed there was a long-standing convention that advice given by the law officers to the government could not be disclosed except with the government's consent.

Then came the counter-attack, directed not against the judges – Cox declared that no improper motives must be imputed to them – but against the Commons whose sovereignty had just been upheld by the Supreme Court. He pointed out that many in the House were setting their faces against leaving the European Union. 'This Parliament is a dead Parliament,' he thundered. 'It should no longer sit. It has no moral right to sit on these green benches.' Uproar, which only made Cox hurl his anathemas with greater indignation:

They don't like to hear it, Mr Speaker. They don't like the truth. Twice they have been asked to let the electorate decide upon whether they should continue to sit in their seats, while they block 17.4 million people's votes. This Parliament is a disgrace . . .

Since I am asked, let me tell them the truth. They could vote no confidence at any time, but they're too cowardly to give it a go. They could agree to a motion to allow this House to dissolve, but they are too cowardly to give it a go. This Parliament should have the courage to face the electorate, but it won't, it won't, because so many of them are really all about preventing us leaving the European Union at all. But the time is coming, the time is coming, Mr Speaker, when even these turkeys won't be able to prevent Christmas.

Cox's rich dark baritone voice filled the Chamber even when, in his wrath, he turned away from the microphone. Nobody on the Opposition benches could stop the bombardment. Attempts to do so made it come on heavier. The turkeys on the Opposition benches gazed at him in stupefaction. They had declared repeatedly that they wanted a general election, but when given the chance they had not voted for one. Cox spotted the inconsistency between those two positions and used it to rout them. He taunted them with cowardice. He accused them of betraying the referendum vote by blocking Brexit: three times they could have voted for Theresa May's deal, but had refused to do so.

If Cox's fulminations had not been based upon fact, they would have sounded ludicrous. As it was, he voiced with all the eloquence of an adornment of the English Bar an argument which could also be heard in any saloon bar: that the people had voted for Brexit and the Commons was now defying the will of the people.

CHARLOTTE JOHNSON WAHL

On 2 October 2019, Johnson addressed the Conservative Party conference in Manchester. He said nothing about the detail of how he proposed to get Brexit done, but instead sought to demonstrate his abounding vitality and foment fear among his opponents that he would be mad enough (as they would characterise it) to leave the EU with no deal. Here was an opportunity for the party faithful to indicate, as they did, that they, like him, would regard this as a perfectly sane course of action.

But Johnson, anxious to avoid any imputation of xenophobia, also got them to applaud the line 'We are European, we love Europe,' and through the applause, which he was perhaps not certain of getting, added, 'I love Europe anyhow.'

The House of Commons received less favourable treatment from him: 'There is one part of the British system that seems to be on the blink. If Parliament were a laptop, then the screen would be showing the pizza wheel of doom. If Parliament were a school, Ofsted would be shutting it down. If Parliament were a reality TV show, the whole lot of us would have been voted out of the jungle by now. But at least we could have watched the Speaker being forced to eat a kangaroo testicle.'

The Speaker, John Bercow, became in these anxious months an ever greater celebrity as he presided over one tempestuous parliamentary occasion after another, seeking with egotistical brio to impose his authority and even to influence the result. For he was accused by Leavers of demeaning his office by showing partiality towards Remain MPs, and one of the latter did tell me he was astonished by the favour Bercow had at times shown them.

Journalists wondered after Johnson's speech whether any previous prime minister had used the word 'testicle' at a party conference, or indeed on some other public platform. The general view was probably not.

Johnson attacked his fellow MPs 'for continuing to chew the supermasticated subject of Brexit', when 'voters are desperate for us to focus on their priorities'. He wanted to 'get Brexit done' on 31 October, 'to answer the cry of those 17.4 million who voted for Brexit. Because it is only by delivering Brexit that we can address that feeling in so many parts of the country that they were being left behind, ignored, and that their towns were not only suffering from a lack of love and investment, but their views had somehow become unfashionable or unmentionable.'

Millions of Remainers, he added, wished likewise to accept the referendum result.

He reached a passage in which he said, 'you are entitled to ask yourselves about my core principles, and the ideals that drive me and are going to drive me as your prime minister'. This could have been followed by so much blather, but Johnson said he was 'going to follow the example of my friend Saj' – Sajid Javid, chancellor of the exchequer, who the day before had talked about his own mother, and indeed greeted her in both English and Punjabi, for she was sitting in the audience, resplendent in a pink scarf.

Johnson's mother, Charlotte Johnson Wahl, who had long suffered from Parkinson's disease and by now was extremely frail, was not in Manchester, but was present in the heart and mind of the prime minister, who told the conference, in tones which at times became religious:

I am going to quote that supreme authority in my family – my mother. And by the way for keen students of the divisions in my family, you might know that I have kept the ace up my sleeve – my mother voted Leave.

And my mother taught me to believe strongly in the equal importance, the equal dignity, the equal worth of every human being on the planet. And that may sound banal, but it is not. And there is one institution that sums up that idea.

The NHS is holy to the people of this country because of the simple beauty of its principle that it doesn't matter who you are or where you come from, but when you are sick the whole country figuratively gathers at your bedside and does everything it can to make you well again, and everybody pays to ensure that you have the best doctors and the best nurses and the most effective treatments known to medical science.

In many ways it is impertinent of me to write about the relationship between Johnson and his mother. I had one long and rewarding conversation with her in 2005, at the end of which she let me borrow a picture she had painted of her children, including Boris, the eldest, and to take it home, rather precariously, on my bicycle, so his head could be photographed and reproduced in my first volume. Her friends have testified that she was an exceptionally sympathetic, truthful and generous woman, and from that single encounter with her I knew this to be true.

My intention was to ask her for a second interview, but the pandemic made me put off this request, for she was by now in an extremely vulnerable state, living in sheltered housing, and to expose her to any risk of infection would be intolerable. I thought I would work round to the family side of things at the end of my researches. This reticence was by no means entirely selfless. I did not want the prime minister to hear I was enquiring into personal matters, and to send out a general order that no one who wanted to remain on good terms with him should have anything to do with me.

While I was hesitating, Tom Bower, equipped with the hobnailed boots that are indispensable when writing his kind of book, plunged in, and obtained an interview with Charlotte. He received ample evidence, from Charlotte, of how unhappy her marriage with Stanley Johnson was. She claimed that Stanley hit her, on one occasion apparently breaking her nose, and that their eldest son, Boris, witnessed this.

This was the only revelation in Bower's biography of Johnson, published in October 2020, and was therefore what appeared in the *Mail on Sunday*'s serialisation of the book. This caused the Johnson family excruciating pain. The general effect of Bower's book was to exculpate Boris by incriminating Stanley. Any ways in which the latter was a good father were obscured by this dreadful revelation.

Bower is a clumsy writer who understands nothing about the Conservative Party, but in some of his previous works he had at least been regarded as an efficient hatchet man. On this occasion, the hatchet was buried in Stanley's head, while Boris got off scot-free. In his acknowledgements, Bower declined to reveal that his wife, Veronica Wadley – who worked with Johnson at the *Daily Telegraph* and for him when he was mayor of London, and backed him to the hilt when she was editor of the *Evening Standard* and he was fighting his first mayoral election – had in the summer of 2020 received, on the recommendation of Johnson as prime minister, a life peerage. Bower did say in his acknowledgements that he had never discussed Johnson with his wife, which showed a remarkable lack of curiosity on his part. Many couples with no connection to Johnson have from time to time asked each other what they think of his latest behaviour. Not the least of his services to his country was his provision of a topic of conversation which occasionally put a smile on the faces even of those who disapproved of him.

When Paul Goodman and I interviewed Johnson for ConservativeHome on the eve of the 2019 general election, we were ushered into a changing room at the Copper Box Arena in the Queen Elizabeth Olympic Park in London. Johnson was about to address an audience of about 3,000 Conservatives, and seemed entirely relaxed. Only he, his press man, Lee Cain, Goodman and I were present. Sandwiches still in their supermarket wrappers were strewn across a makeshift table. We were surrounded by pegs, lockers and showers: the usual furnishings of a changing room. For some reason there was a loud noise of running water.

'We've got to beat the cistern,' Johnson said.

ConHome: In your conference speech you said this: 'I am going to quote that supreme authority in my family – my mother. And by the way for keen students of the divisions in my family you might know that I have kept the ace up my sleeve – my mother voted Leave.'

Did she tell you why she voted Leave?

Johnson [after a pause]: Um. I don't want to go into it. I would rather she spoke for herself. Not that I'm going to encourage her to give you an interview.

ConHome [quoting from the conference speech]: 'My mother taught me . . . to believe strongly in the equal importance, the equal dignity, the equal worth of every human being on the planet.'

Johnson: Yes, that's true.

ConHome: Can you remember an incident that summed that up, something that encapsulated that when you were a kid?

Johnson [after a longer pause, and looking highly emotional]: Yes, um [the noise of the cistern begins to obscure his words], I don't want to go into that too much if that's all right, but my mother certainly believed very strongly in that kind of thing.

ConHome: What has she said to you about the election?

Johnson [after some incoherent spluttering]: That's enough family, Ed.

ConHome: You did mention her in your conference speech.

Johnson: I did. That's perfectly true. That's a very good point, but I think that's enough. The *dea ex machina* has been produced and is now going to disappear behind the proscenium arch or whatever it is.

Characteristic reticence. He won't take us into those personal regions. And yet no other politician refuses to go there while communicating such deep emotion. Even while we are kept at arm's length, we are also allowed in, or perhaps one should say we can't be kept out. Kenneth Tynan wrote that Laurence Olivier, whose mother died when he was twelve, could tap 'a pipeline to some tremendous childhood pain inside him'. So too Johnson. He did not erect the impermeable screen which so many Englishmen place around their emotions. Instead he told jokes, another English stratagem for dealing with pain. While still at school he made himself into a comic actor, and in this way sought, sometimes with a degree of success, to distract everyone, including himself, from his feelings.

VULNERABILITY

'I worry about what the hell he's going to do next,' Johnson's mother said in an interview with the *Radio Times* when her eldest son was still mayor of London, and went on: 'He is interested in the leadership of the Conservative Party, but he could equally well retire and become a painter. He's a very good painter. If he reaches the top, I'd feel very proud, but very anxious. It's a ghastly job being prime minister. He's not as daft as he behaves – and he does behave in quite a daft way. He's late for things and so on, but has a very good sense of what's important. I think he would be a good prime minister. He's a very kind man, very fair.'

There speaks a mother worried her son will suffer if he gets to the top in politics. She wishes he would pursue his artistic vocation, which she believes to be just as genuine.

From the age of five, when she discovered she could paint, which none of her four siblings could, this was her vocation, to which when he was yet a small child she introduced Boris. He too developed a love of painting.

In an interview conducted in 2015 by Mary Killen for the *Tatler*, Charlotte sought to correct some common misconceptions about her daughter, Rachel Johnson, and about Boris: 'Rachel is not the tough person she seems to be. She really minds about things and can become terribly upset and Boris is so soft-hearted.'

Here is a hard thing to understand about Johnson. How can he be so tough if he is also so vulnerable? His mother has given the answer to this question: she said his now well-known desire as a child to be 'world king' sprang from his need to protect himself. His robustness is driven by his vulnerability. Because he suffered so much, he had to make himself strong. Johnson is at once very sensitive and very vigorous; very needy and very protective.

Not everyone likes this mixture of qualities, or trusts it. His performance strikes many people as bogus. A friend of mine, an elderly woman of high intelligence who sat next to him at dinner when he was mayor of London, said later: 'There's a strange thing that's going on. He's both very strong – impenetrable – and really fragile – there's no "there" there – there's a performance he does really well – but underneath he's extremely fragile. The whole thing is so manipulative. Underneath there has to be a terror of being seen through, of falling apart.'

A secretary who worked for many years at the House of Commons was more sympathetic. She was not a member of Johnson's staff, but knew them well, and observed that 'all his staff really liked working for him', which was to his credit, for 'lots of MPs are so shitty to their staff'. Of Johnson himself she said that far from being the 'terribly confident bombastic person' which the world took him for, he was 'very shy, very sensitive'. She recalled that his secretary often 'found it very difficult to get him out of his room to come and address some audience'.

There could, of course, be various reasons for that. He can't bear being alone, and has a deep need for sympathetic feminine company, but he also can't bear being stuck next to unsympathetic people for hours at a banquet. Hence his tendency to arrive just before he is due to speak, and to skip the rest of the proceedings. Sensitivity has something to do with this.

In the spring of 1974, when the Johnson family had just moved to Brussels and Boris, known to the family as Al, was only nine years old, Charlotte had a nervous breakdown and was admitted to the Maudsley Hospital in London, suffering from Obsessive Compulsive Disorder. Professor Raymond Levy, who treated her, said later: 'She suffered from terrible OCD. I was the specialist at the Maudsley and she was one of the worst cases I've seen. She had a phobia of contamination and washed her hands until they bled.'

Her children would visit her in hospital, and then go away again. She felt desolate and so did they. Nor did her treatment work. It consisted of an early form of aversion therapy. Her hands were contaminated with filth, dog shit for example, and she was not allowed to wash.

While in the Maudsley she painted seventy-eight pictures. These works convey contradictory qualities. They are despairing yet hopeful, agonising yet redemptive. She is having a terrible time, she weeps and shows her children weeping, and not for one moment does she try to pretend this is not happening. There is a kind of Englishman who tries so hard to make light of suffering that the suffering itself is never faced, the loss is never mourned, reality is evaded. Charlotte never did this in her paintings.

And yet the Maudsley paintings evince also an inextinguishable love and a wry humour, as if to say, 'I know this is harrowing for us all, but somehow we will come through it.'

Thanks to the researches of Nell Butler, who tracked down hundreds of Charlotte's works, a major retrospective exhibition was held in 2015 at the Mall Galleries. Johnson attempted at this exhibition to buy a charming picture of himself as a small child perched in some branches and gazing intently out, entitled 'Alexander in his Tree', painted in about 1967, when he was three years old. It had been bought in Brussels by the parents of Isabella Di Carpegna, and had always hung in their kitchen. Johnson asked her to ask her father to sell him the picture, but she refused to do so.

These are pictures to which people become deeply attached. After 1978, when Charlotte and Stanley got divorced, she made her living by painting portraits, for which she charged, in the money of those days, between £1,000 and £5,000. In Butler's catalogue a grand, bohemian, left-wing world unfolds before our eyes. This aspect of Johnson's background tends to be ignored by his critics, who long sought to write him off as an out-of-touch Tory toff. He was closely in touch with the racketty, chaotic, generous-minded, unsnobbish but well-connected left-wing intelligentsia. His own mother belonged to it, and he has always sought, and surprisingly often obtained, the approval and even the affection of left-wing women. Charlotte herself said in one of the interviews at the time of her exhibition, 'I find it extraordinary that I should have married a Tory and have four Tory children. I've never voted Tory in my life. My parents were very socialist – rich social-ists with three cars and two houses, but they were socialists in the days when that happened.'

In my volume on Johnson's early life, I sketched Charlotte's family, the Fawcetts, and also Stanley's forebears. Because Stanley attracted more publicity than she did, and had trans-mitted his pale blond hair and the mannerisms of a stage Englishman to his eldest son, people assumed all the influence came from him, and overlooked Charlotte's contribution.

She got married again in 1988, to Professor Nicholas Wahl, an American authority on French politics, and moved with him to an apartment in Washington Square, New York. In 1989 she was formally diagnosed with Parkinson's disease, and in 1996 he died of cancer. Charlotte returned to London and continued to paint. No word of complaint escaped her lips as her Parkinson's got worse. 'She is almost a saintly figure, full of compassion,' her friend Mary Killen said in 2020. 'They all absolutely worship her, her children.'

MARGARET THATCHER

On Monday 7 October 2019 Johnson spoke at the launch party for *Herself Alone*, third and final volume in Charles Moore's biography of Margaret Thatcher. It was held in the Banqueting House, a magnificent double-cube chamber designed by Inigo Jones, the Rubens ceiling commissioned by Charles I, who twenty years later, on 30 January 1649, walked beneath it on his way to the scaffold that had been erected for him just outside in Whitehall.

'I go from a corruptible, to an incorruptible Crown, where no disturbance can be, no disturbance in the world,' the King said after delivering his speech from the scaffold. He laid his head on the block, signalled with his hand that he was ready, and a few moments later the executioner severed his neck with a single blow, calling forth, in the words of a witness, 'such a groan by the thousands then present as I never heard before and desire I may never hear again'.

The Thatcher launch was very enjoyable, and also very instructive. Johnson was in ebullient spirits. He was cheered as he came to the lectern, for many old friends were there from the *Telegraph* and *The Spectator*, publications for which both he and Moore had worked for most or in the latter's case the whole of their professional lives. Johnson's loyalty to institutions to which he himself has belonged is a Tory feeling, though not, of course, limited to Tories. Outside in Whitehall, Extinction

Rebellion protesters were blocking the road. Inside, Johnson began: 'This is a bit like a *Daily Telegraph* leader conference. I'm very glad, Charles, you were so concerned about my security, because my own team didn't want me to come to this event tonight because they said that there were some unco-operative crusties and protesters of all kinds littering the road and they said there was some risk that I would be egged on my way in here, and so I immediately asked the fainthearts in my private office, "What would Margaret Thatcher have done [laughter]? What would Maggie do?"'

After hailing Moore's book as 'the greatest work of modern British history', and saying it showed 'the almost obsessive lust for accuracy and detail that is the hallmark of all great *Daily Telegraph* journalists' (a joke at his own expense, accused as he is of being cavalier with the facts), he went on to talk about Margaret Thatcher.

I am aware that the most embittered enemies of Johnson will be getting a bit fed up – if they have not already cast this book aside in disgust – by the frequency with which I quote at length from his speeches. But a politician's speeches are his or her legacy. When giving a speech, a commitment has to be made to a position (or to a non-position, which is itself revealing of an inability to decide what one can say about some great issue of the day). Here is the chief form of political persuasion since ancient times. Oratory matters. It is not some frill, but structural. Like the Sermon on the Mount, it is a testament of faith, a guide to how, according to the speaker, we ought to live our lives. The fact that it is often done badly, and bores the audience to tears, does not mean it is unimportant. How stupid the politicians are who think that time spent writing speeches is time wasted. Barack Obama became president in 2008 by giving the best speeches, better by far than Hillary

Clinton's. The greatest politicians – Pericles, Cicero, Lincoln, Churchill – were great orators.

Yet Johnson's speeches have been almost totally ignored. This is the first book to take them seriously. I quote at length because I want you to be able to form your own opinion: I don't want to palm you off with a paraphrase, which is unfortunately all you get in most of today's political reports. The newspapers used to print the text of major speeches. Now they don't. The interested citizen is better off with YouTube.

In his speeches we see Johnson working out what he can say about the issues of the day. He tells jokes, for he knows how grateful audiences are to be amused. He cannot bear the self-importance of the prig who supposes that jokes are the enemy of sense. Jokes often illuminate a subject in a way nothing else can.

Here is what he said at the Banqueting House, beneath the Rubens ceiling portraying the apotheosis of Charles I's father, James I:

> Those of us who remember the late 1980s and early 1990s, and a few of you look as though you might [laughter], it is intoxicating to be plunged back into that drama.
>
> And at the heart of it is a single glittering and terrible event. An assassination. A political extinction of a long-serving monarch. And just like Julius Caesar, the drama raises in all our minds the question, 'Were they right, the people who done it? Were the regicides justified in what they did?'
>
> And I know that some of them are possibly here tonight [laughter], or some of them associated with them [half laughs himself], and all I will say is I make no comment on their motives except to say they are all honourable

men, Brutus, Cassius and the rest, they are all honourable men [applause at this pointed joke].

But what comes out so clearly from this book is that she was right and she was so prophetic. She was right to have secret dealings with Nelson Mandela and the ANC to bring about Mandela's release and the end of apartheid.

She was right to try to reform local government finance, by the way, even if the solution that she eventually chose [the poll tax], the one devised with characteristic brilliance by my friend Oliver Letwin [laughter], didn't turn out to be entirely popular.

She was right to oppose communism and to encourage the fall of the Berlin Wall. And right, by the way, to oppose the loony Left in London. One of the few occasions that I actually met her myself, someone, I think it might have been Charles [half turns to Charles Moore], tried to explain who I was, and she said, 'Ah yes, London. Someone really ought to get rid of that dreadful man Ken Livingstone.' And I was too bashful to explain that I just had [laughter].

She was right about the euro. She was right about the ERM by the way, wasn't she? She was right about the euro. Let's face it, she was right in her great 1988 Bruges Speech. And if the continent, if our beloved continent of Europe had followed her proposals then for the development of the EU I believe a lot of our problems would have not arisen and been solved.

And I hope therefore tonight that when we go out from this merry gathering, and when we are waylaid in the streets as I'm sure we will be by importunate, nose-ringed, dreadlocked climate change protesters, we remind them that she was also right before her time about greenhouse gases, and she took it seriously long before Greta Thunberg.

And the best thing possible for the education of the denizens of those heaving, hemp-smelling bivouacs that now litter Trafalgar Square and Hyde Park and the rest of London, the best thing for them would be to stop blocking the traffic and buy a copy of Charles's magnificent book, so that they can learn about a true feminist Green and a revolutionary who changed the world for the better.

One may note how trenchant Johnson is in defence of Thatcher, but how he also portrays her as a feminist, a Green and an opponent of apartheid. He mocks the regicides who overthrew her, and identifies himself strongly with her, but she is presented as a modern woman, whose life could be read with profit by climate change protesters. Thatcherites often attribute to her a stern, unbending, immutable body of economic doctrine. Johnson won't confine himself in that way.

And Shakespeare is there at the heart of what he says. Johnson seizes on 'a single glittering and terrible event', her assassination. He relates it to the crowd of partygoers in the room, already with several glasses of wine inside us. We have among us some of the regicides, or their associates. The question asked in all of Shakespeare's history plays is 'When is it right to rebel?' (see John F. Danby, *Shakespeare's Doctrine of Nature: A Study of King Lear*). It is also a question asked pretty much continuously by Conservative MPs. As I wrote this vignette in February 2022, they were asking it about Johnson, but no full-scale rebellion or coup attempt had been launched, and the will to go for him seemed to have waned a bit. Matthew Parris and many others were shouting encouragement from the sidelines. Parris had just ended his regular Saturday column with words addressed to Tory MPs: 'Your leader is a wrong 'un and must go. We all know that. But who is capable of leading with the guts to say it?'

Lady Macbeth put it more strongly than that, and prevailed. As I revise this book at the end of July 2022, Johnson has been overthrown, and accusations of regicide are once more heard.

All I remembered of the speech by the prime minister at the Thatcher launch was that I had laughed and laughed. Only by watching it again and writing it down have I realised how much there was in it. Johnson had thought carefully about how to praise Thatcher, as any Tory leader must, for to this day she is the figure who impelled many Tories to go into politics.

On the day of her death, 8 April 2013, Johnson, at this point mayor of London, did a camera clip in which he said the country 'has just lost its greatest Prime Minister since Winston Churchill', and described her as 'a revolutionary and . . . a liberator' who 'took on that cosy, clubby, male-dominated consensus, and . . . won'. Who else, one might wonder, could take on that consensus and win? In November of that year, Johnson offered his answer to that question when he delivered the third Margaret Thatcher Lecture at the Centre for Policy Studies, the think tank she and her close allies had set up in 1974 to challenge the post-war consensus. The first lecture in the series had been given by Rupert Murdoch, the second by Charles Moore.

In his lecture we see Johnson quite clearly positioning himself as the heir to Thatcher. He reminds people how low the country had sunk in the 1970s, which he was old enough to remember, and lists some of her achievements, before going on:

> She'd also done something less tangible and more impor-
> tant. She'd changed the self-image of this country. And to
> grasp what she did you have to remember how far we as
> a country felt we had fallen.
>
> Our country, Britain, used to rule the world, almost
> literally. . . . In the period 1750 to 1865 we were by far

the most politically and economically powerful country upon earth.

And then by 1914 we were overtaken by America, we were overtaken by Germany, and we had the world wars. And we ended up so relatively weakened that the ruling classes succumbed to a deep morosity that bordered on self-loathing, and we gave in to the reverse of the fallacy that gripped the Victorian imperialists – the reality of divine providence – that God saw a special virtue in the British people and appointed them to rule the waves . . .

The post-war generation had grown up reading this blimpish stuff . . . they then drew the logical but equally absurd conclusion that the shrinking of Britain must also represent a moral verdict on them all, but in this case the opposite, that we were now decadent, that decline had set in like death watch beetle in the church tower . . .

And Thatcher changed all that . . . She made it possible for people to talk without the slightest embarrassment about putting the Great back into Britain, and she gave us a new idea, or at least she revived an old one, that Britain was or could be an enterprising and freebooting sort of culture with a salt breeze ruffling our hair, a buccaneering environment where there was no shame, quite the reverse, in getting rich.

Freebooting, buccaneering, unashamed about getting rich, liberated from the morbid belief that Britain's relative decline represented a moral verdict on us all: who now could provide such leadership? Johnson did not have to mention his own claim. Nor did he need people to read or watch this now forgotten lecture. He just needed to go on working out the story he himself was going to tell, adding to it, developing it, showing that it was generous and inclusive, modifying it to take account of the ways in which things had changed since the 1980s.

So he warned in his lecture that people were feeling inequality more strongly than they did in the 1980s because inequality had indeed become greater. He said that if Thatcher were around now, she would take social mobility seriously, and would make far greater use of 'that most painful utensil of academic improvement', namely academic competition between children. Johnson is not by instinct a planner. With his magpie eye, he was looking for ideas whose time might have come.

Anyone can see he was not the same as Thatcher. Kwasi Kwarteng, whom Johnson would soon elevate to the Cabinet, has written in his book, *Thatcher's Trial: Six Months That Defined a Leader*:

As a leader, she constantly referred to her upbringing as the daughter of a preacher. Her imagery was infused with Low Church Christian references to the Bible, in particular to the New Testament.

Thatcher saw the world in basic, even simplistic, terms. This binary approach to life was at the core of her being. For her, the conduct of affairs was a series of conflicts between good and evil, between the free market and socialism, between 'people like us' and enemies. This Manichaean mentality was in many ways the source of her conviction and self-belief.

Johnson gave Kwarteng's book a puff: 'A masterpiece of historical reconstruction. I felt I was there.' One of his most amiable characteristics is that he will always find something nice to say about a fellow author's work. By this means he has disarmed more than one writer who had previously been scathing about him.

Some will see, in Johnson's admiration for Thatcher, a preposterous pose. But his attitude to her actually worked rather well. He expressed genuine admiration for her, while seeking also to transcend her Manichaean mentality, her natural inclination, when pressed to do something she believed to be wrong, to reply: 'No! No! No!' Johnson's natural inclination was to find a way to say: 'Yes! Yes! Yes!' But on Brexit, he found himself stuck, at the start of October 2019, in a Manichaean situation.

THORNTON MANOR

On the evening of 8 October 2019, Johnson contacted Leo Varadkar, the Irish prime minister. They agreed to meet on 10 October at Thornton Manor, a hotel just outside Liverpool which advertised itself as a wedding venue. Johnson and Varadkar envisaged a marriage of convenience rather than a full white wedding. There was nevertheless a certain amount of formality involved. Dominic Cummings wore a suit.

The Republic of Ireland, more deeply entwined with the United Kingdom than any other EU member, had much to lose from a No Deal Brexit. The most intractable question in the negotiations was the future of the border between Northern Ireland and the Republic, which would become, after Brexit, one of the EU's land borders, but which both sides had agreed to keep open. Did this mean there would instead be a sea border between Northern Ireland and Britain, with customs controls between two parts of the United Kingdom, and Northern Ireland subjected to EU regulations which it had no part in making? Theresa May had said no British prime minister could agree to such a thing. Prodigious amounts of time and effort had been devoted to this conundrum without solving it.

Varadkar had also, a few months earlier, met the Labour leader, Jeremy Corbyn, in Dublin. But as Gabriel Pogrund and Patrick Maguire relate in *Left Out: The Inside Story of Labour Under Corbyn*, this was for at least one member of the visiting Labour delegation the most embarrassing meeting they had ever attended. Corbyn could answer none of Varadkar's questions about how Dublin and the rest of the EU might help a Labour government get a deal over the line. There was a vacuum in Corbyn's thinking which he sought to fill by saying how anxious he was to protect the rights of the Irish community in Archway, in his constituency.

Johnson and Varadkar met alone. They emerged and said they saw the pathway to a deal. They took a walk round the garden, and were photographed on a path between two rows of lime trees. On his way home to Dublin, Varadkar said at the airport: 'I am now absolutely convinced that both Ireland and Britain want there to be an agreement.'

THE EU AGREES

On Thursday 17 October 2019, EU leaders including Johnson announced at a summit meeting in Brussels that they had reached agreement. David Cameron, appearing at the Harrogate Literature Festival, said of his successor but one as prime minister: 'The thing about the greased piglet is that he manages to slip through other people's hands where mere mortals fail.'

THE COMMONS DISAGREES

On 19 October 2019, the first time the Commons had sat on a Saturday since the Falklands War in 1982, MPs met to vote on Johnson's deal. He needed their support that day, because otherwise the Benn Act would come into force, obliging him to write to Brussels requesting that Brexit be delayed until 31 January 2020. Johnson said:

> Many times in the last thirty years, I have heard our European friends remark that this country is half-hearted in its EU membership, and it is true that we in the UK have often been a backmarker – opting out of the single currency, not taking part in Schengen, very often trying to block some collective ambition. In the last three and a half years, it has been striking that members on all sides of this House have debated Brexit in almost entirely practical terms, in an argument that has focused on the balance of economic risk and advantage. I do not think I can recall a time when I have heard a single member stand up and call for Britain to play her full part in the political construction of a federal Europe. I do not think I have heard a single member call for ever closer union, ever deeper integration or a federal destiny – *mon pays* Europe . . .
>
> With part of our hearts – with half our hearts – we feel . . . a sense of love and respect for European culture

and civilisation, of which we are a part; a desire to co-operate with our friends and partners in everything, creatively, artistically, intellectually; a sense of our shared destiny; and a deep understanding of the eternal need, especially after the horrors of the last century, for Britain to stand as one of the guarantors of peace and democracy in our continent – and it is our continent. It is precisely because we are capable of feeling both things at once – sceptical about the modes of EU integration, as we are, but passionate and enthusiastic about Europe – that the whole experience of the last three and a half years has been so difficult for this country and so divisive.

The divisions remained. Labour refused to play ball, and the Democratic Unionists denounced a deal which, they said, would introduce a customs border down the Irish Sea. The House backed an amendment from Sir Oliver Letwin which was designed to avert the continuing risk of a No Deal Brexit, should the House reject the prime minister's deal. MPs did not trust him anything like enough to allow him to behave as he saw fit. Johnson therefore had to comply with the Benn Act, writing to Brussels to ask for an extension until 31 January 2020, and even though he also sent a handwritten letter explaining why he did not personally wish for that extension, it was granted by the EU.

GENERAL ELECTION

Jo Swinson, since July the leader of the Liberal Democrats, had come to believe the only hope of stopping Brexit was to hold a general election. She expected the Lib Dems, as a whole-heartedly Remain party, to do well: they even produced a leaflet bearing her picture and the words 'JO SWINSON: Britain's next Prime Minister'. The Scottish Nationalists also expected to do well from a general election. They did not, however, have to vote for one, for the Labour leader, Jeremy Corbyn – sensitive to the charge of cowardice, undeterred by opinion polls which suggested Labour would do badly, and deprived by the Letwin amendment of the argument that an election could not be risked because during the campaign Britain might leave without a deal – abandoned his opposition to an election. On Tuesday 29 October the Commons passed a special bill arranging for an election to be held on 12 December, the first election in that month since 1923.

TORY DEMOCRACY

Tory Democracy, espoused with enthusiasm by Johnson in the 2019 general election campaign, is an alliance between a section of the ruling class and the working class, in order to enrage and outwit the middle-class prigs. The programme of this alliance is patriotism plus practical measures to improve the lives of the workers. Tory Democrats proclaim the greatness of Britain, and promise to preserve and increase it. They express with impudent freedom the conservative instincts of the working class: love of country, symbolised above all by the monarchy and the armed forces; contempt for high-minded liberals who claim to be the true guardians of the poor but in fact know nothing about them; respect for family, hard work, cussedness, cheerfulness and saying what the hell you like, especially if it shocks the liberals.

Tory Democrats roar with laughter at the latter-day puritans who wish to subject the country to a joyless rule of virtue, the continuation by other means of the English Civil War, described in *1066 and All That* as the '*utterly memorable Struggle between the Cavaliers (Wrong but Wromantic) and the Roundheads (Right but Repulsive).*'

LOW SERIOUSNESS

Matthew Arnold observed that the poetry of Homer, Dante and Shakespeare was characterised by 'high seriousness', and had no taint of charlatanism. To describe the politics of the Tory Democrats, a new term, 'low seriousness', is needed. Among the Tory Democrats there is, undoubtedly, a taint of charlatanism. They can be written off, if one wishes, as flippant, bogus, immoral, opportunistic.

They offer an attitude, a style, a disposition, which is easier to illustrate than to define, and which cannot be reduced to an ideology. At their best, they display courage, imagination and a sort of spontaneous common sense, emerging under the pressure of events. And they are never wholly frivolous. They maintain a serious commitment to the greatness of Britain and the welfare of the people. A Tory Democrat's instinct, both in politics and in journalism, is to handle some grave theme in so light a manner that it does not weigh on the spirits of the audience. Comedy is placed at the service of a message which can be stated in its baldest form in a sentence or two, and is generally rather serious. Johnson is a man of low seriousness, with more than a touch of greatness about him, but for most of the time it suits neither him nor his critics to admit this.

A DISREPUTABLE PRIME MINISTER

Johnson's opponents had no idea he was a Tory Democrat. Even if one suggested this to them, they thought it was an essentially frivolous thing to be, and therefore not worthy of their attention. But here he was, a Tory member of the ruling class who was going to 'Get Brexit Done' – the patriotism bit of the programme, bitterly opposed by metropolitan types – and employ more police officers, nurses, doctors etc., i.e. improve various public services on which the poor are particularly dependent.

The media was bored by Johnson's programme (which was the intention: the manifesto contained no surprises) and proceeded on the shaky assumption that if only one could uncover enough of the details about the man himself, one would understand him, and would be able to show he was a criminal. Reporters concentrate – it is their job – on what happened today, or yesterday, or at most a few years back. By doing so, they help to keep British politics relatively clean, for none of us is immune to the fear of being found out.

But just as fixing one's eye on the second hand of a watch is of limited value if one wants to know what time it is, so reporting in detail on the latest events does not, on its own, enable one to understand what is going on. Things that have been taking place in various forms for centuries are treated as if they have just happened for the first time. Johnson himself has often been regarded as an inexplicable aberration from an otherwise honest politics.

And yet the Conservative Party has often turned to gifted outsiders for leadership, some of whom have been shockingly disreputable. The most surprising example, and the one who casts the most penetrating shafts of light on Johnson, is Benjamin Disraeli, prime minister for most of 1868 and from 1874 to 1880. He started life as more of an outsider than Johnson. Disraeli was born in 1804 into the Jewish faith, at a time when Jews could not become MPs, a restriction which was not lifted until 1858. Luckily for him, his father, Isaac D'Israeli, well-known as a man of letters, fell out with the Bevis Marks synagogue and had his children, including the twelve-year-old Benjamin, baptised into the Church of England.

Every other prime minister in the nineteenth century went to a famous school, usually Eton or Harrow, and all but one other, Wellington, went to Oxford or Cambridge. This was the path followed by Johnson: those who write him off as a weirdo forget that he is in many respects a traditional figure. Disraeli went to Higham Hall School, Walthamstow, after which his father arranged for him to train as a solicitor.

This was not in accordance with the boy's wishes, for he was an extravagant youth, set on fame and fortune. While yet a teenager he borrowed heavily to invest in South American mining shares and wrote pamphlets to puff those stocks. At the same time he launched a newspaper, *The Representative*, which he intended would compete with *The Times*. These were rasher and more fraudulent speculations than Johnson's fabrication, while a trainee on *The Times*, of a quote about Edward II. The stocks proved worthless, the newspaper collapsed, and Disraeli found himself encumbered with debts of which for most of his life he was unable to get himself clear. In a bid to revive his fortunes, at the age of twenty-one he wrote a novel, *Vivian Grey*, in which he made fun of the investors in the newspaper, who included his father's friend and publisher, John Murray.

The novel, in which Disraeli pretended to a knowledge of fashionable society which he did not as yet possess, made him a laughing stock. Disraeli's biographer, Robert Blake, observes that the character of Vivian Grey, 'with his recklessness, lack of scruple, devouring ambition and impudent effrontery', is a self-portrait. Disraeli proceeded to suffer a nervous breakdown, after which he had an affair with a married woman before marrying, for her money, a widow twelve years older than himself, of whom he became very fond. Like Johnson, he had a deep need for, love of and dependence on women.

Johnson has published only one novel, and took two attempts to get into the Commons, which he managed in 2001 at the age of thirty-six. Disraeli needed five attempts, was elected in 1837 at the age of thirty-two for Maidstone, but was howled down during his maiden speech by some Irish members whom he had annoyed, and was reduced to shouting over the mocking laughter: 'I will sit down now, but the time will come when you will hear me.' Even at moments of acute embarrassment, Disraeli believed in himself. So too Johnson.

In 1841, when Sir Robert Peel came in as Conservative PM, Disraeli wrote to him asking for a job, and was refused. Blake writes of Disraeli that people 'did not trust him personally' and saw him as 'an insolent, mysterious, half-foreign adventurer with a libertine past'. In 1845, with a terrible famine impending in Ireland, Peel decided to repeal the Corn Laws, which kept grain prices artificially high. This infuriated his backbenchers, who were drawn from the landed interest and felt they had been betrayed. They were not eloquent enough to make their case for themselves, so Disraeli became their spokesman. He was unbelievably rude to Peel, ruder than Johnson has ever been to anyone. Peel felt moved to ask why Disraeli had asked him for a job. Disraeli denied asking for a job: a flat lie. From some excess of scruple, Peel, who still had Disraeli's letter, declined to publish it. As Blake remarks, 'It is not an episode on which his admirers care to dwell.' The same words may be applied to various episodes concerning Johnson – perhaps quite a large number of episodes.

Peel got the repeal of the Corn Laws through with the help of the Opposition, but his career was finished. The Conservative Party was very nearly finished too. The split was in many ways even more bitter than Brexit. Except for Lord Derby, who for the next two decades was to lead the Conservative Party from the Upper House, almost all the intelligent, high-minded, reputable people who were capable of transacting public business had sided with Peel. The backwoodsmen, who were far more numerous but also far less intelligent, were with Disraeli. The party was so deeply divided that it took twenty-eight years to win another majority. The lesson of Peel's action for all future Conservative leaders, including Johnson, was that whatever else they did, they must avoid splitting the party.

Readers may object that this comparison of Disraeli to Johnson does not really work, for they are too different. Disraeli in his manners, and admiration for Lord Byron, was a survival from the period before 1837, the year Queen Victoria ascended the throne, after which the rules of acceptable conduct in public life started within a few years to become more strict.

But although one might contend that Johnson too is a survival from a wilder and more hedonistic culture, that of the 1960s and 1970s, I do not for one moment pretend that Disraeli and

Johnson are identical. What I wish to suggest is that there is
something in the British people which for a time, though
perhaps not for very long, responds with joy to leaders like
Disraeli and Johnson. Many of us delight in them precisely
because they are less respectable than we are – less conscientious, less safe. As Paul Bloomfield remarks in *Uncommon People:
A Study of England's Elite*, 'The flamboyant Byron is the darling
of innumerable demure souls for whom he acts as a voluptuary
by proxy.' So too Disraeli: he thrilled Queen Victoria, who in
her widowhood had become the epitome of middle-class
respectability, in part because he himself was not a prude, but
let his imagination run riot and flattered her outrageously. He
poured an unfailing fountain of compliments into the emotional
desert that her life had become since her husband died, and
she blossomed for the first time since Prince Albert's death.
Gladstone, a hundred times more high-minded than Disraeli,
had not the faintest idea how to get on with the Queen, who
complained of him, and treated him unkindly and unfairly.

The art of seduction: the more we disapprove of it, the more
delighted we are when by some lucky chance we find ourselves
seduced. Disraeli and Johnson set out to seduce the British
people. In 1867 Disraeli wangled a bill through the Commons
which enfranchised about twice as many people as the previous
year he had condemned Gladstone for trying to enfranchise.
This, people said, was unscrupulous of Disraeli. Lord Robert
Cranborne, a stern, unbending Tory, denounced him as an
'adventurer' who was 'without principles or honesty', and
resigned from the government.

Johnson has been subjected to strictures at least as severe.
There is a kind of stern, unbending Tory who finds him intolerable. So too do various other stern, unbending critics who
cannot forgive the unscrupulous way in which he wangled

Brexit through. Here he bears a close resemblance to Disraeli. The measure – the Brexit Bill, the Reform Bill – needed to go through, and there was no altogether reputable way to do it. Disraeli and Johnson saw the way the world was moving, and contrived to move with it. This is not one of the most elevated political arts, but if revolution is to be avoided it is one of the most necessary.

Disraeli loved risk, and so does Johnson. Here is another affinity between them. Disraeli could never bring himself to be straight about the dangerous amounts of money he owed. Nor is Johnson inclined to be straight about various inglorious personal matters. Neither of them approaches the American ideal, the young George Washington, confessing to his father that he has cut down the cherry tree with his hatchet (a story which seems, alas, to have been made up by Parson Weems – see *Gimson's Presidents*).

At the end of his great volume, Blake writes:

Where Disraeli excelled was in the art of presentation. He was an impresario and an actor manager. He was a superb parliamentarian, one of the half dozen greatest in our history. He knew how much depends upon impression, style, colour; and how small a part is played in politics by logic, cool reason, appraisal of alternatives. That is why politicians appreciate him. They realise that a large part of political life in a parliamentary democracy consists not so much in doing things yourself as in imparting the right tone to things that others do for you or things that are going to happen anyway. They know how much the art of politics lies in concealing behind a façade of rigid adherence to immutable principle those deviations or reversals which events and responsibility so often force upon governments.

When one looks at those commentators of the present day who suggest that 'rigid adherence to immutable principle' is all that is required to attain political perfection, one cannot help thinking they should go away and read Blake.

DISRAELI'S HEIR

As Disraeli lay dying in the spring of 1881, he was asked if he would like a visit from Queen Victoria, who had often sent him primroses, and this time proposed to deliver them in person. 'No,' he replied, 'it is better not. She'd only ask me to take a message to Albert.' Even at the end, Disraeli's lightness of touch, his ability to see the comic aspect of grave questions, did not desert him. The Queen had a plaque erected to him in the church in the park at Hughenden, Disraeli's house in Buckinghamshire:

> To the dear and honoured memory of
> Benjamin Earl of Beaconsfield
> this memorial is placed by
> his grateful sovereign and friend
> Victoria R. I.
> Kings Love Him That Speaketh Right
> Proverbs xvi 13

It is the only known example of a monument erected by a reigning monarch to one of her own subjects. Disraeli lay side by side with his beloved Mary Anne at Hughenden, and the world moved on without him.

But not long afterwards an extraordinary thing happened. On the second anniversary of Disraeli's death, 19 April 1883, a statue of him was unveiled at Westminster, a ceremony for which many wore bunches of primroses in their buttonholes, no less an authority than the Queen having declared, perhaps erroneously, that 'it was his favourite flower'. Lord Randolph Churchill, a brilliant and rebellious young Tory MP who was already notorious for the rudeness of his attacks on his party leader, Sir Stafford Northcote — 'third-rate', 'apathetic', 'cretin' — wished, at the age of thirty-four, to come before the public as the heir to Disraeli, who almost forty years earlier had been amazingly rude about the then Conservative leader, Sir Robert Peel. Meetings were held at the Carlton Club to plan the formation of 'a new political society which should embrace all classes and all creeds except atheists and enemies of the British nation'. The Primrose League was launched in November 1883, and soon became amazingly popular, by far the largest mass political movement in Britain, within eight years attracting a million members, most of them working class. By 1910 it boasted, with perhaps a touch of exaggeration, that it had two million members, far more than the Conservative Party itself: a massive army of volunteers, much needed after 1883, when, under the Corrupt Practices Act, strict spending limits were introduced for general elections.

Disraeli is the only prime minister ever to have been honoured by the creation of a posthumous cult. When the wife of an Oxford don suggested to Lord Randolph that the members of the Primrose League should be given some solid political education, he replied: 'No, the only way is to amuse them: they're quite incapable of anything else.' Lord Lexden, author of *A Gift from the Churchills: The Primrose League 1883–2004*, remarks of Lord Randolph: 'Churchill may not have been the first to realise that most Tories would rather laugh than think: but he was the first to make politics real fun for them.' They laughed with incredulous joy when in his address in 1886 to the electors of South Paddington, Lord Randolph described Gladstone's plan for Home Rule for Ireland as a 'monstrous mixture of imbecility, extravagance and political hysterics', the product of 'senile vanity', produced 'to gratify the ambition of an old man in a hurry'.

The League offered tremendous opportunities for dressing up, wearing fancy badges and other insignia, playing sports and singing songs, going to dances, picnics, teas and fetes. Yet it was also serious: Lord Randolph's mother, the Duchess of Marlborough, who within the League was President of the Ladies' Grand Council, said the aim was 'to show the nation that the Conservatives are interested in the wellbeing and comfort of the people'. For the first time, women played a large role in a mass political organisation.

Lord Randolph soon blew himself up. Tory Democrats, being risk takers, quite often do blow themselves up. At the end of 1886, he made the error of threatening, after only a few months as chancellor of the exchequer, to resign because of a disagreement over defence spending. The prime minister, Lord Salisbury (previously encountered as Lord Robert Cranborne), to whom Lord Randolph was an exceedingly tiresome colleague, got rid of him by accepting the resignation. In 1895, still only forty-five years old, Lord Randolph died, probably of syphilis.

Why touch on this unhappy figure here? Because Lord Randolph had a son, Winston Churchill, who venerated his memory, kept it alive by writing a two-volume biography which is a model of filial understanding and love, and adopted from his father the politics of Tory Democracy instilled by Disraeli himself.

In 2014, Johnson brought out a book which was intended to introduce Winston Churchill to a new generation. In an early chapter called 'The Randolph Factor', Johnson draws on a curious story written by Winston in 1947, *The Dream*, about Randolph appearing to him, and goes on to explain:

> Both Churchills, father and son, are avowedly working in the tradition of that greatest of all Tory magicians and opportunists, Benjamin Disraeli. Randolph was Disraeli's disciple and his vicar upon earth . . .
>
> As Randolph tells his son in *The Dream*, 'I always believed in Dizzy, that old Jew. He saw the future. He had to bring the British working man into the centre of the picture.' The two Churchills – father and son – were, as Winston put it, the 'bearers of the mantle of Elijah', the heirs of Disraeli.

Churchill today commands so much attention that Disraeli has faded out of the picture. But Disraeli, who laughed at the prigs and in old age told Lord Randolph 'I never was respectable myself', reveals much more about Johnson.

The best of Disraeli's seventeen novels are *Sybil* and *Coningsby*. The latter contains the conversation between two political fixers, Tadpole and Taper, which ends with the immortal words: 'A sound Conservative government,' said Taper musingly. 'I understand. Tory men and Whig measures.'

If one replaces 'Whig' with 'Labour', that is a pretty good description of what Johnson, with breathtaking impudence, has done. He is a joker with a brilliant instinct for power who yearns for immortal fame. He is Disraeli's heir.

VOX PUB IN WEST BROMWICH

On the afternoon of 5 November 2019, I met a woman in her forties in a pub in West Bromwich, in the West Midlands, a pint of lager sitting untouched on the table in front of her, and recorded what she had to say about the general election: 'I have never been for the Conservatives. I have always been for the people. As for Boris Johnson, he is such a fool. He's the most charismatic fool that I have ever met. If I was going to vote, I'd vote for Boris Johnson because he's a fool. I don't care that he's lied and cheated because that is his way and I support Boris. I will definitely vote for Boris, liar, cheat and fool! And for Brexit! I want to get out.'

And here is a man, a bus driver, talking in a calmer tone in the same pub, but sounding just as resolute: 'Boris Johnson is doing what he said he's going to do. He's like Trump, Mr Donald Trump. Trump is sound without the shadow of a doubt. Mr Boris Johnson, I like him. Okay, he's had a bit of argy-bargy with his other half, but that's water under the bridge. Boris is having my vote without a shadow of a doubt. Round here, they're all swinging to the Conservatives. It needs someone to kick Mr Watson off his pedestal. Get a woman in there. We need a strong Labour woman on Sandwell Council.'

'Round here' refers to the parts of the West Midlands nearest to West Bromwich East, the constituency of Tom Watson, deputy leader of the Labour Party. The day before these conversations, the *Sun* reported that the Conservatives were hoping to defeat Watson. This seemed on the face of it a tall order: Watson had a majority of 7,713, and the seat had been Labour ever since its creation in 1974. In 1983, when the Conservative candidate fell only 298 votes short of Labour, the Liberals came a strong third, which was unlikely to happen this time, for the Liberal Democrats had done poorly here in recent years. But the day after these voters offered their opinions, Watson announced that he was standing down both as Labour's deputy leader and as MP for West Bromwich East, held by him for the past eighteen years.

The cut-through issue in the West Midlands was Brexit. It was mentioned without any prompting by almost everyone. Here is a retired builder from Walsall, a borough where the Conservatives already held two out of the three parliamentary seats: 'I'll vote for the one that gets us out [of the EU]. I think it's absolutely disgusting. It's three years now. I will definitely vote for Boris Johnson because he's done more to get us out than anyone else. And all my friends in Walsall feel the same way. Well beyond Walsall.'

On being asked whether he usually voted Conservative, the builder replied: 'Well no. I don't stay with the same one. It's whoever I think is best at the time. If that Labour chap [Jeremy Corbyn] gets in the only thing to do is to leave England and go and live somewhere else. Because it'll be a disaster with him. What's the other one? The Liberal Democrats. If they got in it'd be the end of democracy altogether. They said they'd take no notice of the referendum full stop. What would be the point in voting again?'

A courier broke into the conversation: 'Don't talk about Corbyn in this town. The man who hates Britain. I've voted Labour all my life. I come from a Labour family. But I would never ever vote Labour while Jeremy Corbyn has anything to do with it. And we need to get Tom Watson out of this town. Sixty-seven per cent of people here voted to leave. He's supposed to represent us. This time I'm voting Conservative.'

Nigel Farage's name came up from time to time, but as someone people had voted for in the past. Only one man said he would be voting for Farage this time, while lamenting that this would be a wasted vote. Opinion polls showed Johnson was more popular than Corbyn. But the polls could not convey the way people talked about Johnson, or the strength of their feeling about him, and about the cause which for them he represented. These voters did not regard the prime minister as a saint, but they did regard him as the champion of Brexit, a cause dear to them, and one which they were enraged to see other politicians deserting.

'Obviously he's well educated compared to us plebeians round here,' one man said, in a friendly tone which indicated that, for him, this was no reason not to support the prime minister.

The High Street in West Bromwich contains some fine buildings, including the Central Library, entered beneath stained-glass images of Shakespeare and Milton. One finds oneself in an entrance hall adorned with mosaics, tiles, paintings, busts of local worthies, memorials to the dead of two world wars, an inscription which reads, 'This Building is the Gift of Mr Andrew Carnegie to the Borough 1906', and the arms of the town with its motto, '*Labor vincit omnia*'.

Work conquers all, but in recent decades West Bromwich has not always had enough work. The High Street, some of which was pedestrianised, contained numerous charity shops and lunch cost only two pounds in the Poundbakery – 'Tasty Baking at Tasty Prices'. A pub just along the road was closed and semi-derelict, and there were a number of other empty premises. Out-of-town shopping, the easiest way to pick up supplies by car, has hit streets like this one hard.

I asked the respectable middle-aged lady sitting on the bench beside me, her woollen coat adorned with a metal poppy, how she expected to vote in the general election – a rather personal question, but one she received with friendliness, saying: 'I don't know. What's he done for me anyway? Not a lot. I do vote Labour, yes. I don't know. I ain't got no interest in it. Once they're there [in Parliament], they don't want to know the little people.'

And what does she think of Boris Johnson? 'I don't like him,' the lady replied with a smile. 'I don't like him at all.' Why doesn't she like him? 'I don't know,' she said. 'They're only out for themselves. We don't exist. They're only in there for the money. This country is shit.'

A pollster might put this lady down as a 'don't know', but those words do not do justice to the depth of her disillusion. Five weeks later, the Conservatives took West Bromwich East by 1,593 votes, and also captured from Labour the adjoining seat of West Bromwich West.

BRUTAL LOGIC

The brutal logic of Britain's first-past-the-post electoral system asserted itself. Johnson had united under his leadership all those who, in the words of the Conservative election slogan, wanted to Get Brexit Done. People could see that a second party devoted to that aim would only reduce the chances of achieving it. On 11 November 2019 Nigel Farage, leader of the Brexit Party, recognised this, and announced the withdrawal of its candidates in the 317 seats won by the Conservatives last time.

On 19 November, during a television debate with Jeremy Corbyn, Johnson was asked by the moderator, Julie Etchingham: 'Does the truth matter in this election?'

He replied: 'I think it does, and I think it very important.'

The audience laughed spontaneously, even with enjoyment. He had entertained them. His mishaps entertained them most of all. Meanwhile Labour tied itself in knots on the Brexit issue. It said it would secure a 'sensible' new Brexit deal in Brussels, which it would then put to the people, 'alongside the option to remain'. This meant some of its negotiators, such as Sir Keir Starmer, who were devout Remainers, would campaign in this second referendum against the deal they had just reached in Brussels. 'If the trumpet give an uncertain sound, who shall prepare himself to the battle?' St Paul asked. Labour's trumpet gave an uncertain sound.

THE INSIGNIFICANCE OF
ANDREW NEIL

On 5 December 2019, Andrew Neil attacked Johnson for refusing repeated requests for an interview. Even the most brilliant television interviewers tend to fade quickly from the public mind: who now talks about John Freeman, Brian Walden or Sir Robin Day? But Andrew Neil was at this time still a considerable figure, and had been since 1983, when he became, at the age of thirty-four, editor of the *Sunday Times*, which he remained until 1992. Over the succeeding years he had earned a reputation as perhaps the most formidable interviewer on British television. Neil was also chairman of *The Spectator*, and in 2005 brought to an end Johnson's editorship of that magazine. In the summer of 2019 Neil burnished his reputation by scoring off Johnson during the Tory leadership campaign, in an interview which included the following very funny exchanges, each man striving to patronise the other:

Neil: Only recently you claimed that we could leave on No Deal and we just carry on trading with the EU as now, pending a new trade agreement to be done. You now know that's not true, don't you?

Johnson: Well, it depends what sort of terms you strike with the EU. It might be possible and I accept that this has to be done by mutual agreement but it might be possible, for instance, as we come out to agree under GATT 24 paragraph 5B that both sides agree to a standstill, a protraction of their existing zero-tariff, zero-quota arrangements until such time as we do a free trade deal . . .

Neil: So how would you handle – you talk about Article 5B in GATT 24—

Johnson: Paragraph 5B. Article 24. Get the detail right. Get the detail right, Andrew. It's Article 24 paragraph 5B.

Neil: And how would you handle paragraph 5C?

Johnson: I would confide entirely in paragraph 5B, because that is—

Neil: How would you get round what's in 5C?

Johnson: I would confide entirely in paragraph 5B which is enough for our purposes.

Neil: Do you know what's in 5C?

Johnson: No.

Neil: I thought you were a man of detail.

Johnson: Well, you didn't even know whether it was an article or a paragraph, but—

Neil: But that's not the details you told those Tory hustings . . .

Johnson: There's enough in paragraph 5B to get us the agreement that we want.

Neil: No. 5C says you don't just need the EU's approval; you need to agree with the EU the shape of a future trade agreement—

Johnson: Yes.

Neil: And a timetable to getting towards it. Now can I just point out—

Johnson: But why should that – can I ask you—

Neil: Okay, I'll tell you why.

Johnson: Why, why this defeatism? Why this negativity?

Neil: I'll tell you why – you ask and I'll tell you and you can respond.

Johnson: Why can't we rely on the common sense and good will of both parties to get this done?

Neil: Because you would want the EU to agree to the status quo, for perhaps up to ten years, but you would have walked away from the May agreement, you would have withdrawn the 39 billion—

Johnson: Why do you say ten years?

Neil: You would have – because that's what Article 5B allows. You may have to read it again.

Neil had succeeded in presenting himself as the man with a superior grasp of essential detail, even telling Johnson at one point: 'This bluster may get you through the hustings. It doesn't work with me. I'm trying to pin you down on some facts.'

When the general election was called, Neil applied for another interview with Johnson, and at length felt moved to do a piece to camera describing how things stood:

We have been asking him for weeks now to give us a date, a time, a venue. As of now, none has been forthcoming. No broadcaster can compel a politician to be interviewed, but leaders' interviews have been a key part of the BBC's election coverage for decades. We do them on your behalf to scrutinise and hold to account those who would govern us. That is democracy.

We've always proceeded in good faith that the leaders would participate, and in every election they have. All of them, until this one. It is not too late. We have an interview prepared – oven ready, as Mr Johnson likes to say. The theme running through our questions is trust, and why so many times in his career in politics and journalism, critics and sometimes even those close to him have deemed him to be untrustworthy.

If Neil had been able to interview Johnson, he would have asked him difficult questions about trust, and would have done so in the name of democracy. A note of insufferable self-importance can be detected in Neil's account, and also a sense of being unjustly spurned. As the man with the facts, he believes he is qualified 'to scrutinise and hold to account those who would govern us'.

Who could possibly disagree with this contention? It was surely to Neil's credit that he took the facts so seriously. The image of the noble journalist rises before us, incorruptible, indefatigable, valiant for truth, scrupulous about facts.

But there are actually several objections to Neil's approach to interviewing. One is that hostility to, or at least scepticism about, the subject of the interview is regarded as so great a virtue that it must be maintained continuously, and not just when there is reason to suspect disgraceful behaviour. This means any qualities which can only be understood from a position of sympathy are ignored. It becomes impossible to detect any virtues in Johnson. The presumption of guilt means that even when he behaves with wisdom, kindness or magnanimity, the journalist must not take this at face value, but must regard it as a mere screen for corruption. Believing the worst of Johnson, or of any other leading politician, is how one shows one is a proper journalist. Under these circumstances, it is impossible to report anything good he has done. He can never do anything good, for he is by definition bad. This is journalism's version of the doctrine of original sin.

And Johnson clinging by his fingertips to the edge of the cliff was a better story than Johnson not doing that badly all things considered, let alone Johnson doing well. Neil and many other journalists could be found suggesting at frequent intervals that this time Johnson really was finished, and was about to fall to his death. With unconcealed glee, they stamped on Johnson's fingers, doing all they could to make him plummet to his doom.

Neil's approach entails unquestioning reliance on 'the factual heresy', as it was termed by Sir Wilmott Lewis, for about thirty years the celebrated correspondent in Washington DC for the London *Times*. Claud Cockburn, who served in the early 1930s as Lewis's understudy, has given a brilliant account of this heresy. Cockburn became a communist, indeed by his own account a communist propagandist, and has left, in *Cockburn Sums Up*, one of the best of all journalistic memoirs. He was a friend of Graham Greene, and in the 1930s coined the phrase 'the Cliveden set' to describe an influential group who believed the best way to deal with Hitler was to appease him. Cockburn the commie troublemaker stood outside the liberal consensus, which meant that, like some Tory troublemakers, he saw things which were invisible to the liberal eye. Here is Cockburn's account of the factual heresy:

> To hear people talking about the facts you would think that they lay about like pieces of gold ore in the Yukon days waiting to be picked up – arduously, it is true, but still definitely and visibly – by strenuous prospectors whose subsequent problem was only to get them to market.
>
> Such a view is evidently and dangerously naïve. There are no such facts. Or if they are, they are meaningless and entirely ineffective; they might, indeed, just as well not be lying about at all until the prospector – the journalist – puts them into relation with other facts: presents them,

in other words. Then they become as much a part of a pattern created by him as if he were writing a novel. In that sense all stories are written backwards – they are supposed to begin with the facts and develop from there, but in reality they begin with a journalist's point of view, a conception, and it is the point of view from which the facts are subsequently organised. Journalistically speaking, 'in the beginning is the word'. All this is difficult and even rather unwholesome to explain to the layman, because he gets the impression that you are saying that the truth does not matter and that you are publicly admitting what he long ago suspected, that journalism is a way of 'cooking' the facts. Really cunning journalists, realising this, and anxious to raise the status of journalism in the esteem of the general public, positively encourage the layman in his mistaken views. They like him to have the picture of these nuggety facts lying about on maybe frozen ground, and a lot of noble and utterly unprejudiced journalists with no idea whatever of what they are looking for scrabbling in the iron-bound earth and presently bringing home the pure gold of Truth.

Johnson stands with Cockburn, not with Neil. The facts are 'as much a part of a pattern created by him as if he were writing a novel'. So why not invent them? After all, the only purpose of these facts is to illustrate a wider truth. What pedantry to insist that the facts themselves must be true.

The distinction here is between obtuse high-mindedness, and journalism as actually practised. Chris Moncrieff was by the end of half a century of service such a celebrated figure in the press gallery of the House of Commons that there is now a bar named after him. He was known for the accuracy of his reporting, but this did not mean imagination played no part in his journalism. Here is a line from his *Times* obituary, published on 23 November 2019: 'Sue Cameron, the *Financial Times* journalist, recalled spotting Moncrieff in the lobby and inquired whether he was looking for a story. Moncrieff replied that he already had the story, adding: "I'm just looking for someone to say it."'

That is a perfect account of journalistic creativity. He just had to find someone who would stand the story up. Journalists are dramatists who give shape and narrative to what would otherwise be a heap of meaningless facts. They strive, by skilful storytelling, to create a feeling of excitement, forward movement, the willing suspension of disbelief. Johnson is not such an unusual figure as his most literal-minded critics would have us believe.

One of Johnson's advisers told me why Neil's increasingly desperate demands for an interview were turned down: 'It was a classic example of being able to separate what Westminster thinks important and what actually *is* important. Most people don't know who Andrew Neil is.'

They knew who Boris Johnson was. He had become a bigger figure than any journalist, which was yet another reason why so many members of his old trade felt the urge to prove he was no damn good.

VICTORY

In the general election held on 12 December 2019, Johnson led his party to its best result since 1987, when Margaret Thatcher was leader. Like her, he had led and channelled a popular revolt against the way things were done before. The Conservatives gained fifty-five constituencies from Labour: Ashfield, Barrow and Furness, Bassetlaw, Birmingham Northfield, Bishop Auckland, Blackpool South, Blyth Valley, Bolsover, Bolton North East, Bridgend, Burnley, Bury North, Bury South, Clwyd South, Colne Valley, Crewe and Nantwich, Darlington, Delyn, Derby North, Dewsbury, Don Valley, Dudley North, Durham North West, Eastbourne, Gedling, Great Grimsby, Heywood and Middleton, High Peak, Ipswich, Keighley, Kensington, Leigh, Lincoln, Newcastle-under-Lyme, Penistone and Stocksbridge, Peterborough, Redcar, Rother Valley, Scunthorpe, Sedgefield, Stockton South, Stoke-on-Trent Central, Stoke-on-Trent North, Stroud, Vale of Clwyd, Wakefield, Warrington South, West Bromwich East, West Bromwich West, Wolverhampton North East, Wolverhampton South West, Workington, Wrexham, and Ynys Mon.

The Conservatives also gained three seats from the Liberal Democrats: Carshalton and Wallington, Eastbourne, and Norfolk North.

But the Conservatives lost seven seats to the Scottish National Party: Aberdeen South, Angus, Ayr Carrick and Cumnock, Gordon, Ochil and South Perthshire, Renfrewshire East, and

Stirling. The Conservatives also lost two seats to the Liberal Democrats, Richmond Park and St Albans, and one to Labour, Putney.

So overall the Conservatives gained forty-eight seats, taking their total number of MPs to 365, and giving them a Commons majority of eighty. Labour had suffered sixty losses and was left with 202 MPs. The SNP had risen by thirteen, and now held forty-eight of the fifty-nine seats in Scotland. The Liberal Democrats had gone from twelve to eleven seats, and their leader, Jo Swinson, had lost East Dunbartonshire to the SNP. Her decision to go for an election, and to fight it as a hard-line Remain party, had been a mistake.

Johnson recognised in his moment of triumph that all this could well prove transient. In the speech he gave before dawn on 13 December 2019 to party workers in the Queen Elizabeth II Centre in Westminster, he addressed himself to Labour voters in the north of England, the Midlands and Wales who had switched to the Tories:

I have a message to all those who voted for us yesterday, especially those who voted for us Conservatives, One Nation Conservatives, for the first time. You may only have lent us your vote and you may not think of yourself as a natural Tory.

And as I think I said eleven years ago to the people of London when I was elected in what was thought of as a Labour city, your hand may have quivered over the ballot paper before you put your cross in the Conservative box. And you may intend to return to Labour next time round.

As in so many of his speeches, one has the feeling that he is talking to himself as well as to the nation. Remember, he tells himself, I am mortal. The gods, and the people, could sweep all this away in the twinkling of an eye. I have got to work to keep these Labour voters, and they will like me the better for saying so.

He had won against Jeremy Corbyn, a Labour leader who repelled many traditional Labour supporters. Johnson's other adversaries were a motley crew who were unable to make common cause with each other. And he had a slogan, Get Brexit Done, which appealed even to many Remainers, so fed up were they with three and a half years of not getting Brexit done.

The stars would never again align in quite that way. Nor would his rivals be so likely the next time to underestimate his abilities. They would, indeed, seize on any chance to get rid of him before he could again overpower them on the campaign trail. They were out to get him. This victory might be as good as it would ever get.

'Let's get Brexit done,' Johnson said in his speech before dawn, 'but first, my friends, let's get breakfast done.' Another echo from an earlier success, when he heard on the morning of 8 June 2001 that he had been elected MP for Henley, and urged people to 'go back home and prepare for breakfast'.

CHAOS

'This is great. We can do stuff,' Lee Cain, Johnson's communications chief, said to Dominic Cummings after the election victory.

'We're fucked now,' Cummings replied. 'We've won. We're not needed any more.'

Cummings had been brought in to help solve an urgent and dangerous problem, and had succeeded. Brexit took place on 31 January 2020, by which time it felt like a bit of an anticlimax. A new and difficult negotiation then began, about the trading arrangements between the UK and the EU, which needed to be sorted out by the end of 2020. But the most acute phase of the crisis was over, and the prime minister had won. He was no longer a guerrilla leader who by daring exploits confounded the conventional forces arrayed against him. He had taken command of the regular apparatus of the British state and had to learn how to use it.

And in some ways he was not very good at this. He is not an administrator. That in itself was not a problem: the civil service is there to run the administrative side of things: no prime minister can find enough time for that. The trouble was that Johnson was a poor employer of administrators. As one of his advisers said in the summer of 2021:

He doesn't do his boxes. He doesn't really read his notes. It's very rare that he'll read the things you need to read before the meeting.

It depends what mood he's in. He does play up. If he's in a slightly whimsical mood he will latch on to something and someone, try to make them laugh. Officials can get slightly alarmed, they think the meeting's going badly, they don't understand.

He changes his mind an awful lot. Someone goes in and changes his mind. It does seem to be what sort of mood you catch him in. He will give multiple conflicting steers. The machine doesn't really know what to do. The machine gets into a horrible muddle.

He's terrible at confrontation, and he doesn't like being controlled, or pressured, so he sets up lots of rival camps, and can take soundings from whichever one he wants. It doesn't lead to efficiency. It's quite a dysfunctional court. Just a whole bunch of warring factions briefing against each other.

I don't think he's a very good prime minister, but I like him very much. He's a phenomenal politician. He's got this remarkable ability to connect with people. I've always felt there must be some deep sadness behind his absolute need to be loved. I feel that it's unfair to be cross with him for not being something he never was.

It's very difficult because he's extremely charming. You're often furious, appalled, enraged – you basically hate him and then you go into a room with him, and he's extremely charming, and it drives you mad.

Cummings could not make up for Johnson's deficiencies. A chief of staff was needed who could, in the words of one member of the government, 'glue everything together'. Cummings neither wished to be the Downing Street chief of staff himself, nor allowed anyone else to play that role. He had brilliant shafts of insight, but was brutally rude to those he regarded as useless, a category in which, with increasing frequency, he placed the prime minister.

Cummings sought to exercise complete control over the special advisers in each department. In August 2019 he had sacked in a most public and high-handed fashion Sonia Khan, an adviser to the chancellor of the exchequer, Sajid Javid. In February 2020, when Johnson carried out a Cabinet reshuffle, Javid resigned as chancellor rather than accept that his advisers would be answerable to Cummings rather than himself. The new chancellor, Rishi Sunak, was on good terms with Cummings, and was expected to be more pliable.

UNPREPARED

On 23 January 2020, Matt Hancock, the health secretary, gave the first Commons statement about a new virus that had been detected in China: 'The public can be assured that the whole of the UK is always well prepared for these types of outbreaks, and we will remain vigilant and keep our response under constant review in the light of emerging scientific evidence.'

Johnson's approach to illness was to ignore it. If he felt under the weather, he carried on working, and showed how robust he was by getting better without taking to his bed or seeking medical help. Nor did he appear to notice if someone in his office was unwell: few employers have been less inclined to say, 'You look terrible, do go home and lie down until you feel better.' Nor did he approve of working from home. Before the London Olympics he said: 'Some people will see the Games as an opportunity to work from home, in inverted commas. We all know that is basically sitting wondering whether to go down to the fridge to hack off that bit of cheese before checking your emails again. I don't want too many of us doing that.'

During February 2020 Johnson finalised his divorce from Marina Wheeler, and Carrie announced on Instagram that they had got engaged at the end of 2019, and that she was expecting a child in early summer.

In late February, Dominic Cummings came home one day and told his wife, Mary Wakefield: 'I've seen the plan [for dealing with coronavirus] and I'm afraid it's not a plan at all. It's just a plan to have a plan at some stage.' By the end of that month, the total number of confirmed cases in the United Kingdom stood at twenty-three. On 3 March Johnson said at a press conference that he was maintaining the human contact which came so naturally to him: 'I'm shaking hands continuously, I was at a hospital the other night where I think there were actually a few coronavirus patients, and I shook hands with everybody you'll be pleased to know, and I continue to shake hands.'

From 10 to 13 March, the Cheltenham Festival was allowed to go ahead, and was attended by a quarter of a million people. On 11 March Liverpool played Atletico Madrid at home, before a crowd of 52,000, including 3,000 away supporters, even though Madrid was already badly affected by coronavirus. Many people wondered if it was wise to hold these events, but no clarity yet existed. That came soon afterwards when television pictures were broadcast of intensive care units in Lombardy, the region of Italy round Milan, overwhelmed by Covid cases. The Italians were unprepared for the pandemic, which had so far struck them more severely than any country apart from China. Were the British any better prepared? Would Johnson and his colleagues be able to respond quickly enough? People began, quite suddenly, to feel frightened.

LOCKDOWN!

The pandemic was like a bush fire: it had to be put out, or at least damped down, quickly, or it would get out of control. If Johnson and his colleagues waited for full knowledge before taking action, they would be too late. By 14 March 2020, the number of confirmed cases in the UK had risen to 1,140. Epidemiologists at Imperial College London estimated that if nothing were done, 600,000 people might die. This turned out to be a gross over-estimate, but it helped shape actions at the time. No prime minister who failed to avert or at least palliate such a disaster could expect to remain in office.

On Monday 16 March, Johnson and the government's chief medical and scientific advisers began to hold daily press conferences, and advised people to avoid pubs, restaurants, theatres and 'non-essential travel', and where possible to work from home. On the same day, Johnson hosted, by video link, a conference call with over sixty manufacturers whom he urged to provide more ventilators, of which it was feared the NHS would soon run short. A participant reported that the prime minister had said this exercise should be known as 'Operation Last Gasp'.

Johnson was under immense pressure, and was accustomed to relieve tension by telling jokes. In these early days of the pandemic, he looked like a comic actor unexpectedly required to play the lead role in a tragedy, struggling to strike the sombre note which is required. Nor did he like each day having to impose new rules and regulations. Everyone knew he was not, by temperament, a martinet. He did not enjoy ordering people about. In one of his early press conferences he expressed astonishment that the police might have to be told to enforce these rules and regulations.

There was certainly no question of the rules being observed within No. 10. As one of Johnson's advisers told me later: 'It was awful, the approach in Downing Street to Covid: "I'm doing something important so I don't have to follow the rules everyone else has to follow." The prime minister almost died of that.'

Nor were other parts of the government machine working as they should. Here is Camilla Cavendish's account of conditions at the start of the pandemic in the Department of Health, published later in the *Financial Times*:

> In mid-March . . . I was wading through treacle in the bowels of the department of health as a lowly temporary adviser. I found myself with well-meaning people, some of them seriously clever, trapped in a byzantine web of arm's-length agencies they didn't control. Every bit of the system seemed to think it knew best, and almost no one seemed to look abroad. NHSX, a joint unit of government and the NHS, decided that it should build the NHS Covid app – and failed. Public Health England floundered, while telling ministers everything was fine. The local government department refused to believe for weeks that hard-pressed local authorities were sitting on emergency money which was supposed to save care homes.
>
> The lack of data was astounding, with different agencies presenting conflicting death figures. Gradually, the best

and brightest came to the fore, some of them very
junior . . .

Johnson and others were worried that the measures needed
to slow the spread of the pandemic might kill the economy. If
the economy collapsed, so quite soon would the NHS, even if
it could obtain sufficient supplies of personal protective equip-
ment, a seemingly simple task which for many months was
beyond the capabilities of the British government. A junior
doctor, writing for *Unherd* under the pseudonym Jane Smith,
described her hospital's response in the early stages of the
pandemic: 'A huge gulf developed between those staff members
terrified of the new virus and those who didn't believe it to
be anything more than a normal flu, if it even reached Britain
at all. I was in the "terrified" camp.'

The hospital had no data on how severe the infection was,
or how it was transmitted. The accident and emergency
consultant laughed when Smith asked whether an Italian tourist,
brought into hospital with a fracture, had been screened for
Covid. He accused her of 'racism' against Italians, and exclaimed:
'Whatever next? We test everyone who walks through the doors
for Covid?'

The very design of the hospital helped the virus to spread.
The office for six junior doctors was an old cupboard, meas-
uring two metres by two and a half metres, with no windows,
and had not been cleaned for five years. Fresh air, which turned
out to be an important way of limiting the spread of Covid,
was unobtainable, for the airy hospitals of an earlier era had
been replaced by modern buildings with low ceilings and very
poor ventilation.

The rule of thumb in the early days of the pandemic was at
all costs to get patients out of hospital. Many of them were

instead consigned to care homes, where they died. The disaster of overwhelmed intensive care units was avoided, but at the cost of a disaster in care homes.

In these perturbing or even terrifying weeks, when nobody could see clearly what was happening or how bad things would get, Johnson took on the task of keeping people's morale up. During his press conference on 18 March, he said: 'Now, I cannot stand here and tell you by the end of June we will be on the downward slope. It's possible, but I simply can't say that's for certain. Of course not. We don't know where we are, we don't know how long this thing will go on for. But what I can say is this is going to be finite, we will turn the tide and I can see how to do it within the next twelve weeks.'

To this he added: 'I'm often accused of being unnecessarily boosterish about things and I certainly don't want to strike that note today.'

Johnson learned how to do things by actually doing them, confident that by trial and error he would work things out, not downcast if his first attempts were hopeless. In the pandemic, that was often the only way to proceed. The press kept looking for things the government had got wrong, and often found them. Epidemiologists had never been in such demand, but their predictions seldom matched outcomes.

When Oscar Wilde visited Leadville, a mining town in Colorado, he saw a pianist sitting at a piano, above which was the notice: 'Please do not shoot the pianist. He is doing his best.' This was the attitude many members of the public took at this period to Johnson: 'Please do not shoot the prime minister. He is doing his best.' In such adverse circumstances, it was unreasonable to expect infallibility. But the more frightened people became, the more they demanded and applauded strong measures.

On 20 March the government ordered all pubs, restaurants, gyms etc. to close, and three days later Johnson delivered a televised address in which he announced the start of the lockdown: 'From this evening I must give the British people a very simple instruction – you must stay at home.'

DILYN THE DOG

'You want a friend in this town? Get a dog.' The observation is attributed to Harry Truman, who from 1934, when he was elected senator for Missouri, lived a lonely life in Washington, where he could not afford to rent an apartment big enough for his wife, daughter and mother-in-law to join him. Truman served as president from 1945 to 1953, and in the White House there was room for all three of them to come and live with him, which was perhaps why he evinced no enthusiasm for having a dog too.

Boris Johnson and Carrie Symonds got a dog in 2019, a step many couples take before having children. Dilyn was a Jack Russell cross, rescued by a Welsh animal charity from a breeder who was going to have him put down because he had a misaligned jaw. He was much photographed both with Johnson and with Symonds, who was outspoken in her commitment to environmental causes, including animal welfare. When Symonds went canvassing during the general election of December 2019, and when Johnson himself went to vote, there was Dilyn too, small enough to be held in their arms. Many voters take a more fervent interest in animals than in human beings, and even dog lovers who strongly disapproved of Johnson could not help being delighted to see Dilyn at the centre of the picture. Someone will one day write a history of Johnson's use of images. He has always been brilliant at attracting attention by providing irresistible pictures which also confirm that when, for example, he goes out for his early morning run, he rejoices to wear strange clothes, and is not embarrassed to look podgy. Here, the viewer may think, is a bizarre but also entertaining figure who has the energy to jog, but is not pretending to himself, as so many middle-aged Englishmen do, that he is a professional athlete.

As soon as Johnson and Symonds were known to be a couple, she was attacked in order to have a go at him. This was unfair: he, after all, was the elected politician. But most readers are more interested in girlfriends and boyfriends, in love, romance and sex appeal than in the dry details of a strictly political career. Bagehot, ever the realist, recognised that when he observed, in his essay on the monarchy: 'A princely marriage is the brilliant edition of a universal fact, and, as such, it rivets mankind.'

Even high-minded papers like the *Guardian* could not refrain from commenting on the new woman in Johnson's life, and on what she said about him. Here is Anne Perkins, writing on 1 August 2019, soon after the couple had moved into Downing Street, under the headline, 'Why Carrie Symonds is the embodiment of the Boris Johnson brand': 'Carrie Symonds is not some ingenue blonde playmate of a rich and powerful older man. It is almost worse than that. As the partner of the new prime minister, she has become the visible authentication of the Boris Johnson brand: that's Boris the priapic, convention-busting, law-unto-himself, human bulldozer; a man of as many conflicting opinions as wives and mistresses and more children than principles. For him, moving his girlfriend into Downing Street while he is still married to someone else is one more way of saying that the normal rules don't apply.'

It was also a way of saying that the normal rules were

changing. Only one of the fifty-four prime ministers before Johnson had got divorced while in office: the Duke of Grafton, who did so by special Act of Parliament in 1769. One other, Sir Anthony Eden, got divorced before becoming prime minister, by which point he was happily remarried. So Johnson was by historical standards unusual. On the other hand, for him and Symonds to live together before they got married was, by 2019, when they began to do so, normal practice.

On 14 March 2020, a fortnight after she had announced she was expecting her first child, *The Times* carried a piece under the headline 'Downing Street dog to be reshuffled', which reported that Dilyn was to be got rid of: 'one source said that the couple had already grown weary of the dog before they discovered that Ms Symonds was pregnant. A particular bone of contention was the mess that he created in their apartment above No. 11. "For a while there was dog shit everywhere in the flat," the source added.'

This report caused deep distress to Symonds. According to Dominic Cummings, giving evidence to MPs on 26 May 2021, by which time he had fallen out with Johnson and was doing all he could to destroy him, she called Johnson throughout a meeting of Cobra, the committee which deals with grave emergencies, demanding that he drop everything and ring the editor of *The Times* in order to get the Dilyn story corrected. The prime minister had to decide whether British forces would join an American bombing raid in the Middle East, and what to do about the Covid-19 pandemic: 'And the prime minister's girlfriend was going completely crackers about this story and demanding that the press office deal with that. So we had this completely insane situation in which part of the building was saying "are we going to bomb Iraq?", part of the building was arguing about whether or not we were going to do quarantine or not do quarantine, [and] the prime minister has his girlfriend going crackers about something completely trivial.'

One sees here Cummings' limitations. He thinks that to be accused of wishing to get rid of one's dog is 'completely trivial'. It actually struck at Symonds' whole idea of herself as someone who loves animals. She was held up to the public as a heartless fraud. At her behest a letter of complaint to *The Times* was drafted which stated, 'Dilyn is and always will be a much-loved member of our family,' and went on to say the couple felt they had 'no option but to pursue the matter formally' with the Independent Press Standards Organisation. Johnson declined, however, to sign this letter, which he felt would make him look ridiculous.

Just as his critics tried to get at him via Symonds, so her critics tried to get at her via Dilyn, who was later reported to have committed various crimes, such as damaging valuable books at Chequers, where he also mounted the stuffed foot of an elephant shot by Teddy Roosevelt, and pissed on an adviser's handbag. In the short term, these attacks on Symonds and Dilyn did not succeed in their objective, which was to drive Johnson out of Downing Street. Symonds demonstrated her fighting spirit, while Johnson, by declining to sign the letter to *The Times*, showed he had not gone mad. And many people who were not following the whole thing with obsessive interest felt it was unfair to pick on the prime minister's partner, who was, after all, quite young to be thrown into the spotlight, and might be finding life with the prime minister a bit of a strain.

THERE IS SUCH A THING
AS SOCIETY

On 29 March 2020 Johnson delivered a message from his Downing Street flat which had been shot on a mobile phone. He looked unusually pale, and although his voice was robust, towards the end of the two-minute clip he became almost breathless as he said:

> I want to thank everyone in the NHS, I want to thank all our public sector workers, the roll call of honour . . . Also everybody in the private sector, not just our supermarkets and all the workers in those businesses who help to keep our country going, but our pharmacists as well . . .
>
> And thank you by the way to everybody who is coming back into the NHS in such huge numbers. We have just this evening I can tell you 20,000 NHS staff coming back to the colours, doctors and nurses, it's a most amazing thing, and that of course is in addition to the 750,000 members of the public who have volunteered to help us get through this crisis.
>
> We are going to do it together. One thing I think the coronavirus crisis has already proved is that there really is such a thing as society.

Margaret Thatcher was famous for having said, in an interview in 1987 with *Woman's Own*, that there was 'no such thing' as society, words which her opponents interpreted (unfairly, if one read the whole interview, but understandably, if one wanted to cast her as heartless) as an endorsement of greed, selfishness, untrammelled individualism, a denial of social responsibility and community, a call to leave everything to the free market, with the devil taking the hindmost.

Here was Johnson explicitly repudiating that caricature. 'We are going to do it together,' he said. His language was inclusive and as usual he went out of his way to thank many people in unsung roles who were helping us to get through the pandemic, and used military expressions ('the roll call of honour', 'return to the colours') to convey the stirring message that we were going, by working together, to beat this illness.

Johnson recorded a lot of messages during the pandemic, and I had slightly forgotten about this one until I read *Boris Johnson: Porträt Eines Störenfrieds (Boris Johnson: Portrait of a Troublemaker)* by Jan Ross, of the Hamburg weekly newspaper *Die Zeit*, published in October 2020. Johnson's words sound weightier and more thoughtful in German. In English he is afraid of sounding dull. In translation, that fear is purged: he is no longer able to distract us from his seriousness by putting in all sorts of Wodehousian flourishes.

INTENSIVE CARE

At eight o'clock on the evening of Thursday 26 March 2020, members of the public stood outside their houses and showed their appreciation for NHS staff and other carers by clapping. This ritual, suggested by a Dutchwoman resident in London, Annemarie Plas, met a widespread desire to find some way to say thank you, though some people disliked feeling compelled to join in. The prime minister stepped that evening into Downing Street, where he was joined by Rishi Sunak, the chancellor of the exchequer. Johnson looked unwell but, as if to prove he was fit as a fiddle, clapped with gusto.

'Are you okay, boss?' an adviser asked Johnson at about this time.

'Strong like bull,' Johnson replied.

'Are you okay, boss?' the same adviser asked a day or two later.

'Strong like bull,' Johnson said again, banging his chest, but burst out coughing and was dripping with sweat.

'I've developed mild symptoms of the coronavirus,' Johnson admitted in a broadcast on 27 March, with heavy emphasis on the word 'mild'. He said he would self-isolate and work from home in his Downing Street flat. Viewers should 'be in no doubt' that he could continue 'to lead the national fightback'. A week later, he had not recovered, and admitted in a broadcast that 'I still have a minor symptom, I still have a temperature'.

Nadine Dorries, MP since 2005 for Mid Bedfordshire, could see that his symptoms were not minor. She was a fervent Johnson supporter, loyal to him through thick and thin, and in early life had trained as a nurse.

In July 2022, when I asked her whether she had saved the prime minister's life, she said: 'I spoke to him every day. I noticed the daily deterioration.'

Dorries raised the alarm: 'I was always bothered by the fact he didn't have a GP. He never has. What I did then, I put in place the process to get him seen by a doctor.' It was discovered that 'his blood oxygen levels weren't in a good place – he needed to go to hospital.'

So did she save the PM's life? 'I suppose I did actually,' she replied.

Johnson's condition was getting worse, and on the evening of Sunday 5 April he was taken by car, having refused to go by ambulance, to St Thomas' Hospital, which faces Parliament across the Thames, and was admitted as a patient.

The following evening he was transferred to an intensive care unit. About 46 per cent of Britons in the 50–69 age group who were admitted at this time to intensive care because of coronavirus died. The BBC prepared special broadcasts and newspapers got ready to publish special editions. Sir Keir Starmer, elected three days earlier as Labour leader, sent his best wishes for a speedy recovery, as did Jeremy Corbyn, whom he had replaced. Tony Blair, prime minister from 1997 to 2007, said on the *Today* programme on Radio 4: 'I have every sympathy and solidarity with him. I know it must be a hellish situation to be in.' Donald Trump said at his daily coronavirus press conference, 'All Americans are praying for him,' and added: 'He's a great friend of mine. I'm sure he is going to be fine. He's a strong man, a strong person.'

Carrie Symonds, who was heavily pregnant and while Johnson self-isolated could not live with him, went through torments. 'She did say to me she was terrified. She thought he was going to die,' a friend of hers told me. She herself had coronavirus, but her symptoms were genuinely mild. She was twenty-four years younger, and did not weigh 17 stone.

Some time later, I asked another close observer, 'Is Johnson Roman Catholic?' She replied, 'I don't buy it for a moment,' and then added of Symonds: 'His near death inspired her return to the faith.'

Once Johnson was on the mend, Symonds sent Dorries some photographs: 'I got some lovely pictures from the oxygen tent when he was back on Planet Earth.'

Johnson came out of intensive care on 9 April, and on 12 April, which happened to be Easter Sunday, was discharged from hospital and delivered the following message: 'I have today left hospital after a week in which the NHS saved my life, no question. It's hard to find words to express my debt, but before I come to that I want to thank everyone in the entire UK for the effort and the sacrifice you have made and are making . . . I thank you because so many millions and millions of people across this country have been doing the right thing . . . We're making progress in this national battle because the British public formed a human shield around this country's greatest national asset, our National Health Service.'

Johnson expressed, as a Tory Democrat, his pride and confidence in the nation and its people, who have protected, and are themselves protected by, the NHS. Some Tories found this continual praise for the NHS a bit hard to take. They thought the NHS was a much more flawed organisation than he implied, and that to praise it in this way was the sort of thing a socialist would do. In this they were right. There is a socialist element in Tory Democracy. As Harold Macmillan had said in 1936, 'Toryism has always been a form of paternal socialism.'

Johnson's Easter Sunday message lasted five minutes, unusually long for him, and when I listened to it again on Twitter in April 2022 had been watched 12.5 million times. He went on to describe his own experience:

> I want to pay my own thanks to the utterly brilliant doctors, leaders in their fields, men and women, but several of them for some reason called Nick . . . I want to thank the many nurses . . . I'm going to forget some names so please forgive me, but I want to thank Po Ling and Shannon and Emily and Angel and Connie and Becky and Rachael and Nicky and Ann.
>
> And I hope they won't mind if I mention in particular two nurses who stood by my bedside for forty-eight hours when things could have gone either way. They are Jenny from New Zealand – Invercargill on the South Island to be exact – and Luis from Portugal – near Porto . . .
>
> We will win because our NHS is the beating heart of this country. It is the best of this country. It is unconquerable. It is powered by love.

Johnson had never been more popular. He convalesced for a fortnight at Chequers, which many people feared was not long enough. When he returned to work, Rachel Sylvester, a columnist on *The Times* who had often expressed her disapproval of him, felt moved to write: 'This is Mr Johnson's chance to transform himself from populist rabble-rouser to national statesman. The question is, will he seize it?'

On Wednesday 29 April, a few days after Johnson returned to work, word went round that he would be missing prime minister's questions, and there was brief, feverish speculation about why this might be, before the news broke that Carrie Symonds had given birth to their first child. He was named Wilfred, after Boris's grandfather, Laurie after Carrie's grandfather, and Nicholas after Dr Nick Price and Dr Nick Hart who had saved the prime minister's life. There was, one might say, a lot going on, and though many people congratulated the couple, many also wondered how Johnson's convalescence would be affected.

BARNARD CASTLE

On the afternoon of Friday 22 May 2020, the *Daily Mirror* and the *Guardian* revealed that Johnson's chief adviser, Dominic Cummings, had driven on 5 April from London to County Durham with his wife, Mary Wakefield, and their four-year-old son. This looked like a clear breach of the lockdown rules. Millions of people had since 23 March observed those rules and stayed in their own homes, unable even to visit family members who were dying. Meanwhile, Cummings had driven 260 miles. He seemed to think there was one rule for people like him and another rule for everyone else.

This blew up over the weekend into a major storm. There was a great hue and cry against Cummings, led by figures such as Alastair Campbell, Tony Blair's former head of communications, and Piers Morgan, presenter of *Good Morning Britain*. Remainers who regarded Cummings as the evil genius of the Leave campaign saw the chance to take revenge. Tory MPs were inundated with complaints from furious members of the public who thought Cummings had behaved abominably and must go. Many MPs already detested Cummings, and yearned to see the back of him.

'It's not a good look, is it, Mr Cummings?' a reporter said to him outside his house in Islington, as Cummings put his son's bike in the back of the car.

'Who cares about good looks?' Cummings retorted. 'It's a

question of doing the right thing. It's not about what you guys think.' He insisted that he had 'behaved reasonably and legally'. If he and his wife both fell ill with Covid, there was no one in London who could look after their son, whereas in Durham, where they stayed in a house on land belonging to Cummings' parents, his sister and her children had offered to help with childcare.

When it emerged that, while in Durham, Cummings had driven on 12 April with his wife and child to Barnard Castle, a distance of about 30 miles, he said this was to test his eyesight, to see whether it was good enough for the long drive back to London. This explanation provoked incredulous anger.

One of Johnson's advisers said later: 'It wasn't our finest hour. You could feel the pressure in the building. The PM is incredibly loyal in these situations.'

A few moments later, the adviser repeated: 'It wasn't our finest hour.'

Johnson's instinct, when called on to sack someone, is to stand by them. He has probably noticed over the years that having in a few moments torn their first victim limb from limb, the feral beasts of the media return to the attack with sharpened blood lust. The prime minister informed the *Sunday Times* that he would not throw Cummings 'to the dogs', and at a press conference on Sunday afternoon, continued to defend him: 'I think he followed the instincts of every father and every parent and I do not mark him down for that.'

But once total intransigence was judged to have become impracticable, Cummings was told he would have to give a press conference in the Downing Street garden. For this curious ceremony, held on the afternoon of 25 May, bank holiday Monday, he sat at a small table, one of his legs hooked round the leg of his chair, plainly making a great effort not to lose his temper as he set out his case to journalists seated on widely spaced chairs. A year after these events, while giving evidence to MPs in May 2021, Cummings revealed that security threats made against his family were the real reason they drove to Durham, and admitted that not telling the full story at the time, and appealing for the public's sympathy, had been 'a terrible misjudgement'.

Cummings stayed in No. 10, but at heavy cost to Johnson, who lost all the popularity he had won when he was at death's door in early April. On Tuesday 26 May, Douglas Ross, a junior Scottish Office minister, resigned in protest at Cummings' continuation in office, and by 10 p.m. that evening, thirty-seven Tory MPs had called for Cummings to go.

The survival of Cummings, with his gift for picking fights, made it impossible to see how harmony could be restored within No. 10, or between No. 10 and the parliamentary party. Tory MPs felt spurned by Johnson, and feared he was leading them to disaster. If they became completely disillusioned with him, they would do to him what they had done to a number of his predecessors, including Iain Duncan Smith in 2003, Margaret Thatcher in 1990, and Edward Heath in 1975. They would sack him.

STATUES

On 7 June 2020 a statue of Edward Colston (1636–1721), erected in Bristol in 1895 in recognition of his philanthropy, was pulled down and tipped into the harbour, in protest against his connections to the slave trade. On the same day, the words 'is a racist' were daubed on the plinth of Winston Churchill's statue in Parliament Square in London. These events occurred during the Black Lives Matter protests which had been set off by the murder in Minneapolis of George Floyd, a Black man killed by a white police officer who pressed down on his neck for nine minutes.

Johnson took some time to respond to the Black Lives Matter protests. He sometimes found it expedient to wait, in a case like this where very strong feelings had been engaged, before making his own position known. He at length wrote a piece for the *Daily Telegraph*, published on 15 June, in which he said that 'rather than tear some people down, we should build others up', including the many men and women, most of them Black and minority ethnic, who had helped to make 'our modern Commonwealth and our modern world'. Johnson contended: 'If we start purging the record and removing the images of all but those whose attitudes conform to our own, we are engaged in a great lie, a distortion of our history – like some public figure furtively trying to make themselves look better by editing their own Wikipedia entry.'

The prime minister had thought more carefully about this than his critics gave him credit for, and had commissioned research by Munira Mirza, who had worked for him at City Hall and was now head of the No. 10 policy unit, and her colleagues. He wanted to make it as easy as he could for reasonable people on both sides of the argument to agree with him, and for those who abused him to sound unreasonable. He said it was time for a cross-governmental commission to look at all aspects of inequality. On his forays as prime minister into the culture wars, Johnson was desperately anxious not to be seen as nasty.

After the Barnard Castle affair, many people who had believed in Johnson when he was the great election victor broke cover and said they no longer believed in him. The story now was of a dysfunctional Downing Street which would not take advice and made unforced errors. The government picked a fight about free school meals with Marcus Rashford, a brilliant and charming young footballer, and lost. The first lockdown came to an end, but the easing of restrictions was frustratingly slow, and there were many things, such as testing for coronavirus, of which the government made an expensive and conspicuous hash.

The never absent tendency to believe the worst of Johnson as an administrator became more marked. It was fashionable to praise Rishi Sunak, the chancellor of the exchequer, as a much more capable figure, who at the start of the pandemic had within a few days devised a furlough scheme which averted mass unemployment. Tory MPs felt spurned, and were furious that Cummings was still in post. Within No. 10, warring factions leaked against each other to the press, and anyone who failed to get what they wanted blamed Carrie Symonds.

CAR CRASH COMING

'I could see the car crash coming,' Tim Montgomerie wrote in the *New Statesman* on 10 June 2020, 'and I couldn't bear to be part of it.' That was why, he said, in February he had refused a post at No. 10 as an adviser working on a 'grand project' to help the poorest, long a passionate interest of his. Montgomerie, once a warm supporter of Johnson, thought 'the turbulence in his private life does a great deal of the explaining' of what had gone wrong.

The car crash took longer to happen than Montgomerie expected, but in the summer of 2020 things did look pretty bad. A minister who took a comparatively benign, even admiring, view of Johnson said of the latter's illness: 'It has taken the stuffing out of him. The *joie de vivre* is lacking.' This same minister added: 'I think the money worries are true.' Divorce is a fearfully expensive business, and Johnson as prime minister was earning far less, about £160,000 a year, than he did when he could sell his services as a writer and speaker, which brought in at least four times as much.

But there were happier moments. *The Times* reported that on 19 June the prime minister had celebrated his fifty-sixth birthday with a small gathering in the Cabinet room, where Rishi Sunak and a group of aides 'sang him Happy Birthday before they tucked into a Union Jack cake'.

And there were also quite a few moments which it was hard

to imagine occurring under any of his fifty-four predecessors. So keen was he to show the world that he had recovered from his illness that while being interviewed at the end of June 2020 by the *Mail on Sunday* he said, 'I'm as fit as a butcher's dog now', and did a press-up on the floor of his study to prove it.

MESSAGE TO SCHOOL LEAVERS

At this low point in his fortunes, the prime minister issued a message on 10 July 2020 to young people leaving school at a time of 'the greatest crisis our country has faced since the Second World War': 'Your journey forward will not always be easy. There are always going to be people who want to pour a bucket of cold water on your ideas. People who like to sit on the sidelines, and criticise, sometimes with good cause, sometimes for the sake of criticising. And, of course, you may make some mistakes. But the important thing is to get out there, to keep picking yourself up, to keep trying again and again.'

Here is a particularly clear example of a speech addressed not just to the outside world but to himself. Johnson exhorted school leavers, and himself, to 'rugby tackle that opportunity to the floor'. Life is like rugby, a rough, skilful, exhilarating game which Johnson played, both at school and at university, like 'an absolute berserker', in the words of one of his own most respected teachers, Martin Hammond.

PATRONAGE

Sir Robert Walpole, prime minister from 1721 to 1742, defined 'the gratitude of place-expectants' as 'a lively sense of *future* favours'. Most politicians yearn to rise higher. They crave office, and then higher office. Who can gratify their ambition? The prime minister, who three centuries later was Johnson. Ministerial office was nothing like as profitable as it had been in the eighteenth century, but was just as keenly desired.

And so were peerages, many of which were handed out on the recommendation of the prime minister. A batch of these were announced on 31 July 2020. They included Kenneth Clarke, a distinguished parliamentarian, holder of many ministerial offices, several times a contender for the leadership of the Conservative Party, one of the twenty-one rebels on 3 September 2019; Philip Hammond, like Clarke a former chancellor and rebel; Jo Johnson, former universities minister and the prime minister's brother; Ed Vaizey, former culture minister and Gove supporter; Ed Lister, chief of staff to Johnson at City Hall and an adviser in Downing Street; Daniel Moylan, Johnson adviser on transport in the mayoral period; Veronica Wadley, who as *Evening Standard* editor backed Johnson to the hilt during his first mayoral campaign; James Wharton, a former MP who helped run Johnson's 2019 leadership campaign; Charles Moore, biographer of Margaret Thatcher and former editor of *The Spectator*, *Sunday Telegraph* and *Daily Telegraph*; and Evgeny Lebedev, owner of the *Independent* and the *Evening Standard*. Lebedev attracted more attention than the rest of them put together, and will be touched on later.

SCOTLAND

In August 2020 Johnson, Symonds, their son Wilfred and Dilyn the dog spent a few days on holiday on the Applecross peninsula in Wester Ross. They stayed in the Old School House, a small, isolated, white-painted building with views over the sea to Raasay, Rona and Skye. While there, Johnson annoyed the local farmer, Kenny Cameron, by erecting a tent without permission and lighting a fire. Cameron said: 'Mr Johnson is meant to be leading the country and yet he is not setting a great example. Usually if people want to go inside a fenced area, they ask for permission first, but I was not asked at all. It is only polite to ask.'

Johnson and Symonds had planned to stay for a week, but cut short the trip after the media discovered their whereabouts. To the question of Scotland he had as yet devised no very convincing solution, and was widely regarded as part of the problem. His ebullient Merry England persona was repugnant to the many Scots who preferred the evident moral seriousness of a figure such as Gordon Brown, son of a Church of Scotland minister from Kirkaldy, in Fife, and the last Labour leader under whom, at the general election of 2010, that party managed to retain most of its Scottish seats.

The Scottish National Party, now led by Nicola Sturgeon, had gained power in Edinburgh in 2011 and was still there, dominating the political landscape north of the border, for she communicated far more successfully with the Scots than Johnson did. He denied her the second referendum on Scottish independence which she demanded: the first one, in 2014, had been supposed to settle the question for a generation. But the danger still existed that having achieved Brexit, he would go down in history as the prime minister who lost Scotland.

LAW BREAKING

On 8 September 2020 Brandon Lewis, the Northern Ireland Secretary, said in the House of Commons of the Internal Market Bill, which overruled the part of the Brexit deal which introduced customs checks on goods moving from Britain to Northern Ireland: 'Yes, this does break international law in a very specific and limited way.'

His statement dismayed many Conservatives, including Lord Howard, party leader from 2003 to 2005, in which period he had become so infuriated by Johnson's misbehaviour that he sacked him. Howard said on Times Radio: 'It's very bad because it damages our reputation for probity and the rule of law. To hear a minister say at the despatch box you are passing legislation in breach of international law is a very sad day. I never dreamt I'd hear a minister, still less a Conservative minister, say such a thing.'

Sir Jonathan Jones, head of the government's legal service, and Lord Keen, advocate general for Scotland, resigned in protest. Geoffrey Cox, who until February had served as attorney general, said the Internal Market Bill was 'unconscionable'. Ed Miliband, for Labour, taunted Johnson about the bill in the Commons, mocking him as 'a details man' who 'doesn't know his stuff' and telling him: 'For the first time in his life, it's time to take responsibility.'

Two former prime ministers, Sir John Major and Tony Blair,

were among many others who condemned the bill, which was rejected several times by the House of Lords and before being passed into law was toned down in its application to Northern Ireland. Here, it seemed, was a provocation devised by Dominic Cummings and his gifted protégé Oliver Lewis which had been a bit too provocative. But as Charles Moore observed in the *Daily Telegraph*: 'The truth is that no independence struggle can be conducted with perfect decorum.'

WHERE'S BORIS?

A stormy sea, two abandoned oars, a small boat in danger of being upended by a wave, and within that boat, at the centre of the illustration, a hunched figure identifiable by his bright blond hair. This was the cover of *The Spectator* for 19 September 2020, painted by Morten Morland, and bearing the headline 'Where's Boris? *Fraser Nelson* on a government at sea'.

The editor of the magazine once edited by the prime minister reported that 'MPs who bumped into Johnson in the chamber last week said he looked exhausted, broken'. That is what others said too. Johnson was overburdened, underpaid, miserable, had not recovered properly from his illness, and was resisting the imposition of a second lockdown to avert a new wave of coronavirus.

At the back of the magazine, Toby Young, who had known Johnson since they were at Oxford together, wrote that 'I too have given up on Boris', who is 'no longer fit to be prime minister'.

One could multiply such testimony many times over. 'He reaches for acolytes, not friends,' one old friend lamented. Many who had once been close to him watched the unfolding shipwreck with dismay.

BOREDOM

How difficult it is to give a true sense of what it felt like to live through the Brexit negotiations. They lasted for years, and prompt the thought that the role of boredom in political life has not been sufficiently studied. Scholars and journalists have tended, understandably, to assume it would make a boring theme for an article, let alone a book. While working as parliamentary sketch writer for the *Daily Telegraph*, I tried never to say a debate had been dull, and attempted to make even the dreariest day amusing.

Just as the true eccentric is unaware of being unusual, so the true bore has no sense of being dull. Geoffrey Madan remarks somewhere in his *Notebooks* on the blast area round the club bore. *Private Eye* had a column called Great Bores of Today by Michael Heath, which caught to perfection the latest fashionable way in which to hold forth in some unstoppably dreary manner. Michael Wharton, while serving as an intelligence officer in India during the Second World War, thought of writing an *Anatomy of Boredom*, on the lines of Burton's *Anatomy of Melancholy*, and later, while writing the Peter Simple column in the *Daily Telegraph*, invented several world-famous bores who competed in competitions organised by the British Boring Board of Control.

The political bore seeks, like the expert bore, to bore us into submission. He or she (usually he) sets out to dominate us by being dull. We cannot bear to go on listening, so decide to leave the whole thing in the hands of the politician or the expert.

Walter Bagehot, with his marvellous alertness to politics as actually practised, wrote in his essay on *Mr Lowe as Chancellor of the Exchequer*, published in 1871, that one of the secrets of getting a piece of legislation through Parliament 'is to make the whole discussion very uninteresting – to leave an impression that the subject is very dry, that it is very difficult, that the department has attended to the dreary detail of it, and that on the whole it is safer to leave it to the department, and a dangerous responsibility to interfere with the department. The faculty of disheartening adversaries by diffusing on occasion an oppressive atmosphere of business-like dullness is invaluable to a parliamentary statesman.'

Many politicians and experts sought to dishearten their adversaries in the Brexit debate by being unbearably dull. I have lost count of the number of articles I have not read, or if read have not had the stamina fully to digest, on such questions as the single market and the customs union. For a short time, if I concentrated, I could hold in my mind the difference between those two entities. But my memory refused to retain the information. If a day or two later I opened, as it were, that computer file, I found I had somehow managed to wipe it, and if I wanted to understand the single market and the customs union I was going to have to start all over again, beginning perhaps with the useful account of the whole damn business on Wikipedia.

Politicians who play this kind of game like to say, to an opponent who is already feeling demoralised, 'Have you actually read the Irish Protocol?', or even, 'Have you actually read the Belfast Agreement?'

Johnson adopted the opposite approach. He strove to make

dull things interesting, and was often brilliant at doing so. This was his game as the *Telegraph*'s correspondent in Brussels from 1989 to 1994. He routed members of the pious Brussels Establishment by holding them up to public ridicule. To them, the details were sacred, especially as only they had a full grasp of the details, which were too profuse and tedious for anyone else to master. To Johnson, the details could if necessary be exaggerated or even made up, vivid embellishments to whatever story he was telling.

And this is what he was doing now with Brexit. He was bringing the story alive. It became in his hands a performance. But all the same, there were long periods, omitted from this account, when the experts just repeated their views *ad nauseam*. They loved to tell us what disasters would befall us in the near future if we failed to take their advice. Here was another reason to close our ears to their joyless imprecations. They intended to coerce us into agreeing with them on the basis that they were in possession of superior knowledge, and superior morals too. They looked down on us from a great height. Johnson didn't.

BOUNCED

On Saturday 31 October 2020 Boris Johnson was bounced by a leak from Downing Street into announcing a new four-week lockdown, a move he had long resisted and which he intended to go on thinking about over the weekend. His conduct looked chaotic, many Tory MPs thought he had adopted the wrong policy, and people said it 'could be his Suez'. Some months later, it emerged, thanks to Dominic Cummings, that while resisting the lockdown, Johnson had said: 'No more fucking lockdowns – let the bodies pile high in their thousands!' Many people professed to be shocked that he had spoken in this crude, unfeeling way, and a rather smaller number actually were shocked, against whom could be set a number of people, including many Tory MPs, who deeply disapproved of lock-downs, as being an offence against liberty, and who admired Johnson for at least having the argument, even though this time he lost it.

LORD LEXDEN'S LETTER

On 8 November 2020 the *Sunday Times* printed, under the headline 'Tories have no faith in Johnson', a letter from Lord Lexden, the Conservative Party's official historian: 'In the Commons and the Lords, despair reigns. Would someone of even modest parliamentary talent have given such a huge hostage to fortune by crudely dismissing Keir Starmer's call for a national lockdown? Or pushed ahead with the Internal Market Bill, which the Lords will reject? Perhaps if Johnson had accepted my invitation to join the Conservative Research Department in 1988, something might have been made of him.'

THE VACCINE CAVALRY

On 9 November 2020 Pfizer and BioNTech announced the development of a coronavirus vaccine which was over 90 per cent effective, and Johnson declared at a press conference: 'We have talked for a long time, or I have, about the distant bugle of the scientific cavalry coming over the brow of the hill. And tonight that toot of the bugle is louder. But it is still some way off.'

Not that far off, for Oxford AstraZeneca soon announced the creation of a second vaccine, and on 8 December the first British patients were vaccinated, before any other country in the world, even Israel, had reached that point.

What had gone right? For in many other respects, the United Kingdom's response to the pandemic had been alarmingly and embarrassingly inept, with the central bureaucracy unable either to perform well itself, or to make productive use of offers of help. The test and trace programme cost huge amounts of money and did not work properly. Nightingale hospitals were opened amid great fanfare, to take the overflow from NHS hospitals, but were scarcely used. There was a dreadful level of mortality in care homes, strict lockdown rules meant family members were not allowed to visit the dying, and in January 2021 the UK became the first European country to record 100,000 deaths from coronavirus.

From the earliest stages of the pandemic it was clear that the development of effective vaccines would transform things for the better, and scientists started work on these. How could the government enable them and all the others whose participation would be needed to work together at top speed? Dominic Cummings and the government's chief scientific adviser, Patrick Vallance, were among those who realised it would be fatal to entrust such a complicated project, a matter quite literally of life and death, to the Department of Health. A special team would be required. Vallance reckoned the right person to lead it was Kate Bingham. She was a woman of phenomenal energy, intellect and strength of character, with thirty years' experience of investing in new drugs, and knew everyone of any significance in the pharmaceutical industry, where Vallance had himself worked as head of research and development at GlaxoSmithKline.

In early May, Vallance, Cummings and the Cabinet secretary, Simon Case, put the case for a vaccine task force led by Bingham to the prime minister. According to Cummings, Johnson 'just decided in 90 seconds: "Fine. Do it."' There was no need for long debate or formal structure. On 6 May 2020, Johnson rang Bingham to recruit her to head the vaccine taskforce. 'I absolutely fell off the chair,' she later related. She told the prime minister, 'I'm not a vaccines expert': she knew about therapeutics, ways of treating diseases rather than averting them, and 'started off with a classic imposter syndrome as a woman – my first reaction was that I'm not qualified to do the job.'

Bingham 'got told off by my daughter', recipient in the past of maternal pep talks on the theme of 'don't do yourself down'. After consulting a number of experts in order to satisfy herself that she would in fact be able to do the job well, she accepted, without pay, a role in which she would find herself working harder than she ever had in her life.

Johnson had given her a clear goal: to save lives as soon as possible. She put together a taskforce which commissioned all the different stages of developing a new vaccine simultaneously. The six most promising out of hundreds of possible vaccines were selected, many millions of doses were ordered before it was known whether these six would work, hundreds of thousands of volunteers were recruited on whom the new vaccines would be tested, and manufacturing capacity in Britain was prepared.

In normal times, these tasks would be performed one after the other, for the later work would be a waste of time and money if the vaccines did not actually work. Indeed, in normal times a slow process would have been gone through in order to recruit the head of the task force, and Bingham herself might have decided she did not wish to sacrifice her previous career for the dubious pleasure of becoming entangled in the public sector bureaucracy.

Johnson himself had shown, since becoming prime minister, no capacity for getting that bureaucracy to work in a harmonious way. He was a disruptor, and so was Cummings, his chief adviser, who had announced, indeed, that he wished to recruit 'weirdos and misfits' to work for him in Downing Street, and was intent on root-and-branch reform of the civil service, so that at long last it recruited senior people who knew about science, mathematics, data, computing and how to get things done, rather than generalists whose forte was explaining why things could not be done.

During the pandemic, Johnson had to promulgate rules about how people should behave: he who had always held that rules were made to be broken. Within No. 10, the rules went on being broken, something for which he himself would later incur ferocious criticism.

But the vaccine taskforce was actually intended to operate

outside the rules, in order to bring together all sorts of things Britain was brilliant at, ranging from vaccine research to large-scale clinical trials on hundreds of thousands of volunteers, a field in which the NHS was a world leader, and then getting those vaccines into millions of arms, at which the NHS was also excellent. Johnson saw all this in a flash. No prime minister could have grasped more quickly the point of setting up the taskforce, and many might have paused to wonder whether it would be more prudent to go with the European Union's vaccine programme.

The EU authorities had far greater buying power than the British, but were much less clear about what they were trying to do. Rather than treat speed as the key objective, they picked fights with the pharmaceutical companies. Brussels soon stood convicted of retarding the progress that the member states might have made on their own.

Throughout the pandemic, British journalists searched with patriotic tenacity for things the British government was getting wrong. Bingham had been at St Paul's Girls' School with the prime minister's sister, Rachel Johnson, and at Oxford with both the Johnsons; was married to Jesse Norman, a Conservative MP, Treasury minister, Etonian and friend of the prime minister; and was herself the daughter of Lord Bingham, widely regarded as the greatest lawyer of his generation.

In November, the *Sunday Times* published a series of stories which suggested that her appointment was a stitch-up, and that she was behaving in various disgraceful ways, including the appointment of PR advisers at a cost of £670,000. There was no truth in the suggestion that she was spending extravagant sums, or indeed any sums, to embellish her own reputation, but she could not respond directly: any response had to be approved by No. 10 and the business department, and it became evident that there had been briefing against her from within the government machine.

'I was incredibly cross, I was incredibly frustrated, I was hurt,' she said later. She was doorstepped by camera crews, and Sir Keir Starmer, the Leader of the Opposition, joined in and said the £670,000 'cannot be justified'. Bingham, it turned out, had never approved any expenditure – that was done by ministers and officials – and the so-called PR advisers were in fact promoting the NHS Registry, which by the end of 2020 had recruited 360,000 volunteers to take part in vaccine and other studies.

In December 2020, as the vaccine rollout began, Bingham began to be acclaimed as one of the heroes who had made it all happen. In the summer of 2021 she was appointed DBE in the Queen's Birthday Honours. In her various public appearances she took care to pay tribute to the many other people who had played key roles, and who saw what needed to be done, and started doing it, well before she came on board. She also said that with hindsight, she could see 'we should have done cross-party briefings'. She refused to be drawn into any kind of political point-scoring.

Members of the public exchanged happy stories of going to be vaccinated, with the oldest and most vulnerable invited first. The whole process felt good: quick, informal, friendly, expert and efficient. The vaccine cavalry had arrived, and maintained a discipline and cohesion which cavalry often do not show. An almost miraculous deliverance was taking place.

CUMMINGS AND GOINGS

On Friday 13 November 2020 Dominic Cummings left Downing Street carrying a cardboard box. He and Johnson parted company after several months of increasingly acrimonious leaks in which the friends of Cummings and the friends of Carrie Symonds tried to destroy each other.

The downfall of Cummings was presaged by the downfall, the previous day, of Lee Cain, who had got to know Johnson while working for Vote Leave and had worked for him since Foreign Office days. Several other allies of Cummings departed soon after.

All this seemed, at the time, completely gripping. If one read or better still wrote for the newspapers and websites which published the leaks from the rival camps at the court of King Boris, one became hooked on the soap opera, anxious not to miss the next thrilling instalment, in which one or other character could be relied on to plumb new depths of rudeness. Journalists became the mouthpieces of the rival camps. Symonds was cast as the Mad Queen, or Lady Macbeth: the evil and designing woman leading Boris astray. Cummings was first the sworn enemy of the Remainers, for he had steered Leave to victory, and then, suddenly, their ally as he denounced Johnson. Implausible twists in the plot were constantly occurring, but in retrospect, the series came to seem a bit less thrilling, and one felt no pressing desire to watch the whole thing all over again, consisting as it mostly did, one realised, of the tittle-tattle of the servants in an ill-run house.

Vote Leave had left the building, insisting loudly, in the manner of a cook who has just been dismissed, that Johnson would be unable to manage without its services. Cummings a few months later began his campaign to get the prime minister sacked, which will be touched on in due course, and seemed a poor return for the loyalty the PM had shown him during the Barnard Castle affair. A Downing Street admirer of Cummings said he was 'missed' at No. 10, remarked that his subsequent disclosures were 'not very dignified', and admitted that 'he does go mad'.

But Cummings was in some ways wonderful. He was particularly good on the weaknesses of his opponents, their inability to conceive that anyone could disagree with them, let alone that those disagreements might lead to the world being turned upside down. In his long account of the EU Referendum, *Branching histories of the 2016 referendum and 'the frogs before the storm'*, published on 9 January 2017, he remarked with justice: 'Most educated people are not set up to listen or change their minds about politics, however sensible they are in other fields.'

And who can resist a writer like Cummings who quotes 'a wonderful passage in *Anna Karenina*' because it sums up better than any political scientist has done what he is trying to say:

Oblonsky never chose his tendencies and opinions any more than he chose the style of his hat or coat. He always wore those which happened to be in fashion. Moving in a certain circle where a desire for some form of mental activity was part of maturity, he was obliged to hold views in the same way he was obliged to wear a hat. If he had a reason for preferring Liberalism to the Conservatism of many in his set, it was not that he considered the liberal outlook more rational but because it corresponded better with his mode of life . . . . The Liberal Party said that marriage was an obsolete tradition which ought to be reformed, and indeed family life gave Oblonsky very little pleasure, forcing him to tell lies and dissemble, which was quite contrary to his nature. The Liberal Party said, or rather assumed, that religion was only a curb on the illiterate, and indeed Oblonsky could not stand through even the shortest church service without aching feet, or understand the point of all that dreadful high-flown talk about the other world when life in this world was really rather pleasant . . . Liberalism had become a habit with Oblonsky and he enjoyed his newspaper, as he did his after-dinner cigar, for the slight haze it produced in his brain.

Cummings sees that 'the conformity of the educated', though in some ways a good thing, leads to 'a collective lack of imagination', a tendency to believe that their own view is the only possible one, an inability to foresee what Stalin, Hitler or Putin will do.

One detects in Cummings something of the spirit of the young Disraeli, who in 1833, four years before he entered the Commons, confided to his diary: 'My mind is a revolutionary mind. It is a continental mind. I am only great in action. If ever I am placed in a truly eminent position I shall prove this.'

During the referendum campaign, Cummings proved himself great in action. So too from July to December 2019, when his audacity was exactly what Johnson needed. But in 2020 his audacity became, in most respects, a liability, as he sought through a network of special advisers loyal to himself to enforce his will across Whitehall, regardless of the views of the prime minister, the Cabinet and the parliamentary party. Johnson had reached, after much painful experience, the right conclusion, namely that Cummings must go. The prime minister hated falling out with people. He poured some of the drinks at the leaving party for his director of communications, Lee Cain, Cummings' ally, held in the Downing Street press office that Friday evening. And there was a celebration in the Downing Street flat. Spadocracy, in the sense of rule by the unelected Cummings, was over. Cummings had gone.

PRITI PATEL

On 20 November 2020, Johnson declared that he had 'full confidence' in Priti Patel, the home secretary, after Sir Alex Allan, the prime minister's independent adviser on ministers' interests, had reached a somewhat unfavourable view, published by the Cabinet Office, of allegations that she had bullied her staff:

> My advice is that the Home Secretary has not consistently met the high standards required by the ministerial code of treating her civil servants with consideration and respect. Her approach on occasions has amounted to behaviour that can be described as bullying in terms of the impact felt by individuals. To that extent her behaviour has been in breach of the ministerial code, even if unintentionally. This conclusion needs to be seen in context. There is no evidence that she was aware of the impact of her behaviour, and no feedback was given to her at the time. The high pressure and demands of the role, in the Home Office, coupled with the need for more supportive leadership from the top of the department has clearly been a contributory factor. In particular, I note the finding of different and more positive behaviour since these issues were raised with her.

Johnson, writing on a WhatsApp group, told Tory MPs the time had come to 'form a square round the prittster'. Sir Alex issued a final statement, given here in its entirety: 'I recognise that it is for the prime minister to make a judgement on whether actions by a minister amount to a breach of the ministerial code. But I feel that it is right that I should now resign from my position as the prime minister's independent adviser on the code.'

Sir Alex clearly took a very low view of the way Johnson had behaved. Argument raged about whether the prime minister was right to defend Patel. Bullying was a serious matter, the Ministerial Code a serious document, and Sir Alex a serious person – more serious, some people thought, than Patel. On the other hand, the Home Office was a bloody incompetent department, and maybe Patel was just being picked on because she was a woman, and indeed a woman of immigrant descent. To reshuffle the Cabinet just as talks on reaching a new trade deal with the EU by the end of 2020 approached the moment of decision would have been extremely difficult for the prime minister, who might well judge that it would weaken Britain's negotiating position.

Lord Wilson of Beriton, Cabinet secretary from 1998 to 2002, felt moved to write a letter to *The Times*: 'Sir, The prime minister's rejection of Sir Alex Allan's report into the home secretary's behaviour is worrying. It seems he does not hold his colleagues responsible for their actions where they have got things wrong but it would be inconvenient to accept it.'

An accurate summary of the situation, except Johnson did not think Patel had got things all that wrong, and 'inconvenient' was an understatement. If Johnson had sacked Patel, Remainers and a large part of the press would have said the whole government was falling to pieces. It is easy to say in a case like this,

'Let justice be done though the heavens fall.' But when Patel herself was showing (as Sir Alex conceded) 'more positive behaviour', and the falling heavens might render Brussels more intransigent, there was also something to be said for giving her another chance. This, at least, was how Johnson chose to play it. He defied his critics, and for the time being his luck held.

DINNER WITH VON DER LEYEN

On 9 December 2020 Johnson had a three-hour dinner with Ursula von der Leyen, president of the European Commission, in Brussels. A short clip was released of them on their way in to this meal. They entered stage right to a susurration of cameras, she an elegant, gamine figure beside this vast, shambolic John Bull of a man, laughing at something he had said, both of them wearing masks, for this was negotiation in the time of Covid. He came to a halt in front of the Union Jack, she in front of the EU flag.

Johnson: Do we take our mask off, Ursula?
    Von der Leyen: Well, keep distance.
    Johnson [taking a pace away from her]: Face mask off? [removes his mask, addresses the waiting press] How are you? Good evening, everybody.
    Von der Leyen [apologetically]: So we put it back on.
    Johnson [putting his mask back on]: We put it back on immediately. You run a tight ship here, Ursula. Quite right too.
    Von der Leyen [pointing the way they are to go]: *Allons-y!*
    Johnson: Okay, *allons-y. Voila!*

They exited stage left. The prime minister wore an air of perfect geniality combined with disruptive mockery. What friendliness! What ridicule! What paucity of information! We still did not know what was going to happen. David Frost, for the British, and Michel Barnier, for the EU, had been negotiating for many months, but the final deal, if there was one, would be done at the last moment and at a higher level. If the negotiation was about to fail, why had Johnson gone to Brussels? But he had warned before going that 'it's looking very very difficult at the moment', and afterwards von der Leyen tweeted: 'We understand each other's positions. They remain far apart.' Neither party wished to look like a pushover. Both were keen, when the dance ended, to find they had reached an agreement.

UNMERRY ENGLAND

On 19 December 2020 Johnson held a press conference at which he said: 'It is with a very heavy heart that I must tell you we cannot continue with Christmas as planned.' Johnson as a Merry England conservative has always attached great importance to Christmas, the festival the Puritans tried to ban. One of his friends was surprised to hear him say, at a moment of acute domestic difficulty at the end of 2004, 'Put on a good Christmas and it'll all be all right,' a remark recorded on page 228 of my earlier volume.

Sixteen years later, Johnson as prime minister had promised everyone they would be able to put on a good Christmas, telling Harry Cole of the *Sun* on 17 September 2020: 'Christmas we want to protect, and we want everyone to have a fantastic Christmas. But the only way to make sure the country is able to enjoy Christmas is to be tough now.'

As it turned out, he was not tough enough, and now had to introduce strict new limits on mixing with people outside one's own household over Christmas. His last-minute change of approach once again divided opinion, with some feeling that his heart had been in the right place, and others putting it down to bottomless incompetence.

THE PATISSERIE DEPARTMENT

On 24 December 2020 Johnson announced that Britain had reached a deal with the EU. He strove to make it, if not as easy as possible to agree with him, then at least as difficult as possible to disagree with him while not sounding grumpy: 'although we have left the EU this country will remain culturally, emotionally, historically, strategically, geologically attached to Europe, not least through the four million EU nationals who have requested to settle in the UK over the last four years and who make an enormous contribution to our country and to our lives.'

He said there would be no tariffs and no quotas on trade between the UK and the EU. This was true, but not the whole truth: many traders found, when the new rules were introduced, that selling goods to EU countries had become much more complicated and expensive. While answering a question from Robert Peston, political editor of ITV News, Johnson said: 'And for people at home who've zoned out while I've been talking about this, let me tell you . . .'

As it happens, I was just nodding off, as no doubt were other viewers. Johnson's awareness of when he became dull, and determination to do something about it, helped create a feeling he was on the side of the ordinary person who was not obsessed by politics. Johnson toyed with the idea that 'this is a cakeist treaty'. He returned to this notion when he spoke on 30

December 2020 at the start of the debate on the EU (Future Relationship) Bill, which passed its first reading in the Commons by 521 to 73 votes. Johnson stayed in the chamber for longer than usual, enjoying the compliments that were paid to him. Sir Bill Cash, the veteran Tory Eurosceptic, compared him to Pericles and Alexander the Great. In a piece for the New Year's Day edition of the *Daily Telegraph*, Johnson portrayed himself as a pâtissier, or pastry maker: 'You couldn't have your cake and eat it, we were told. Maybe it would be unduly provocative to say that this is a cakeist treaty; but it is certainly from the patisserie department.'

THE MEANING OF CHRISTMAS

'At the end of this extraordinary year,' the prime minister declared, 'I want to say something about the meaning of Christmas.' Some of us felt this was a bit of a cheek. Johnson had, admittedly, made videos about the meaning of every other major world religion. But could he not leave Christianity safe in the hands of her majesty the Queen and the clergy?

'It's about hope,' Johnson said as he got into his stride. Over his left shoulder there was a Christmas tree. Hugh Grant is among Johnson's most implacable enemies, and here was Johnson doing a send-up of Grant in *Love Actually*: 'I still think that feeling of hope is all around us this Christmas, because there really is a star in the sky and it is glowing brighter and brighter, and you know what it is, it's thanks to the efforts of wise men and wise women in the east and elsewhere, we have a vaccine . . .

'And by the way, this night, on Christmas Eve, I have a small present for anyone who may be looking for something to read in that sleepy post-Christmas lunch moment, and here it is . . .'

He bent down to pick up something from the foot of the tree, which turned out to be a thick, scruffy bundle of papers, and went on: ' . . . because this is a deal, a deal to give certainty to business and travellers and all investors in our country from the first of January . . . You remember the oven-ready deal, by which we came out on January the 31st. That oven-ready deal

was just the starter. This is the feast, full of fish by the way . . .
That's the good news from Brussels. Now for the sprouts, and
a happy Christmas to you all.'

Shameless, utterly shameless, this harnessing of the gospel
to the Johnson bandwagon.

SURPRISE AT BRACKEN HOUSE

On 30 January 2021, the *Financial Times*, edited from Bracken House in the City of London and fiercely critical of both Brexit and Johnson, reported in an incredulous tone (one notes the repetition, perhaps by a disorientated sub-editor, of the word 'position'): 'After being pilloried for his handling of the Covid-19 pandemic, Mr Johnson finds himself in the unusual position of having manoeuvred Britain into the position of being a global leader in the purchase and distribution of vaccines. "We gambled and it paid off," said one ally of Mr Johnson on Friday. Britain now has orders for 367m doses of seven different vaccines in production or development and the good news kept coming this week for the prime minister. The UK has vaccinated more than 10 per cent of adults, compared with the EU's 2 per cent . . .'

GREED

In a speech on the evening of Tuesday 23 March 2021 to Conservative MPs, Johnson said: 'The reason for our vaccine success is capitalism – greed, my friends.' After uttering those words, he added: 'Forget I said that.' But it was too late. His remark was reported first in the *Sun*, and the following morning by the BBC, which led on it.

The prime minister had spoiled, by this gross error of taste, the heartening sense that we had come through the pandemic by all working together, something he himself had stressed earlier in the day at a press conference. His defenders said he was making a jokey reference to the film *Wall Street*, famous for the speech in which Gordon Gekko, played by Michael Douglas, declares: 'Greed, for lack of a better word, is good.' They pointed out that Johnson went on to say the development of the vaccines 'was driven by big pharma – and I don't just mean the chief whip.' This joke was at the expense of Mark Spencer, a farmer from Nottinghamshire who was rather on the tubby side, and who was serving as chief whip.

But when Johnson told jokes, he often did so in order to render whatever underlying argument he was making more acceptable. Here was a man who could only moralise by pretending not to be a moralist. In his speech at the Centre for Social Justice on 7 August 2015, he defended the 'pointless ostentation' of the rich, for it 'produces employment for chauffeurs, tailors, tutors, trainers, chiropodists, teachers, divorce lawyers and so on'. In Johnson's words, 'it is a sad fact that the wheels of the economy are turned all the faster by a greedy and competitive desire to consume'. He praised 'the more elegant formulation' of this argument in Bernard Mandeville's poem 'The Grumbling Hive', published in 1705, and, being Johnson, went on to quote a passage on the springs of industry in human nature, how private vices lead to public benefits, as seen in the role played by greed in wealth creation:

> The Root of Evil, Avarice,
> That damn'd ill-natur'd baneful Vice,
> Was Slave to Prodigality,
> That noble Sin; whilst Luxury
> Employ'd a Million of the Poor,
> And odious Pride a Million more:
> Envy itself, and Vanity,
> Were Ministers of Industry;
> Their darling Folly, Fickleness,
> In Diet, Furniture and Dress,
> That strange ridic'lous Vice, was made
> The very Wheel that turn'd the Trade . . .
> Thus Vice nurs'd Ingenuity,
> Which join'd with Time and Industry,
> Had carried Life's Conveniences,
> It's real Pleasures, Comforts, Ease,
> To such a Height, the very Poor
> Liv'd better than the Rich before,
> And nothing could be added more.

Earlier in his speech, Johnson, who at this point was drawing towards the end of his second term as mayor of London, tackled with admirable directness the question of inequality: 'We One Nation Tories accept that for all the triumphs of the modern London economy, and it is sensational at generating wealth, it is still a lamentable fact that for the past thirty years the gap has opened yet further between rich and poor.'

He observed that the multiple of average pay to top pay had risen over the last forty years from 25 times to 130 times. One Nation Tories needed to go beyond trickle-down economics and ensure 'that in a dynamic market economy there is real cohesion, a real sense of shared interest'. He declared that the wealth gap was only tolerable if three conditions were met:

1. The rich pay their fair share of taxes.
2. People who work hard doing 'indispensable' jobs 'are properly and decently rewarded'.
3. There must be the possibility of change and advance and there must be openness and there must be permeability in the affluent classes.

Johnson pointed out that social mobility had declined in the last three decades, the professions were dominated by the children of professionals, and the most recent Oscars were 'a competition between an Old Etonian and an Old Harrovian – it was like some sort of bad joke'.

He went on to argue that 'we should be giving the poorest the chance to compete on an equal footing with the affluent bourgeoisie'. The three great equalisers, he said, were home ownership, cheap mass transit and education. He emphasised that as a One Nation Tory, he did not wish to 'eat the rich'. Johnson, himself an insatiable competitor, communicated his enthusiasm for enabling the poor to compete on equal terms.

When I mentioned this speech to one of Johnson's critics,

she replied: 'But surely he doesn't really believe in all this. He's just saying what people want to hear. He hasn't done any of it.'

She is right that it is a thousand times easier to talk about equality of opportunity than to take serious steps towards attaining it. She is also right that he was speaking to the Centre for Social Justice, who wanted to hear a message about equality. But as a man coming towards the end of his time as mayor of London, he had no need to give such a speech. It only makes sense as an attempt to prepare himself for being prime minister.

When some harmless drudge in the Conservative Research Department is told to compile a volume of Johnson's speeches, this one will have to be included. So far as I can see, no text of it is available on the internet. It can, however, be watched on YouTube.

JENNIFER ARCURI

On 28 March 2021, the *Sunday Mirror* published an interview with Jennifer Arcuri about her affair with Johnson while he was mayor of London. The world had known since September 2019 of this relationship, which lasted from 2012 to 2016, but Arcuri, who was hurt and angry that he no longer returned her calls and had even on one occasion got someone to answer her in a Chinese accent, from time to time offered further revelations. On this occasion she said that when they first met for a drink, at the Tavistock Hotel in Bloomsbury, he returned from the bar in order to borrow £3.10 off her. She also described as 'perfectly inedible' the pasta that he cooked for her in the kitchen of his family home: 'It was horrible. It was soggy and limp. This man was completely useless in the kitchen.'

In earlier interviews, she had revealed that he was amazingly good at reciting Shakespeare – 'I had never had a man be able to keep up with me on Shakespeare like he had' – and that his seduction technique included reciting Sonnet 29:

> When, in disgrace with fortune and men's eyes,
> I all alone beweep my outcast state,
> And trouble deaf heaven with my bootless cries,
> And look upon myself and curse my fate,
> Wishing me like to one more rich in hope,

Featured like him, like him with friends possessed,
Desiring this man's art and that man's scope,
With what I most enjoy contented least;
Yet in these thoughts myself almost despising,
Haply I think on thee, and then my state,
(Like to the lark at break of day arising
From sullen earth) sings hymns at heaven's gate;
For thy sweet love remembered such wealth brings
That then I scorn to change my state with kings.

Before Johnson became prime minister, he was working on a book about Shakespeare. He had reluctantly concluded he could not finish it while in Downing Street, but one trusts that now he has been thrown out of power, and the book can at last be expected to appear, some enterprising literary editor will ask Arcuri to review it.

Alice Thomson testified, when interviewing Arcuri for *The Times*, that she is 'clever, articulate, funny, engaging and enraged', and knows a lot about Shakespeare. Arcuri had unfortunately helped to obscure these qualities by going public about the affair. The lower the view Johnson's opponents were able to take of her, the more discreditable her liaison with him could be made to appear. Her tech company had received £120,000 from public funds, and she had gone on three trade missions led by Johnson. Surely, his critics thought, there was something here which could be used against him? The Greater London Assembly referred the matter to the Independent Office for Police Conduct, which in May 2020 reported that it would not be initiating a criminal investigation into the former mayor for misconduct in public office, as it had found no evidence that he 'influenced the payment of any sponsorship monies to Ms Arcuri or that he influenced or played an active part in securing her participation in trade missions'. It added that under the Nolan principles of public life, it would have been 'wise' of him to declare his relationship with Arcuri 'as a conflict of interest'.

HARTLEPOOL

The Hartlepool by-election, held on 6 May 2021, was an astonishing triumph for Johnson. The Conservatives won 15,529
votes to only 8,589 for Labour. Hartlepool, a port on the coast
of County Durham, had elected its first Conservative MP since
1959, and the swing of 16 per cent from Labour to the
Conservatives was the biggest to an incumbent governing party
since the Second World War.

Sebastian Payne has described, in *Broken Heartlands: A Journey
Through Labour's Lost England*, Johnson's visit to Hartlepool on
a cold, wet bank holiday three days before the poll:

At midday, the prime ministerial motorcade pulled into
the car park, Range Rovers with blue sirens, and Johnson
leapt out onto the campaign trail. With Jill Mortimer, the
Tory candidate, he paced up the seafront in his trademark
blue suit – sans coat, despite the weather. He was mobbed.
Soon, the traffic piled up as every car stopped to point
and shout, 'Boris!' He was the Pied Piper in the middle
of a hurricane. He asked each voter he stopped to talk to
if the party could count on their support. Bar some who
were uncertain, everyone answered in the affirmative. No
one said they were backing Labour. The response was
unlike any I have seen to any politician on the campaign
trail, in any election: dozens of Hartlepudlians wanted

selfies and elbow bumps [which had replaced handshakes during the pandemic] with the prime minister.

Johnson and Sir Keir Starmer, the Labour leader, each visited Hartlepool three times during the campaign. Starmer quite rightly shut up about Brexit, which was popular in Hartlepool, but Johnson was still the man who could make a connection with Labour, or former Labour, voters in the north of England. Nor did those voters yet appear to be much concerned about the story running in the press since February 2021 about a lavish refurbishment of the Downing Street flat where Johnson and Symonds lived, and Johnson's hope that donors could be found who would fund this extraordinarily expensive work, carried out by an interior designer called Lulu Lytle, whose work looked preposterously ornate. The money was going to flow through a charitable trust run by Lord Brownlow, a philan-thropist whose good causes included the Conservative Party. In a blog published on 23 April 2021, Dominic Cummings related a conversation he had on the subject with Johnson in 2020: 'I told him I thought his plans to have donors secretly pay for the renovation were unethical, foolish, possibly illegal and almost certainly broke the rules on proper disclosure of political donations if conducted in the way he intended.'

The media devoted vast amounts of space and energy to the story, but the public did not yet seem very concerned by it. In the local elections, also held on 6 May 2021, the Conservative vote rose by 8 per cent compared to 2019, the local elections of 2020 having been postponed because of the pandemic.

LORD GEIDT

Lord Geidt, formerly the Queen's private secretary, succeeded Sir Alex Allen as the independent adviser on ministers' interests, and on 28 May 2021 brought out a report which focussed mainly on the redecoration of the Downing Street flat. Anyone who wishes to study the Establishment's opaque yet incisive use of language is referred to this report, of which the following three extracts convey the flavour:

> Lord Brownlow behaved in a confidential manner consistent with his own experience of blind trusts.
>
> the Prime Minister — unwisely, in my view — allowed the refurbishment of the apartment at No 11 Downing Street to proceed without more rigorous regard for how this would be funded.
>
> These possible mitigations notwithstanding, however, it cannot be right to assert that the duty attaching to all ministers, and not least to the prime minister to observe the high standards of what is, after all, his ministerial code is anything other than absolute.

Johnson had got away with it, but was reminded by Lord Geidt of his 'absolute' duty to observe the Ministerial Code. He had received, with the words 'unwisely, in my view', a slap on the wrist, a punishment which had never been known to alter his behaviour by one iota.

BATLEY AND SPEN

At the next by-election, held on 17 June 2021 in Chesham and Amersham, the Liberal Democrats scored a thumping victory, turning the Tory majority of 16,223 at the 2019 general election into a majority for their candidate of 8,028. This result unsettled Tory MPs in the south of England, many of whom were vulnerable to a Lib Dem resurgence. Johnson might have some special pull with voters in the midlands and the north, but the home counties didn't think much of him.

Even in the north, he was far from invincible. Lord Salisbury, Conservative titan of the late nineteenth century, once said, 'English popularity, like an English summer, consists of two fine days and a thunder storm'. Voters do not like their leaders to get cocky. The longest period of unbroken popularity in modern times was enjoyed by Tony Blair after becoming Labour leader in 1994, but he paid for it with an even longer period of unpopularity after in 2003 taking Britain to war in Iraq.

The next northern by-election was due on 1 July in Batley and Spen, West Yorkshire, where Labour would be defending a majority of 3,525, almost identical to the majority, 3,595, which had just been overturned in Hartlepool. In the middle of May, I interviewed drinkers in the Union Rooms, a pub at the top of Hick Lane in Batley. The first person I met was Mick Carter, a retired painter and decorator, who said: 'I vote Labour.

I can't vote Conservative. They tell too many lies.' He regarded Sir Keir Starmer as a great improvement on Jeremy Corbyn, and said of Johnson himself: 'You know what he is. He's a dictator.' Carter objected also to Johnson's extravagance: 'Then he redecorates his flat. How much does it cost? £500,000 [an exaggeration – in 2020 the cost was £112,549]. She wants gold doorknobs. That's what it says in the paper the other day. I would have done the job for about four grand.'

Batley contains many handsome stone buildings, some of which look as if they have seen better days. The Union Rooms, run by Wetherspoons, has inscribed over its fine gothic porch the words 'West Riding Union Bank 1877'. On the other side of the road stands a tremendous Wesleyan Chapel, now occupied by Europabeds, whose slogan is 'Sleep in Style, Wake in Comfort'. One of Carter's friends said: 'It used to be a good place, Batley. Everything's gone now. It used to be buzzing. We've had them all here, the top stars, at Batley Variety Club. Shirley Bassey, the Drifters, Tom Jones. They couldn't get Elvis. They offered him £50,000 a night. Louis Armstrong, Neil Sedaka, Showaddywaddy, Gene Pitney.'

This sense of abandonment – of having once been world class but now not worth visiting – is found in many of the northern towns captured by the Conservatives. But I did not get the impression they would capture Batley. In the Union Rooms, several people said unprompted they would vote for a well-known local figure, Kim Leadbetter, who they expected, rightly, would be adopted as the Labour candidate, and who was the sister of Jo Cox, murdered in 2016 while serving as the Labour MP for Batley and Spen.

A woman aged twenty-five, employed as a retail assistant and drinking a Sex on the Beach cocktail (vodka, peach schnapps, cranberry juice, orange juice), said she would 'most likely' vote for Leadbetter. When asked what she thought of Johnson, she said:

He's a buffoon. I can't stand him. His priorities have been elsewhere. He cares more about how he looks [laughter]. This whole pandemic, he could have done more, sooner, like New Zealand [which shut down foreign travel].

My father passed away last year when it peaked, in April. My dad, he barely went out. He went out to the hospital, we thought he had cancer, unfortunately he contracted coronavirus. He did have additional health problems. If only he [Johnson] had done it sooner like New Zealand. He's a joke, he's an embarrassment.

My dad were only sixty when he passed away. Not being able to see him, to be around him, we didn't even see him in the chapel of rest, apparently his body was contaminated, he was put in a plastic bag, which we didn't need to know. It happened on day eight of the hospital admission. He left behind three children, five grandchildren, his wife.

Reverting to Johnson, she said: 'In five to ten years we'll be a military-led country. He's a dictator. He is literally a clone of Donald Trump. He and Donald Trump are the same person.'

The man sitting next to her, pouring himself drinks from a jug of Godfather (whisky, amaretto, Pepsi), said: 'Everyone thinks that.'

The woman did a rather good imitation of Johnson, 'I, I, I, I, I'll be going down to get a drink myself,' and went on: 'I don't like him but he makes me laugh.'

There was much laughter during these conversations. Nobody seemed to mind an ignorant southerner coming into a pub in

West Yorkshire and asking people about their politics. A sort of friendly defiance of the prime minister prevailed. On the basis of these and other conversations, I predicted that Labour would hold Batley and Spen, which Leadbetter proceeded to do by the slender margin of 323 votes.

WEDDING

Saturday is often a quiet day for news, and on this particular Saturday those journalists who were at work only found out about the big story six hours after it had happened. Here is how Westminster Cathedral reported the event: 'On Saturday 29 May, the wedding of Carrie Symonds and Boris Johnson took place in Westminster Cathedral. The bride and groom are both parishioners of the Westminster Cathedral parish and baptised Catholic. All necessary steps were taken, in both Church and civil law, and all formalities completed before the wedding.'

Johnson's capacity to achieve total surprise had once more been demonstrated. The press were under the impression that the wedding would not take place until the summer of the following year. The ceremony was carried out by Father Daniel Humphreys, who had also baptised the couple's son, Wilfred, on 12 September the previous year: another event missed by the press, and only revealed after erroneous reports began to circulate that on that day, Johnson had been spotted at the airport in Perugia, opening up the exciting possibility that he had been visiting his friend Evgeny Lebedev.

A number of Catholics were furious that Johnson was allowed to get married at Westminster Cathedral, despite having been married twice before, whereas many Catholics are denied a second wedding in church. But Matt Chinery, an ecclesiastical and canon lawyer, pointed out on Times Radio that the Catholic Church does not recognise weddings which have not been performed by Catholics, so Johnson, having himself been baptised (like his mother) a Catholic, and having had one Anglican wedding and one registry office wedding, was in the eyes of the Church a Catholic who had never been married.

Thirty people were invited to the wedding. The reception was held in the Downing Street garden, with hay bales, bunting and a fiddle band. James Cleverly, a Tory MP who had worked for Johnson at City Hall, posted a picture on Twitter of the Johnsons (for Symonds took her husband's name), he in shirt sleeves, she bare-footed in her wedding dress, a garland of flowers about her head. One of the guests was Hugo Dixon, photographed resplendent in a fancy gold waistcoat as he came out of No. 10. He was a close friend of the prime minister, with whom he had been at Ashdown House, Eton and Balliol. In recent years, they had been on opposite sides, with Dixon, the deputy chair of People's Vote, spending 'every waking hour' campaigning for Britain to stay in the EU, and on 19 July 2019 addressing an open letter to the prime minister elect, published in the *Guardian*:

You love Churchill [Johnson had written a book about Churchill, while Dixon was a descendant of the great man]. You must know one of his favourite poems, *The Clattering Train*. The last verse goes:

For the pace is hot, and the points are near,
And sleep hath deadened the driver's ear;
And signals flash through the night in vain.
Death is in charge of the clattering train.

You're like that driver on the clattering train, except you're not asleep. Jacob Rees-Mogg and Nigel Farage have persuaded you to sabotage the brakes – and you are hurtling towards the abyss with 66 million people in the back. So some of us are going to have to stop the train for you.

Like you, I'm a fighter. But I don't want to fight fire with fire. I prefer to fight fire with water. I prefer Gandhi to Machiavelli. The ends don't justify the means. If we pursue the wrong means, we'll corrupt the ends. Democracy so easily descends into demagogy, as the ancient Greeks knew so well.

Dixon's open letter conveys the agonised sincerity of the Remainers. Many a leader, on being accused by an old friend of leading 66 million people into the abyss, might have decided the friendship was over. Johnson made Dixon one of the handful of guests at his wedding.

G7 AT CARBIS BAY

From 11 to 13 June 2021 Boris and Carrie Johnson hosted the G7 leaders and their spouses at Carbis Bay, in Cornwall. This was feel-good politics at the seaside. Cornwall looked wonderful. We saw pictures of Carrie Johnson and Jill Biden, wife of the American president, sitting on the stone steps at the Minack Theatre, and paddling on the beach together, with Wilfred taking a few steps towards them. Johnson took an early morning dip in the sea, swimming in an old-fashioned way with his head out of the water. He went running, greeted leaders, did interviews, stood in the middle of the front row for the group photographs. Fears that Joe Biden, inaugurated as president in January, would spurn Johnson had long been forgotten. The Europeans sat together at some of the social events, as if demonstrating their solidarity. The Queen cut a cake with a sword. The Duchess of Cornwall was photographed with a large glass of red wine.

The press sought to disturb this unnewsworthy harmony by playing up differences between Johnson and the French president, Emmanuel Macron, about the Northern Ireland protocol. Johnson asked how Macron would like it if the French courts stopped him moving Toulouse sausages to Paris. Macron retorted that this was 'not a good comparison, because Paris and Toulouse are part of the same country'.

Johnson said Northern Ireland and Britain are likewise part of the same country. Lord Frost, the Brexit minister, attended Johnson's three meetings with Macron, and wore Union Jack socks.

LEVELLING UP

On 15 July 2021 Johnson delivered a speech in Coventry about levelling up. The media said it contained too few novelties to be a success. David Gauke, one of the twenty-one rebels in September 2019 and an astute critic of Johnson, remarked that the Treasury, where he had worked as a minister, would consider the speech 'a triumph', as it contained 'a spending commitment of just £50 million'. Dominic Cummings dismissed 'levelling up' as 'a vacuous slogan'.

Many people wanted to cut Johnson down to size, or indeed to chuck him out. He must not be allowed to become, as the voters in Batley had said, a tyrant. But this admirable determination not to have an over-mighty prime minister could tip into a wilful under-estimate of his ability. Comforting though it was to dismiss his speech, and to conclude that in this key area of policy he had nothing to say, this was a caricature of what was actually quite a thoughtful position.

The media were right to remark on a lack of novelty. The expression 'levelling up' was not invented by Johnson. It is found in *The Right Approach*, a 23,000-word statement of Conservative aims published in 1976, the year after Margaret Thatcher became leader: 'Conservatives are not egalitarians. We believe in levelling up, in enhancing opportunities, not in levelling down, which dries up the springs of enterprise and endeavour and ultimately means that there are fewer resources for helping the disadvantaged. Hostility to success, because success brings inequality, is often indistinguishable from envy and greed, especially when, as Alexander Solzhenitsyn has pointed out, it is dressed up in the language of the "class struggle".'

Forty-five years later, at the UK Battery Industrialisation Centre in Coventry, Johnson said: 'We don't want to level down. We don't want to decapitate the tall poppies, we don't think you can make the poor parts of the country richer by making the rich parts poorer.'

He lamented the 'basic half-heartedness' of the forty different schemes or bodies in the last forty years which had tried to boost local or regional growth. The country was over-centralised: 'That's because for many decades we relentlessly crushed local leadership and we must be honest about why this was necessary, it was because we were in the grip of a real ideological conflict in which irresponsible municipal socialist governments were bankrupting cities . . . Now, with some notable exceptions, that argument is over and most of the big metro mayors know that private sector investment is crucial.'

Johnson celebrated the end of ideological conflict. His tone was boosterish as he declared: 'there is one final ingredient, the most important factor in levelling up, the yeast that lifts the whole mattress of dough, the ketchup of catch-up, and that is leadership.'

But would the British continue to accept his leadership?

PARANOID AND EXHAUSTED

There was something not quite done about praising Johnson. Even people who were fond of him, and admired his gifts, tended to refrain from saying so. In August 2021 one of them said to me, 'I think he is unhappy and would like to get a grip on it – he knows in his heart it's not working.' And speaking almost as one might of a child: 'I look at him and wonder if he's happy.'

Some old friends had fallen out with him in a more definitive way. They felt deserted, and wanted to convince themselves that it was Johnson's fault, which often, no doubt, it was. 'He's desperate, bitter, unhappy, paranoid and exhausted,' one of them told me in the summer of 2021. 'Can you imagine being PM without being able to trust anyone?'

But Rory Stewart, in September 2019 one of the twenty-one rebels and in November 2020 the author of a celebrated denunciation of Johnson as a liar which has been quoted earlier, said in an interview with the *New Statesman*, published on 28 July 2021: 'I'm beginning to see the ways in which he has a kind of political genius. I find him infuriating, but there is something mesmerising about him. With all the things that appal me about his moral character, he is much more interesting, obviously, than David Cameron or Theresa May.'

Stewart added, while Michael Berkeley's guest on *Private Passions* on Radio 3 on 24 October 2021, that Johnson 'brought out the worst moralising side of me' when they were both Foreign Office ministers. It is unusual for someone who has fallen out with Johnson as badly as Stewart to admit, or even to realise, that this is very often the effect Johnson has on his critics.

AFGHANISTAN

On Sunday 15 August 2021 the Taliban captured Kabul without a shot being fired. Although the Americans had indicated eighteen months earlier that they would be withdrawing their forces, neither in Washington nor in London had such a rapid and total collapse been foreseen. As recently as 8 July 2021, Johnson had said: 'I do not think that the Taliban are capable of victory by military means.' As Kabul fell, the foreign secretary, Dominic Raab, was spotted on a beach at a five-star hotel in Crete. In Afghanistan, too, the speed of events took members of the regime by surprise. The governor of the central bank expressed indignation that the president, Ashraf Ghani, had fled without letting him or anyone else know.

On Monday 16 August, Johnson was seen at Taunton station, returning to work after one day's holiday on the family farm on Exmoor. Raab had abandoned his holiday the night before, though only after fierce criticism for not coming back sooner. Almost unbelievably, Sir Philip Barton, the permanent secretary at the Foreign Office, remained on holiday, even though his department was trying to organise the evacuation from the airport at Kabul, still in American hands, of British nationals and of Afghans who had worked for the British.

On Wednesday 18 August, the Commons returned from holiday and debated Afghanistan. Johnson said it was 'an illusion' to think we could send 'tens of thousands of British troops to fight the Taliban' in the place of the Americans. He took a realist view: 'we must deal with the position as it now is'. Tom Tugendhat, chairman of the foreign affairs select committee, made the most moving speech of the day:

> Like many veterans, this last week has seen me struggle through anger, grief and rage – through the feeling of abandonment of not just a country, but the sacrifice that my friends made. I have been to funerals from Poole to Dunblane. I have watched good men go into the earth, taking with them a part of me and a part of all of us. This week has torn open some of those wounds, has left them raw and left us all hurting. And I know it is not just soldiers; I know aid workers and diplomats who feel the same. I know journalists who have been witnesses to our country in its heroic effort to save people from the most horrific fates.

Tugendhat and others who had served in Afghanistan felt appalled at the abandonment of Afghans who had worked for the British and were now in mortal danger from the Taliban. Frantic efforts were made to get as many as possible of these people out, but nothing in the way of advance planning had been done, and chaos reigned. On Saturday 28 August the last British soldiers flew out of Kabul. The Ministry of Defence said 15,000 people had been saved. The Foreign Office stood accused of gross negligence: it was reckoned that with proper contingency planning another 9,000 people could have been flown out. In the midst of all this, a cargo of animals belonging to a charity was rescued, with only one human passenger on the plane.

On Monday 6 September, when the Commons returned

from its summer recess, Johnson gave a statement on Afghanistan: 'The whole House will join me in commending the courage and ingenuity of everyone involved in the Kabul Airlift, one of the most spectacular operations in our country's post-war military history.'

He made a defeat sound like a victory: just what Harold Macmillan had done after the Suez debacle of 1956, and just what many people wanted to hear. Tugendhat was not deceived. In May 2022 his committee produced a report which said: 'The fact that the Foreign Office's senior leaders were on holiday when Kabul fell marks a fundamental lack of serious-ness, grip or leadership at a time of national emergency.' It examined the case of the evacuated animals, admitted it had been unable to discover who had ordered this, and went on: 'Multiple senior officials believed that the Prime Minister played a role in this decision. We have yet to be offered a plausible alternative explanation for how it came about.' Johnson did not emerge well from this episode, but British shortcomings were less significant than the American decision to cut and run from Kabul.

A JUNTA OF
BELGIAN TICKET INSPECTORS

On 4 September 2021, *La Repubblica* published an interview with Hilary Mantel, celebrated author of a trilogy of novels about Thomas Cromwell, in which she announced she was planning to leave England: 'I feel the need to be packing my bags, and to become a European again.'

Many Remainers felt this yearning to become European again, and would tell you with deep emotion that they had exercised their right to acquire, say, an Irish or a German passport. The more highly educated they were, the more dissatisfied they were to be British. It was so obvious that Johnson was unfit to be prime minister, they generally saw no need to produce any further evidence. When asked whether she had met him, and what she thought of him, Mantel said: 'I have met him a number of times, in different settings. I agree he is a complex personality, but this much is simple: he should not be in public life. And I am sure he knows it.'

This inclination to believe the worst of one's own country, and of those running it, has been around for longer than Brexit. Johnson himself had noted its existence in his first book, *Friends, Voters, Countrymen*, published in 2001:

I was recently waiting for some chips in a seaside tavern
in Devon with my brother-in-law, Ivo Dawnay, and when,
after forty minutes, the chips were still not there, Ivo

launched into a fiery attack on British waitressing, culture, economic habits and all the rest. 'And that's why,' he concluded, 'we should just shut up and allow ourselves to be integrated into Europe. Christ, man, the Portuguese are better than us at this kind of thing. We need the Europeans to teach us a lesson.'

Well, we all feel like that from time to time, when the chips are down, or absent; but you don't believe, surely, that you can improve the standards of waitressing in Woolacombe by demolishing a thousand years of parliamentary democracy? Do you? Perhaps you do.

It is a chronic vice of the British middle classes to think that their country would be better off run, in Auberon Waugh's phrase, by a 'junta of Belgian ticket inspectors'. That is, in my view, a delusion, and I say that not just because I have some knowledge of Belgian ticket inspectors.

In the 1790s, George Canning, a junior minister and future prime minister, helped set up a paper, *The Anti-Jacobin*, in which he poured scorn on the kind of person who supported the French Revolution:

A steady patriot of the world alone,
The friend of every country but his own.

George Orwell was to identify the same mentality in left-wing intellectuals in the mid twentieth century.

From 2016, this hostility became bound up with an almost demented hatred of Johnson. One should not mistake Twitter for real life, but Philip Pullman, author of *His Dark Materials,* is a real writer, and on 12 October 2021 tweeted: 'Saying this

as clearly as I can: Boris Johnson is removing the Covid restrictions because he WANTS the NHS to collapse, so that he has
a political excuse for privatising it. Nothing else, not even
stupidity, can explain what's going on.'

The NHS did not collapse, but had it done so would almost
certainly have precipitated the collapse of Johnson's prime ministership. The idea he was deliberately trying to destroy the NHS
is preposterous, but how ready Pullman is to believe it. In the
same month Martin Fletcher, a former foreign editor of *The Times*,
wrote in the *New Statesman*: 'It gives me no pleasure to say it, but
my daughter is right. She should raise her children in Germany
rather than Boris Johnson's increasingly debased Britain.'

I agree with Fletcher about the attractions of Berlin, a city
where I lived for almost six years, and of course he is right to
back his daughter's decision to live there. But was he also right
to describe Britain, under Johnson, as 'increasingly debased'?
There was, however, a thriving market on the left for this sort
of stuff. Fletcher's articles were among the most popular pieces
published at this time by the *New Statesman*. Oddly enough, at
about the same time a friend of mine, a thoughtful German
journalist, visited London and expressed concern that so many
on the left in British politics seemed to hate their own country.
This was an excruciating problem for the Labour Party. Its
working-class voters felt deeply proud of being British. Many
of its middle-class activists were, on the contrary, deeply
ashamed of being British, particularly in the wake of Brexit,
and yearned, like Mantel, to pack their bags and become
European again.

CHARLOTTE'S FUNERAL

The following notice appeared in *The Times* on 14 September 2021:

> JOHNSON WAHL Charlotte Maria Offlow, née Fawcett. Died suddenly and peacefully St Mary's Hospital, Paddington, 13 September 2021, aged 79. Painter. Mother of Alexander, Rachel, Leo, and Joseph; grandmother of Ludovic, Lara, Charlotte, Milo, Oliver, Cassia, Theodore, Rose, Lula, William, Ruby Noor, Stephanie and Wilfred. Private Funeral.

At the funeral, held at the Church of St John the Evangelist, Notting Hill, Alexander (better known as Boris), Rachel, Leo and Joseph carried the coffin in. Boris, Carrie and Wilfred were in the front pew on the right. Rachel, Leo and Jo were in the front pew on the left. There was then 'a buffer zone', as one mourner described it, two pews deep, of grandchildren, in which was found Boris's previous wife, Marina Wheeler, 'very solicitous and friendly' to all of them.

All this was observed with interest by the rest of the congregation. Some thought it 'very poor form' that Carrie, 'in a tremendous hat, large and black', from time to time 'thrust the baby in Boris's lap', where he had to feed Wilfred his bottle. How could he mourn his mother while he was doing this? But others said he 'obviously rather enjoyed it', and he remarked afterwards with pleasure that it 'had been rather a wrestling match'.

Charlotte's grandchildren read the passage from *Cymbeline* which begins 'Fear no more the heat o' the sun', and her exact contemporary and lifelong friend Rachel Billington delivered a eulogy which everyone described as excellent, and which had been prefigured by a piece in *The Times* which described the two of them being pushed by their mothers, Elizabeth Pakenham and Beatrice Fawcett, through Oxford in 1942.

Andrew Knight, once the editor of *The Economist*, and painted by Charlotte looking uneasy in a family group, gave a second eulogy which received less good reviews, for it contained 'an odd attack on Stanley', Boris's father, who was sitting quite far back in the church with Stephanie, Boris's daughter by Helen Macintyre. Knight looked hard at Stanley and, talking as if Charlotte were there, addressed her as the brilliant mother who had produced four wonderful children, and told Stanley this was nothing to do with him.

Stanley, looking ancient and befuddled, started laughing.

Her brother, Edmund Fawcett, read 'If I Could Tell You' by W. H. Auden. The choir sang passages from Fauré's *Requiem* and Mozart's *Great Mass in C Minor*. One of her sisters, Sophia, read the Prayer of St Julian of Norwich, which ends with the words, 'All shall be well, and all shall be well, all manner of things shall be well.'

The hymns were 'The day thou gavest, Lord, is ended' and 'The Lord's my shepherd, I'll not want'. The Fawcett family song, 'My Brother Sylvest', was sung – 'funny, raucous' according to a non-Fawcett – and the service ended with 'When the Saints Go Marching In' by Louis Armstrong.

As soon as he had helped carry the coffin out, Boris 'bounded back in, glad-handed everyone, stayed for a good hour or hour and a half' at the party after the service, which was held in the church. In the words of one mourner: 'He talked to absolutely everyone, great or small, and was clearly enjoying it. Carrie didn't stay. He didn't want to talk politics but was quite happy to have a bit of a gossip. It wasn't glitzy. There were no paparazzi. There was also an almost complete absence of politicians. There were journalists. It was genuine family friends, mainly Charlotte's friends. Everyone felt she'd had a wonderful life. It was one of the happiest funerals I can remember.'

Few things gave Charlotte's children greater pleasure than to hear her acclaimed as a great artist by Daniel Johnson in a piece for *The Article*.

The prime minister took no compassionate leave after his mother's death. How could he? There was a lot to do, and in any case, he does not enjoy inactivity. But it seemed to me that in the months after his mother's death his judgement was worse than normal. He appeared unable to think straight about how to handle such awkward problems as Partygate, but instead tried first one tack, then another contradictory one, hoping always to throw off his enemies by refusing to play by their pettifogging rules, relying more than ever on his spur-of-the-moment resourcefulness and blind, recklessly bold determination to find a way through. At a time when it would have been expedient to play things in a more responsible way, he doubled down and become more mercurial.

A month after Charlotte's death I remarked to Miriam Gross that I was astonished by Johnson's seeming ability to keep going at full throttle. Gross has a wonderful ear: see her memoir, *An Almost English Life*, which includes her interviews, first published in *The Observer*, with Philip Larkin, Francis Bacon, Harold Pinter and Anthony Powell. She is unusual, in literary London, for having admired Boris ever since she first met him, and for having expressed that admiration quite openly. In my earlier volume she says that on meeting him over New Year 1986–87, when he was in his last year at Oxford, she was 'completely bowled over by' him and 'thought he was exceptionally charming, sophisticated, witty, erudite at that age, and he didn't have that slightly bumbling thing which he has now, which is a defence mechanism'.

Gross became, in the last twelve years of Charlotte's life, a good friend of hers, and gave the following reply:

I was astonished that Boris was able to continue so energetically with his public duties, not showing any outward signs of distress or shock. But on further reflection it occurred to me that it was precisely because his mother was so much his role-model that he was able to do this. Charlotte was incredibly stoical and resilient – she never complained, whinged or gave in, despite the endless succession of illnesses and tragedies that afflicted her for so many years.

I had many conversations with her in the last decade or so of her life, often about Boris (or Al as she called him). She seemed very happy about this because, I gather, most of her friends had been Remainers and avoided mentioning him, while I'd been a friend and admirer of his for ages.

It was clear that they were extremely close. Of course Charlotte adored all her children, but I think she felt particularly protective and anxious about Boris and regarded him as very vulnerable. She must have been a huge support for him, because she completely understood him, including his weaknesses. Charlotte was totally unsnobbish, unpompous, straightforward and always kind. Boris, in my view, was inspired by her example.

After losing one's mother, one feels one has been thrown into the front line; that one has lost a protector, a tower of strength, however weak she may have been in body, who gave one unconditional love and support; who knew one's faults, and did not condemn one for them.

Also at the funeral were Allegra Mostyn-Owen, Johnson's first wife, and Alexa de Ferranti, his first girlfriend. Their presence was a compliment to Charlotte which could not be faked.

NARCISSISM AT THE UN

In a speech at the United Nations in New York on 22 September 2021 Johnson postulated, as he lifted off into one of the flights of fancy which come so frequently to him and so seldom to most politicians, that the average mammalian species exists for about a million years before evolving into something else or vanishing into extinction. He contended that *Homo sapiens* has been around for about 200,000 years, which if you imagined that million years as the lifespan of an individual human being, about eighty years, meant that 'we're now sweet sixteen':

> We have come to that fateful age when we know roughly how to drive and we know how to unlock the drinks cabinet and to engage in all sorts of activity that is not only potentially embarrassing but also terminal for ourselves and others.
>
> In the words of the Oxford philosopher Toby Ord 'we're just old enough to get ourselves into serious trouble'.
>
> And I'm afraid we believe, we still cling with part of our minds to the infantile belief that the world was made for our gratification and pleasure and we combine this narcissism with an assumption of our own immortality.
>
> We believe that someone else will clear up the mess, because that is what someone else has always done.
>
> We trash our habitats again and again with the inductive

reasoning that we've got away with it so far, and therefore we'll get away with it again.

My friends, the adolescence of humanity is coming to an end, and must come to an end . . . It's time for humanity to grow up.

Johnson delivered this speech a week after his mother died. He was addressing the United Nations, and was getting ready to host COP26, the climate change conference, in Glasgow. He was also quite plainly addressing himself. It was time for him to grow up, and to put away the 'infantile belief' that the world was made for his gratification, and someone else would always clear up the mess he left behind.

The death of a parent makes one grow up, or at least try to grow up. We are mortal. A friend of mine pointed out that it is narcissistic to come out as a narcissist in a speech to the whole world. This is true, but perhaps he was becoming more candid because that is what his mother would have done.

MACRON SPURNED

On 23 September 2021 Johnson said a few words in Washington about the anger felt by the French president, Emmanuel Macron, about AUKUS, the recently announced deal between Australia, the United Kingdom and the United States to build nuclear submarines, which supplanted a previous deal under which France worked with Australia to build conventionally powered subs. Johnson said: 'I just think it's time for some of our dearest friends around the world to "prenez un grip" about this and "donnez-moi un break". Because this is fundamentally a great step forward for global security.'

His use of expressions such as 'prenez un grip', though a long-standing Johnson tradition, was a subversion of the language of diplomacy all the more insulting because he speaks fluent French. In an attempt to explain why Australia had given France minimal notice of the change, Johnson said: 'It's a very human thing to delay the frank conversation until the last possible moment. I don't know if anyone has been in that situation in their emotional life but it's very human to put it off.'

No one doubted here that he knew what he was talking about.

COP26

Johnson had once written articles in which he mocked climate change and said wind power 'would barely pull the skin off a rice pudding'. He now promoted with a convert's zeal measures to save the planet. Just before COP26, he flew to Rome for the G20 summit and said on the plane: 'Humanity, civilisation and society can go backwards as well as forwards and when they start to go wrong, they can go wrong at terrifying speed. You saw that with the decline and fall of the Roman Empire: people lost the ability to read and write and the ability to draw properly. They lost the way to build in the way that the Romans did.'

He said that only after becoming prime minister, when he was briefed by government scientists, did he become convinced of the need for action: 'I got them to run through it all and, if you look at the almost vertical kink upward in the temperature graph, the anthropogenic climate change, it's very hard to dispute.'

Johnson's conversion risked annoying many Conservatives, and millions of voters, who were sceptical about climate change and reckoned that even if it was occurring Britain might spend vast sums on reducing carbon emissions without doing anything appreciable to save the planet. The prime minister promised *Sun* readers this would not happen: 'While we're going to have to make some pretty major changes to the way we heat our homes, the Greenshirts of the Boiler Police are not going to kick in your door with their sandal-clad feet and seize, at carrot-point, your trusty old combi.'

Cakeism was liberally applied to the problem. Far from impoverishing us, going green would provide well-paid jobs in every part of the country, levelling up the land. Johnson's gifts as a propagandist helped him to make a propaganda success of COP26, which lasted from 31 October to 13 November. He allied himself with progressive opinion, but made it sound less pious and dull. It was hard to see how anyone could have hosted the event better. But this was the last event of its kind which went well for him, and success had been achieved at the cost of annoying many in his own party who thought the environmental commitments he had espoused with such enthusiasm would inflict unacceptable economic damage.

THE *DAILY TELEGRAPH* DINNER

The *Daily Telegraph* Leader Writers' Dinner was held at the Garrick Club on the evening of Tuesday 2 November 2021. About thirty-two people who had at one time or another written editorials for that paper came to the dinner, including Johnson, who arrived hot-foot from the climate conference in Glasgow just after the meal had begun. He sat between Dean Godson (who since his leader-writing days had become director of the think tank Policy Exchange, and a Conservative life peer) and Harry Mount (editor of *The Oldie*), and opposite Charles Moore.

Johnson gave a short speech in which he praised the 'stubborn, truculent refusal to go along with received opinion' that had characterised leading articles in the *Telegraph*. This anarchic element, he suggested, had been transmitted from the columns of that newspaper to the Tory membership, and from them to Tory MPs, with Brexit the result. He became impassioned as he made this case, and was very good at including everyone in the room, so that he gave no sense of having ascended into a higher sphere. I attended this dinner because I had at one time or another contributed a handful of leaders to the paper. Johnson made us feel we had helped to create a climate of opinion which had ended up changing things. No doubt he exaggerated for effect, but anyone acquainted with the paper knew that, as Nicholas Garland, the political cartoonist, put it in a piece for *The Oldie* which appeared soon after the dinner,

'There was something about *Telegraph* leader-writers. As soon as one was appointed, he or she became infected by a kind of unruly spirit.'

Garland gave some examples of this unruly spirit. The proposal that the distinguished leader-writer and columnist T. E. Utley (1921–88), who was blind, should become the TV critic, 'to get a new point of view on television programmes', was characteristic.

So there was much hilarity at the dinner, and Johnson went on his way rejoicing, seen out of the club and thanked by Moore, who was photographed with him on the front steps.

The following afternoon a debate was held in the Commons before MPs voted on whether to accept a report by the Committee on Standards, which had sentenced Owen Paterson, former minister and since 1997 Conservative MP for North Shropshire, to suspension from the House for thirty sitting days, as punishment for breaking the rules on lobbying. He had been paid £100,000 a year by Randox, a drugs firm in Northern Ireland, on whose behalf he had lobbied ministers. Paterson and his allies had complained for a long time that the process to which he had been subjected was unfair, and that he had no right of appeal, but nothing had been done about this. Many people felt desperately sorry for Paterson, whose wife, Rose, had committed suicide in June 2020.

During the debate, the government allowed a fatal conflation to occur between Paterson's case and changing the rules. Andrea Leadsom put forward an amendment, supported by the govern-ment, which proposed the setting up of a new committee to look in to how, in cases where an MP had been censured, the right of appeal could be upheld. Aaron Bell, since 2019 Conservative MP for Newcastle-under-Lyme, said it 'looks like we're moving the goalposts'. Many Conservative MPs agreed with Bell, and refused to support the Leadsom amendment. They felt that Paterson's mates, a group of older, well-established, well-organised Eurosceptics, had gathered round to defend him. Paterson himself sat stony-faced and silent through the debate. Christian Wakeford, since 2019 Conservative MP for Bury South, went up to him in the division lobby and called him 'a cunt'.

Because of the pandemic, during much of which the Commons held virtual rather than face-to-face proceedings, new MPs had not generally got to know long-serving ones. Nor had the Conservative whips prepared the ground: had they done so, they would have reported back that the Leadsom amendment was unacceptable. On Thursday morning, at business questions, Jacob Rees-Mogg, the Leader of the House, conducted a U-turn, and said that any reforms would have to be bipartisan. On Thursday afternoon, Paterson resigned his seat.

This was a debacle. The Labour leader, Sir Keir Starmer, said the Tories were 'yet again wallowing in sleaze'. The press noticed that on Tuesday evening Johnson had dined with Lord Moore, one of Paterson's staunchest defenders. This made it easy to assume, as many in the media did, that the dinner had been arranged so Moore could talk Johnson into supporting Paterson. This was wrong: the decision to support Paterson had already been taken by the time of the dinner, which had been arranged as a reunion of old colleagues by Neil Darbyshire and Stephen Glover, both formerly at the *Telegraph* and now at the *Mail*.

Johnson was accused by his own troops of behaving like the Grand Old Duke of York. He marched them up to the top of the hill and he marched them down again. What is more, he kept on doing this. Sir John Major, prime minister from 1990 to 1997, felt moved to appear on the *Today* programme at ten past eight, the prime slot, on Saturday 6 November, when he was interviewed by Nick Robinson:

I have been a Conservative all my life, Nick, and if I'm concerned at how the government is behaving I suspect lots of other people are as well. And it seems to me as a lifelong Conservative that much of what they're doing is very unconservative in its behaviour. There are many strands of this that go far beyond the Standards Committee imbroglio of the last few days. There's a general whiff of 'we are the masters now' about their behaviour. And I think this is cutting through to the public, it has to stop and it has to stop soon.

Parliament cannot be the plaything of any prime minister or indeed any government. This government has done a number of things that concern me deeply. They have broken the law, I have in mind the illegal prorogation of Parliament for which I went to the Supreme Court; they have broken treaties, I have in mind the Northern Ireland Protocol; they have broken their word on many occasions, the one that I find most odious was the cut in overseas aid . . .

Robinson put it to Major that this was personal animus, because he had lost the argument on Brexit. Major replied: 'I'm very well aware that the extreme Brexiteers will say, well there he is, bitter old Remoaner. That old mantra will be repeated. And let me say it's partly true. I am old, and I'm most certainly a Remainer. But I'm not bitter. But I am angry and disappointed at the way the government has behaved. I'm angry about the trashing of our reputation.'

Major had been hostile to Johnson for a very long time. In 1993 he had summoned Andrew Mitchell, then MP for Gedling and vice-chairman of the Conservative Party with responsibility for drawing up the list of parliamentary candidates, and had greeted him with the words, 'Ah, Andrew, thanks for coming: what the fuck do you mean by putting Boris Johnson on the candidates list?'

People who had been hoping for a long time to get rid of Johnson reckoned now might be the time to do it. As Labour moved ahead in the opinion polls, Matthew Parris assured readers of *The Times* that 'Flight Bojo 2019 has begun its final descent.' A speech Johnson gave to the CBI in South Shields, during which he lost his place and dwelt at length on a visit he had made to Peppa Pig World, increased the suspicion that he had lost his touch and was on the way out.

NORTH SHROPSHIRE

On Saturday 11 December 2021 the *Daily Telegraph* published the following report from the North Shropshire by-election, which had been caused by Owen Paterson's resignation:

For Neil Shastri-Hurst, the Conservative candidate for North Shropshire, it should have been the easiest of door-knocks.

Lifelong Tory voter Pearl Morris not only had a campaign poster of Mr Shastri-Hurst in the window of her detached home in Oswestry, she also lives next door to a party activist.

'Thank you so much for putting my poster up,' said Mr Shastri-Hurst cheerily as 77-year-old Mrs Morris answered her door. But she didn't return his smile.

'That's quite alright,' she said, 'but I must say to you, this year I can't vote for that charlatan you have got in charge. Next time round, he'll have gone, won't he? And you can have [my vote] back. But I really can't vote for him.'

When the crestfallen candidate asked why his campaign poster was in her window, Mrs Morris replied: 'My husband put it up. But I will add that he has got dementia.'

This was no isolated case of an angry Tory voter. On 16 December, Paterson's majority of 22,949 at the general election was converted into a Liberal Democrat majority of 5,925.

PARTYGATE

On 1 December 2021 the *Daily Mirror* reported that staff at No. 10 had held parties in the run-up to Christmas 2020 which broke lockdown rules. This was the start of a stream of revelations about possible breaches of the rules by Johnson and others which continued for many weeks. The prime minister was unable to find any satisfactory way to respond to these stories. People pointed out that since he and his colleagues had made the lockdown rules, they were under a moral as well as legal obligation to observe them. Johnson himself realised that many people had followed the rules with self-denying conscientiousness, to the point of not visiting sick or dying relatives, or had been forbidden, by hospitals and care homes, to visit those relatives, so were incandescent with rage that he had broken the rules.

On 8 December, after a video had come to light of No. 10 staff making light of lockdown measures at a mock press conference, Johnson said at the start of PMQs:

> May I begin by saying that I understand and share the anger up and down the country at seeing No. 10's staff seeming to make light of lockdown measures. And I can understand how infuriating it must be to think that the people who have been setting the rules have not been following the rules, Mr Speaker. Because I was also furious to see that

clip. And, Mr Speaker, I apologise unreservedly for the offence that it has caused up and down the country, and I apologise for the impression that it gives. But I repeat, Mr Speaker, that I have been repeatedly assured since these allegations emerged that there was no party and that no Covid rules were broken, and that is what I have been repeatedly assured. But I have asked the Cabinet secretary to establish all the facts and to report back as soon as possible. And, Mr Speaker, it goes without saying that if those rules were broken there will be disciplinary action for all those involved.

Johnson's critics had every incentive to prove that he himself had broken the rules. They had high hopes of achieving this, for he was a known rule-breaker. Johnson's defenders found themselves in an awkward position. They could argue that much of the evidence of wrongdoing by which the media set such store was laughably trivial: who cared if a bottle of prosecco had been opened at the end of a long, hard day? But if they did this, they could be accused of making light of others' sufferings during the pandemic, and of seeking to justify law-breaking.

It soon turned out that the Cabinet secretary could not look into the parties, because one of them had apparently occurred in his office. The task was therefore handed over to Sue Gray, a senior civil servant with long experience of looking into cases where politicians were accused of unethical behaviour. On 19 December 2021, a photograph was published of nineteen people, including the prime minister and his wife, drinking in the Downing Street garden on 15 May 2020. On 11 January the Metropolitan Police said they were looking into alleged breaches of Covid rules in Downing Street and

Whitehall, many of which had by now been reported. Gray's report could not be published in full until the police had concluded their enquiries, so it was impossible to see when the affair would close.

On 19 January 2022, David Davis, a senior Tory backbencher, flung at Johnson the words used by Leo Amery as the Tory Party turned against Neville Chamberlain in 1940, and before that by Oliver Cromwell to the Long Parliament: 'You have sat there too long for all the good you have done. In the name of God, go.' But Davis had not quite caught the mood of his Tory colleagues, and unlike Chamberlain, Johnson survived, at least for the time being.

THESE TORIES ARE LIARS

On 18 January 2022, Marianne Dashwood, a young woman of arresting presence, powerful intellect and strong Conservative convictions, undertook the vital task of obtaining from a nearby supermarket chocolate biscuits for herself and her colleagues in one of Westminster's leading think tanks. As she approached the till, she noticed there was a bit of a hold-up, the cashier and a customer being deep in conversation:

Cashier [a woman]: 'Boris is terrible! He's been lying so much all this time! I'm fed up with him.'

Customer [a man]: ''E's bloody awful, 'e is. I can't believe 'e's still there. They should kick 'im out! [turning to Dashwood] 'E should go, shouldn't 'e?'

Dashwood [avoiding the question]: 'Who do you think should come in? Who could replace him?'

Customer [in a conspiratorial tone]: 'Someone from the Labour side. These Tories are liars!'

Cashier: 'They think they can have parties while everyone else is suffering!'

While Dashwood was paying for her biscuits, the original customer lingered and a second customer joined the conversation:

Second customer [a woman]: 'You know, I used to like Boris, but I think he has to go now.'

The cashier and the first customer nodded, while Dashwood remained silent.

Second customer [turning towards Dashwood, in an accusatory tone – not vicious but disbelieving]: 'You *like* him!'

All eyes turned to Dashwood, who replied: 'No! No, I don't!'

She paid as quickly as she could and left. Afterwards she said: 'Even though, as you know all too well, I am not even a Boris fan, I still felt as though I was somehow betraying the party by so readily denouncing him to a bunch of strangers without thinking twice. I almost felt like Peter denying Jesus!'

That comparison is too hard on Dashwood and indulgent to Johnson, but indicates the depth of feeling stirred by the crisis. Where did Conservatives' loyalties now lie? With their embattled leader? Or should they as quickly as possible sever their connection with a man who had become a liability?

For the avoidance of doubt, Marianne Dashwood is a pseudonym, but the dialogue in this story is exactly as her original recounted it to me.

SLAVA UKRAINI!

The Russian invasion of Ukraine began before dawn on 24 February 2022. Johnson was the first Western leader to whom Volodymyr Zelenskyy, the president of Ukraine, spoke, soon after 4 a.m. London time. The prime minister at once expressed the most energetic and heartfelt support for the Ukrainians in their struggle for freedom. In this he expressed the view of most people in Britain, who saw the invasion as an utterly unjustifiable act of aggression.

Many people had assumed that Vladimir Putin, the president of Russia, would not be so reckless as to launch the attack, but British and American intelligence had correctly predicted what would happen. Johnson and the British defence secretary, Ben Wallace, had already over-ruled objections from other parts of the British security establishment, and had supplied anti-tank weapons to the Ukrainians. Putin thought his forces would be able to seize Kyiv, the capital of Ukraine, within days. The bravery and skill of the Ukrainians, and incompetence of Russian commanders, meant that did not happen. A month later, when the Russians retreated from the outskirts of Kyiv, they left behind them the evidence of heinous war crimes. They had conducted themselves like savages.

The crisis required Western nations to do all they could to arm the Ukrainians and impose sanctions on Russia. Johnson was in the forefront of these efforts, seizing the chance to form alliances with like-minded countries, while refraining from criticising those who were slower to get the point. Zelenskyy addressed the Commons by video link, quoting Shakespeare and Churchill, and thanking Johnson by name. The Kremlin complimented Johnson by calling him 'the most active anti-Russian leader'.

On 9 April 2022, Johnson became the first leader of a G7 country to visit Kyiv, walking the streets of the city with Zelenskyy, and being greeted with joy by Ukrainians. This was one of his finest hours as prime minister, and even some of his fiercest critics at Westminster conceded that now was not the moment to get rid of him.

ARISE, SIR GAVIN

On the afternoon of 3 March 2022, I received a text from Marianne Dashwood, already quoted in the vignette about Tory Lies: 'Gavin Williamson knighted!!! What on earth for??!!'

She reflected the widespread view that Williamson was an undeserving recipient of this honour. He had been sacked by Theresa May from the post of defence secretary after she became convinced he had leaked details from the National Security Council about a plan to allow Huawei, a Chinese telecom company, a role in building Britain's new 5G network. He had been sacked by Johnson from the post of education secretary after taking the blame during the pandemic for the exams fiasco which proceeded from the introduction of an algorithm which he had favoured.

I texted Dashwood my explanation for Williamson's knighthood: 'He helped Johnson win the leadership election, and Johnson doesn't want him to help anyone else to do that.'

Dashwood: Hmmmm.

Gimson: Patronage – shocking to an idealist such as yourself.

Dashwood: Well, this is surely taking the biscuit. A colleague asking me for permission to eat a biscuit as I was texting inspired that turn of phrase!!

Gimson: Yes, a good way of putting it – I admire your

indignation, and feel it too in a way. But BJ wants to go on being PM.

Dashwood: Yes, I think he makes that incredibly obvious . . . Far too obvious when the country has not yet forgiven him for the Downing Street parties. People like Williamson are widely loathed and despised and I don't think it helps his image to be rewarding them for obviously personal gain.

Gimson: The country likes to see the PM suffer a bit, and admires his keenness. As for Williamson, well, I don't like the look of him, but this will not rescue his reputation.

Dashwood: No, but it makes unhelpful headlines. With such patent incompetence as Williamson has demonstrated it is difficult not to attract charges of cronyism. 'The country . . . admires his keenness' – perhaps, but one should not be complacent. Is there any evidence?

Gimson: Just my instinct – we want to see the PM energetic, full of fighting spirit, anxious to go on serving us, himself not complacent but straining every sinew.

Dashwood was more in tune with Conservative opinion than I was. By this stage, his own side were ready to be cross about any lapse by Johnson. He had consumed whatever reserves of good will he possessed. But for a time, the harrowing scenes from Ukraine drove out all other news.

LORD LEBEDEV

In the early weeks of the war, as Russian troops behaving with grotesque cruelty and astonishing strategic and tactical ineptitude strove to conquer Kyiv, Johnson's friendship with Evgeny Lebedev came under renewed scrutiny. On 6 March 2022, the *Sunday Times* began a long report by reminding its readers that in March 2020 British intelligence had warned the prime minister against giving a peerage to Lebedev, owner of the *Independent* and *Evening Standard* newspapers, and son of Alexander Lebedev, a former KGB agent who had become a billionaire oligarch, owner of the National Reserve Bank.

When offered this advice, Johnson was said to have replied: 'Hang on a second. What's the problem? Why haven't any of you told me there was a problem before? Because I've been talking to him for ages. How come it's okay for him to own our newspapers and talk to everybody?'

The nomination proceeded, in July 2020 the peerage was announced, and in November Baron Lebedev, of Hampton in the London Borough of Richmond upon Thames and of Siberia in the Russian Federation, took his seat as a crossbencher in the House of Lords, introduced by Lord Clarke, who as Ken Clarke had been a prominent Tory minister, and Lord Bird, who as John Bird had co-founded the *Big Issue*.

Lebedev was a giver of parties, both in London and at his two grand houses in Umbria, reached by flying to Perugia.

He enjoyed dressing up and loved meeting actors, and not just posh ones: his enthusiasm extended to Blackpool and the music hall. While Johnson was mayor, he saw Lebedev frequently in London, and in October would usually visit him in Umbria. A fellow guest recalled a party there after the Conservative Party conference which included the actress Barbara Windsor and the chief executive of Lloyds Bank, Antonio Horta-Osorio. 'Oh, you're Portuguese,' Windsor said, 'my cleaner's Portuguese.' On another occasion, Lebedev wished to entertain both Katie Price, reality TV star, and Johnson to dinner in Umbria on the same evening, and this was arranged. Johnson's then wife, Marina Wheeler, usually accompanied him on these jaunts, but in 2018, while foreign secretary, he was spotted alone one morning at the airport in Perugia, looking more tired and dishevelled than usual, as if he might have slept for an hour or two in his clothes after the revels ended.

'Boris does reward loyalty,' a friend of both men said, 'and Lebedev has always backed him.' This friend said Lebedev is 'very sociable, but also slightly solitary. He is observant and he listens.' Lebedev was at the dinner in February 2016 in Johnson's house when Oliver Letwin tried and failed, by telephone, to persuade Johnson and Gove to back Remain. Johnson and Symonds attended the grand party given in London by Lebedev on the night after the general election victory in December 2019.

The *Sunday Times* headlined its piece on 6 March 2022, 'THE PEER WHO COULDN'T STOP APOLOGISING FOR PUTIN', and cited a number of occasions when Lebedev had sought to explain or justify Russian policy, for example after the annexation of Crimea in 2014. A few days later, Lebedev responded with a statement in the *Evening Standard*:

I am a British citizen. I first moved here as a child and was educated in the United Kingdom at primary and secondary level. I am proud to be a British citizen and consider Britain my home.

I have publicly made clear my condemnation of the war in Ukraine and called on President Putin to end the invasion of the country in the most public way possible through a letter to him published on the front page of the *Evening Standard* . . .

At the moment many with Russian roots are under scrutiny, including myself. I understand the reason for this as it is inevitable when events of such magnitude occur and the world order as we have known it in recent decades suddenly gets torn up.

But I am not a security risk to this country, which I love. My father a long time ago was a foreign intelligence agent of the KGB, but I am not some agent of Russia.

Lebedev making these protestations on his own account was not immensely persuasive, and parts of the British press continued to regard him with suspicion. But on 18 March, a piece by Dmitry Muratov, founder and editor in chief of *Novaya Gazeta*, appeared in *The Times*:

The current narrative about the Lebedev family in the British press is unfair and inaccurate. I urge my UK readers to rethink what they are being told about the Lebedevs, who I believe have had unfair accusations levelled against them in recent weeks.

Novaya Gazeta, one of the last independent Russian free speech institutions, survives to this day thanks to the Lebedevs, who took on great risks to keep it alive. My work at *Novaya Gazeta* was recognised when I won the Nobel peace prize last year on behalf of the newspaper.

Novaya Gazeta wouldn't have survived, and I couldn't possibly have won the Nobel peace prize, if Alexander Lebedev hadn't financed it. The paper was established in 1993 thanks to Mikhail Gorbachev, the former Soviet leader, who used funds from his own Nobel peace prize to set it up. Despite this, there was hardly any money. Sometimes, salaries would go unpaid and there were serious questions about whether we could continue. We survived in large part because of the help we received from the Lebedevs.

I do not exaggerate when I say the paper has been one of the last bastions of free speech in my country. It has enabled me and countless others to report on contentious topics in Russia for decades.

Such testimony was harder to ignore.

LORD PALMERSTON

The accusation of being pro-Russian, made against Johnson because of his friendship with Lebedev, has been made against earlier prime ministers too. Karl Marx, among other things a brilliant polemical journalist, accused Lord Palmerston of pretending to be 'truly English', while actually being pro-Russian. Here is Marx's opening sketch of Palmerston for a series of articles about him written in 1853:

> Although a septuagenarian, and since 1807 occupying the public stage almost without interruption, he contrives to remain a novelty, and to evoke all the hopes that used to centre on an untried and promising youth . . .
>
> If not a good statesman of all work, he is at least a good actor of all work. He succeeds in the comic as in the heroic – in pathos as in familiarity – in tragedy as in farce; although the latter may be more congenial to his feelings. He is not a first-class orator, but an accomplished debater. Possessed of a wonderful memory, of great experience, of consummate tact, of never-failing presence of mind, of gentlemanlike versatility, of the most minute knowledge of parliamentary tricks, intrigues, parties and men, he handles difficult cases in an admirable manner and with a pleasant volatility, sticking to the prejudices and suscepti-bilities of his public, secured from any surprise by his

397

cynical impudence, from any self-confession by his selfish dexterity, from running into a passion by his profound frivolity, his perfect indifference, and his aristocratic contempt. Being an exceedingly happy joker, he ingratiates himself with everybody. Never losing his temper, he imposes on an impassioned antagonist. When unable to master a subject, he knows how to play with it. If wanting in general views, he is always ready to weave a web of elegant generalities.

Endowed with a restless and indefatigable spirit, he abhors inactivity and pines for agitation, if not for action. A country like England allows him, of course, to busy himself in every corner of the earth. What he aims at is not the substance, but the mere appearance of success. If he can do nothing, he will devise anything. Where he dares not interfere, he intermeddles. When unable to vie with a strong enemy, he improvises a weak one. Being no man of deep designs, pondering on no combinations of long standing, pursuing no great object, he embarks in difficulties with a view to disentangle himself from them in a showy manner. He wants complications to feed his activity, and when he finds them not ready, he will create them. He exults in show conflicts, show battles, show enemies, diplomatical notes to be exchanged, ships to be ordered to sail, the whole ending in violent parliamentary debates, which are sure to prepare him an ephemeral success, the constant and the only object of all his exertions. He manages international conflicts like an artist, driving matters to a certain point, retreating when they threaten to become serious, but having got, at all events, the dramatic excitement he wants. In his eyes, the movement of history itself is nothing but a pastime, expressly invented for the private satisfaction of the noble Viscount Palmerston of Palmerston.

Marx detests Palmerston, but does not make the mistake of undervaluing him. Unlike our latter-day moralists, who were bent on getting rid of Johnson by proving him immoral, Marx recognises that cynicism, impudence, selfishness, frivolity, indifference and contempt may be valuable qualities for a practising politician.

My contention is not, by the way, that Palmerston and Johnson are identical: of course they are not. Palmerston by the time he became prime minister in 1855 at the age of seventy – the oldest anyone has attained that office for the first time – was a minister of enormous experience in foreign affairs, in which, as Marx notes, he had been active since 1807, for in those days the most promising members of the political class were given work experience in their twenties as ministers rather than as special advisers. One may note Palmerston's amazing stamina. From 1855 he held office for most of the next ten years, and died in 1865, two days short of his eighty-first birthday, having just won a general election.

Why did he have to wait until 1855 to get his chance? Because his colleagues distrusted him and considered him reckless. The outbreak of the Crimean War changed everything. The British Army's shameful unpreparedness, revealed to the public by William Howard Russell of *The Times* by way of the newly installed telegraph, forced the resignation of the prime minister, Lord Aberdeen, and the appointment in his place of Lord Palmerston, the one person the public knew to possess the energy and drive needed to defeat Russia.

Johnson's colleagues likewise distrusted him, and considered him reckless. The public trusted him to get Brexit done, and insisted only he was equal to the crisis. In any mid-nineteenth-century suburb in the country one is likely to find Alma, Balaclava and Inkerman Roads, commemorating the costly victories of the Crimean War, and a pub called the Lord Palmerston, in celebration of the prime minister credited with winning it. How the people loved this bold, jaunty, high-handed patriot, known also for his love affairs. At the age of seventy-nine, his popularity rose to new heights after he was accused by the wife of an Irish journalist of having committed adultery with her.

Florence Nightingale, whose transformation of the army's medical services had been supported by Palmerston, said of him after his death: 'He will be a great loss to us. Tho' he made a joke when asked to do the right thing, he always did it.' Here too, Palmerston was an English figure: a man who would not adopt a serious tone of voice, even when he was doing serious and well-calculated things.

FIXED PENALTY NOTICE

On 12 April 2022 the Metropolitan Police issued Johnson with a fixed penalty notice for having attended a party held in the Cabinet room on 19 June 2020 to celebrate his fifty-sixth birthday. Johnson had earlier let it be known that he had only attended this event, which had not been planned by him, for nine minutes. He issued an apology from Chequers. Some commentators, including Daniel Finkelstein in *The Times* and Nick Timothy in the *Telegraph*, said he should resign, but although many Conservative MPs remained silent, there was as yet no general call for a leadership contest.

On 19 April 2022, the first day the Commons met after Easter, Johnson came to the chamber and uttered the word 'sorry' forty-two times, after which he sounded much less penitent while addressing a closed meeting of Conservative MPs. By such changes in tone he continued to try their patience, and made an increasing number of them feel he was never going to change.

THE SUE GRAY REPORT

On the morning of Wednesday 25 May 2022, Sue Gray's report into the various Downing Street parties was at long last published. At first sight, it did not appear to be particularly damning, or to add much to the story. Johnson made a statement about it in the House which was received by Conservative MPs in embarrassed silence.

Most of them slipped away early to lunch, wishing neither to defend nor to denounce him. They were getting fed up with the whole business, and with his inability to bring it all to an end, and they could not pretend to find his displays of penitence convincing. Some photographs of him raising a glass at Lee Cain's leaving party on 13 November 2020 had been published the day before. There were also some photographs of him at what looked like a miserable surprise birthday party in the Cabinet room on 19 June 2020, the event for which both he and Rishi Sunak, who had arrived early for a meeting, were given a fixed penalty notice by the Metropolitan Police, which had handed out a total of 126 such notices. The opinion polls showed the Conservatives clearly behind Labour, with many Tories doubting whether he any longer had the ability to make this ground up.

Rory Stewart, still one of Johnson's most eloquent critics, testified on television that he was an impossible man to work for, cited instances of this from the period when Johnson was foreign secretary and Stewart a junior minister in that department, and remarked that 'you end up feeling like a sort of aggrieved partner or wife'. He said the PM's staff were 'sacrificing everything . . . to try to keep this monstrous ego floating around in Downing Street', and suggested that hundreds of small things mounted up 'to make our country feel like Berlusconi's Italy'.

In the days after the Gray report, a number of Conservative MPs said they had put in letters to Sir Graham Brady calling for a confidence vote to be held. The prime minister's situation was, as so often, precarious, which in a free country was as it should be.

NEGATIVE CAPABILITY

On Sunday 22 December 1817, the poet John Keats, aged twenty-two and living in Hampstead, then a village to the north of London, wrote this passage in a letter to his brothers: 'Several things dovetailed in my mind, & at once it struck me, what quality went to form a Man of Achievement especially in Literature & which Shakespeare possessed so enormously – I mean *Negative Capability*, that is when man is capable of being in uncertainties, Mysteries, doubts, without any irritable reaching after fact & reason.'

Johnson cannot be understood by those who demand certainty. Thoughts, feelings, jokes, images, snatches of verse and bizarre turns of phrase crowd in upon his fertile mind. He is a dramatist, a storyteller, a man of Negative Capability.

So Johnson is strong and weak, truthful and dishonest, loyal and fickle, bold and timid, buoyant and depressed, friendly and distant, generous and selfish, unifying and polarising, educated and vulgar, old-fashioned and modern, wholesome and toxic, innocent and guilty, flexible and intransigent, a believer and a sceptic, determined to be in charge and unconcerned to be out of control.

James Forsyth observed of him in *The Times* on 28 May 2021: 'He can adopt all sides of any argument. Discombobulating as this may be for his ministers, it is part of Johnson's decision-making method. He likes to inhabit positions, to try them on for size, to work out what he actually thinks.'

Dominic Cummings remarked in his blog on the EU Referendum, published on 9 January 2017, that 'the most effective person in politics for whom we have good sources, Bismarck, operated always on the principle of "keep two irons in the fire".'

A footballer does not show his opponent until the last moment which way he is going to go, and often does not know himself until that moment.

THE JOHNSONIAN NATION

What is the nation to which Johnson for a short time appealed so successfully? It is free, tolerant, spontaneous, instinctive, intuitive, energetic, hopeful, competitive, courageous, hardworking, bold, piratical, playful, comic, witty, generous, passionate, scruffy, shameless, randy and rude. It is fairminded but self-indulgent. Often it is tasteless, and generally speaking it is unfashionable. Intellectually, it is lazy, for it sees no value in abstractions.

The Johnsonian nation enjoys a bewildering range of sports, books, plays and films. It is amused by most forms of eccentricity, hates being ordered around and can't bear being told what words it can use or thoughts it can have. It has no time for Victorian values and is closer in spirit to the licentious eighteenth century, and before that to Chaucer. It thinks people should be left alone to live their lives as they wish, but demands collective action when there is an obvious need for it. It loves going on foreign holidays, but is intensely patriotic and thinks Britain is the best country in the world.

It is keen on bangers and mash, fish and chips and chicken tikka masala. It has an idealised vision of the pub, to which many real-life pubs do not live up. It abhors any form of pretention. It tries to hide its feelings by making jokes, but those feelings keep bursting out. It loved Johnson, or found in him a kindred spirit, because he too is a man of feeling, who tries to repress those feelings, but cannot manage it. As I wrote earlier in this volume, 'there is something in the British people which responds with joy to leaders like Disraeli and Johnson. Many of us delight in them precisely because they are less respectable than we are – less conscientious, less safe'.

This book is not only about Johnson. It is about the British nation, its instincts and affections and hatred of ideology; its high-spirited feeling that to take a flutter on Johnson was more fun, and might bring greater returns, than making a supposedly safe bet on some more conventional politician.

The early stages of Johnson's national leadership, the 'shocking the grown-ups' phase in which he led Leave to a narrow victory in the referendum campaign, and (after the Theresa May interlude) won a handsome general election victory and got Brexit done, were exhilarating for everyone who liked to see the Establishment confounded. But no sooner had he won the election than the pandemic impelled a more serious tone. It depleted the nation's coffers, showed how inefficient many parts of the British state were, and was followed by a cost of living crisis. Could Johnson the troublemaker rise to these grave new challenges?

His own colleagues doubted whether he could. Many of them had never supported him: in the final round of the parliamentary stage of the Tory leadership contest, held on 20 June 2019, he received the support of only 160 MPs, barely more than the total of 152 votes divided between his two remaining opponents, Jeremy Hunt and Michael Gove. Almost half the parliamentary party had rejected him before he even started, a weakness obscured at the time by the enthusiastic backing of the party membership. Nor had his record in office obliged his colleagues to change their minds. Johnson had not, in the eyes of his own MPs, emerged as the steady, sober, competent figure who was now required. 'Many of them were waiting for an excuse to drop him,' an MP loyal to Johnson observed in the summer of 2022, 'and he provided excuses faster than Cadbury's turn out Smarties.'

DEEPENING PERIL

On Saturday 23 April 2022, St George's Day, as I returned home on my bicycle with some bread and fruit from the local market, I was told by my cheery Labour neighbour: 'Your man is fucked, I'd say.' This belief rendered him even cheerier than normal, and I did not seek to spoil his morning by arguing with him. After all, he could well be right. According to the front page of that morning's *Guardian*, 'Boris Johnson is facing deepening peril over the Partygate scandal after a source said a fine had been issued for a second event attended by the prime minister, while senior Conservatives warned he could face a leadership challenge within weeks.'

Peril, in news reports, is always 'deepening', and a number of senior Conservatives were indeed fed up with Johnson. One of them, Steve Baker, a man of high principle, impressive organisational ability and passionate sincerity, had declared two days earlier in the Commons that 'the gig is up', and in Saturday's *Daily Telegraph* went on to say: 'I am a comprehensive kid and many of the unspoken rules about the way our system works, the way that loyalty to the party is supposed to work, the gradations of hierarchy, they're all very public school. And I regard all this stuff – I'll use the word though I don't like to swear – as such bullshit. And I'm willing to urinate all over their conventions.'

Johnson faced a revolt by backbenchers who felt he had a

'morally disintegrating effect' on all who dealt with him. Those words were spoken in 1922 by Stanley Baldwin, an obscure but emerging Conservative MP who led the revolt which in October of that year toppled Lloyd George. It looked as though a century later, the same was going to happen to Johnson. The Conservative Party exists to do the country's bidding, and it had sensed that the country wanted a steadier and less flamboyant leader than Johnson.

My own preference, as a man happiest supporting lost causes, was to carry on with Johnson, whose energy, benevolence and flashes of genius in my opinion outweighed his appalling flaws. This Tory Democrat had the imagination, I thought, to give the nation a new idea of itself, the judgement often to find the right way forward, and the stamina to be a ten-year prime minister. And I was not much pleased, to borrow a phrase coined by Edmund Burke in 1770 in *Thoughts on the Present Discontents*, with the 'professions of supernatural virtue' made by the prime minister's critics.

But the destinies of a great nation do not depend on the predilections of a shy, retiring biographer living in north London. They depend on public opinion refracted through the House of Commons, in which, thanks to Johnson's leadership in 2019, the Conservatives enjoyed a substantial majority. Would they be so ungrateful as to overthrow a leader to whom they owed so much? On past performance, they would do this as soon as they believed it to be in their own interests.

NOBODY'S PERFECT

Politics is often written about as if it were perfectible. The pundit gazes down on the politician from a position of superior wisdom and integrity. If only, it is implied, the politician were as wise and incorruptible as the writer, all would be well.

Johnson has long invited such treatment. By taking Britain out of the European Union he inflicted agonising pain on devout Remainers and became in those circles a hate figure. He added insult to injury by cultivating a style which defied accepted norms: cavalier with the facts, provocative in use of language, dishevelled in personal appearance.

How, then, did he persuade so many people to vote for him? The longer I studied him, the more I concluded that people warmed to him precisely because he was subversive. They too felt themselves scorned by the Establishment for defying its line on the EU, and its prissy and illiberal views about many other things too. Johnson's imperfections placed him on the side of the underdog. As my friend Russell Middleditch, who calls himself 'a Suffolk coast boy' and has lived his whole life in Thorpeness, including a spell as a fisherman, put it when Johnson was under sustained attack from the Opposition and the media: 'The more they try to trip him up the better the people of this country like him.'

His genuine and undoubted flaws became, for a time, a strength. While the going was good, they made him more likeable. It is hard to be fond of a censorious person, and Johnson was never censorious. He instead sought, rather mischievously, to provoke his adversaries into being censorious. Hence the description of him in the title of this book as 'a troublemaker'. Although himself a Tory troublemaker, he has more in common with left-wing troublemakers – Karl Marx and Claud Cockburn have been cited – than with such pious figures as Sir Keir Starmer. We live in a fallen world, which rebels and comedians may understand better than moralists do. Nobody's perfect.

A grand Washington lady said of Bill Clinton during the Monica Lewinsky scandal, when great but unavailing efforts were being made to evict him from the White House: 'Bill Clinton is not the first man I've had to forgive and I hope he won't be the last.' Politics is a test not only of our politicians, but of our willingness, or otherwise, to forgive them. Are we strict or lax, merciless or tolerant? In the case of Johnson, by the end even his own colleagues felt there was simply too much to forgive.

CONFIDENCE VOTE

Pretty much everyone who has ever had anything to do with Johnson has at some point felt goaded beyond endurance and has gone into opposition. In the first five months of 2022, so many arrows were shot at him, not only by his inveterate enemies but by his former friends, and hit the target, that he came to resemble a corpulent Saint Sebastian. The press speculated with mounting excitement that fifty-four Conservative MPs, 15 per cent of the total, were going to send in letters to Sir Graham Brady, chairman of the 1922 Committee, which would trigger a vote of confidence.

The four days from Thursday 2 June to Sunday 5 June, during which the nation celebrated the Queen's Platinum Jubilee, appeared to offer some respite to the prime minister. It was generally assumed that however many letters Sir Graham received in this period, he would wait until after the celebrations before making an announcement. But on Friday 4 June Boris and Carrie Johnson were booed as they arrived at St Paul's Cathedral for a service of thanksgiving for the Queen's reign. Cheers were sufficiently mingled with boos for viewers to dispute which side won, but this was an ominous portent.

At 7.30 on the morning of Monday 6 June, Jesse Norman MP, an old friend of the Prime Minister, published a letter denouncing him. Half an hour later, Sir Graham said the threshold of fifty-four had been reached, and a ballot of

Conservative MPs would be held that evening. In Committee Room 14, a splendid chamber overlooking the Thames, Sir Graham announced the result: 211 votes in favour of Johnson, 148 against.

A strange, low whistle of amazement was heard the moment the figures were known, followed by a great drumming of desks, the traditional way in which the Tory tribe demonstrates its approval. But many Tories stood in silence, and were not applauding. Johnson's performance was worse than most people had expected. We found ourselves watching a blood sport, and the quarry, a 57-year-old man, had been wounded, not just by the fifty-four of his followers who had put in letters against him, but by almost three times as many who cast their ballots against him.

'It's not very good, is it?' I remarked to a colleague as we traipsed back to the Press Gallery in a less gilded part of the Palace of Westminster.

'It's very bad,' the colleague replied.

That certainly was how it felt, and the blow was the worse because only a few hours earlier Johnson had been given the chance to defend himself in a speech to Conservative MPs in the Boothroyd Room in Portcullis House, the modern part of the palace above Westminster Underground Station. He had appealed for their support, and 148 of them had rejected him. At some moments in this narrative, I may have suggested that only clueless liberals, out of touch with public opinion, could see no further use for Johnson. But here were 148 Conservative MPs who had observed Johnson at close quarters, and could be presumed to be alert to the views of their constituents, deciding it was time for him to go.

About an hour after the result had been declared, Johnson came on the television. He wore a shell-shocked smile as he claimed he had more support from Conservative MPs than he did when he became leader. 'I don't think that people want to talk about stuff that goes on at Westminster,' he asserted. That was the media's agenda, in which the public were not interested.

But he stumbled over the words as he said them, and all the world knew 148 of his own MPs had just knifed him, albeit in a secret ballot. This was getting serious in the way that the fall of Margaret Thatcher in 1990 got serious. A blood-letting had begun, so that the party of government could be renewed. William Hague, a former Conservative leader, used his column in the following morning's *Times* to urge Johnson to step down.

In these febrile days, I spoke to a Cabinet minister who said the Conservative Party, and the wider public, had suffered 'an attack of doubt and distrust'. He added that Johnson 'has the mentality of a Greek or a Roman', like them 'regards life as a competition or a race', considers that 'daring and courage and panache' are virtues, is 'addicted to adrenalin', and although 'personally kind, if people get in his way will take the necessary steps to get them out of his way. He can be ruthless.'

The Conservatives can be ruthless too, but had yet to agree among themselves who should take over if they defenestrated Johnson. Nor did Sir Keir Starmer, the Labour leader, look like a prime minister in waiting. During the Partygate scandal, he had adopted an increasingly pharisaical tone, congratulating himself on being more upright than Johnson, and declaring he would resign if the police found he had broken lockdown rules by drinking, as photographic evidence suggested he had, from a bottle of beer while with Labour colleagues in Durham. Nor was Starmer able, at prime minister's questions on the Wednesday following the confidence vote, to score off the weakened Johnson. The police at length decided not to proceed against him, but meanwhile, Starmer's weakness encouraged the Tories to think, rightly or wrongly, they could afford to indulge in an argument among themselves.

Nine days after the confidence vote, Lord Geidt, Johnson's adviser on the ministerial code, resigned, saying that he had been placed by the government in 'in an impossible and odious position' when asked to approve in advance 'a deliberate and purposeful breach of the Ministerial Code' in connection with trade rules: strong language for this usually reticent figure. Here was yet another member of the Establishment whose patience had at length snapped under provocation from the prime minister. Had Geidt's resignation occurred just before the confidence vote, it might have meant Conservative MPs seized that moment to get rid of Johnson.

Not one member of the Cabinet had yet moved against Johnson in the way they moved to finish off Thatcher in November 1990. He lived to fight another day, and bent all his energies to regaining control. The drama was not over, he was still at the heart of it, and although he was weak, with every day that he remained in office his chances of lasting through the summer improved. It was possible to believe Johnson was about to be thrown overboard, or that he would last for a good time yet. He himself spoke defiantly in the Commons, two days after the confidence vote, of 'a long political career . . . barely begun'.

DOWNFALL

On Thursday 23 June 2022 the Conservatives lost two by-elections, at Wakefield, in West Yorkshire, and Tiverton and Honiton, in Devon. In the former seat, the sitting Conservative MP, Imran Ahmad Khan, had resigned after he was convicted of sexually assaulting a fifteen-year-old boy, and his general election majority of 3,358 became a Labour majority of 4,925. In the latter seat, the sitting Conservative MP, Neil Parish, had resigned after admitting watching pornography on his mobile phone in the Commons chamber, and his general election majority of 24,239 became a Liberal Democrat majority of 6,144.

These defeats were deeply perturbing for Conservative MPs, for although they knew that governments often lose by-elections, it was only just over a year since Johnson had led them to a famous victory in Hartlepool. They now faced the danger that in the south the Lib Dems would come and get them, while in the north scores of seats would return to Labour.

An increasing number of Conservatives had lost faith in Johnson's ability to turn things round. His poll ratings were poor, and why, they wondered, should these improve? Having got the unconventional but essentially popular Brexit done, perhaps he had exhausted both his usefulness and his reserves of trust. They noted that when difficulties arose, he was inclined to steer a zig-zag course, darting first in one direction, then in another, heedless of the inconsistencies and inaccuracies this entailed. The Tory tribe watched with alarm his ducking and diving. Nor was this just a question of style. Hard economic problems faced the nation. The pandemic had required a vast increase in public spending and borrowing, with no idea of how it was to be paid for. Energy prices had soared, food was more expensive and property prices were so high the young despaired of home ownership, and instead contemplated paying extortionate rents for the rest of their lives. Interest rates were rising and would need to go up further in order to squeeze inflation out of the system, which would make life harder for borrowers. To none of this did Johnson have anything useful to say. Never had the contrast between him and Thatcher been more apparent. Where she would have admitted the gravity of the nation's predicament and insisted on stern measures which would in time bring their well-earned reward, Johnson seemed to offer only boosterism.

A week after the by-election defeats, the government's deputy chief whip, Chris Pincher, wrote a letter which began 'Dear Prime Minister' and went on: 'Last night I drank far too much. I've embarrassed myself and other people which is the last thing I want to do and for that I apologise to you and to those concerned. I think the right thing to do in the circumstances is for me to resign as deputy chief whip.' He was reported, while in his cups the night before, to have groped two men at the Carlton Club, a venerable Tory institution founded in 1832. One of these men reported his behaviour to a Tory whip, Sarah Dines, who was also in the club, and she in turn reported it the following morning to the chief whip, Chris Heaton-Harris.

Downing Street was not disposed, once Pincher had resigned, to think any further action was required. Johnson takes a relaxed view of sexual relations, is not inclined to fling accusations of sexual harassment about, and during the Monica Lewinsky affair had leaped to the defence of President Bill Clinton (see chapter 22 of my previous volume). The prime minister appears to have decided that Pincher had suffered enough.

Johnson's inaction appalled many. It opened him to the charge that he did not take sexual harassment seriously, and that by tolerating Pincher, he was betraying Pincher's victims. Only under pressure, and after a formal complaint had been lodged, did the prime minister agree that the Tory whip should be withdrawn from Pincher while an investigation was carried out. Nor was this the end of the matter. Earlier allegations against Pincher now emerged, and Dominic Cummings testified that Johnson used to refer 'laughingly' to 'pincher by name, pincher by nature'. Pincher, people pointed out, was a Johnson loyalist, who had campaigned for the PM in recent months.

Downing Street insisted Johnson had not known of any specific earlier allegations against Pincher. Lord McDonald, who had served as permanent under-secretary at the Foreign Office while Johnson was foreign secretary, said he 'watched with incredulity' on Sunday 3 July as Thérèse Coffey, the work and pensions secretary, promulgated this line on the airwaves. 'I knew that wasn't the case,' McDonald stated. There had been a complaint of a similar nature against Pincher, then a Foreign Office minister, in the summer of 2019, and McDonald was certain that Johnson, by then prime minister, was told about it. By his own account, McDonald got in touch with Downing Street, asking that the line be changed. It was not, so at 7.30 a.m. on Tuesday 5 July he tweeted: 'This morning I have written to the parliamentary commissioner for standards – because No 10 keep changing their story and are still not telling the truth.' He accompanied the tweet with a copy of his letter, in which he admitted that 'it is unusual to write to you and simultaneously publish the letter', but explained that 'I act on behalf of the victims'. Forty minutes later he appeared in the prime 8.10 slot on the *Today* programme, on Radio 4, where he declared: 'Things get to a point where you have to do the right thing.'

We found ourselves watching a power struggle as well as a morality tale. The Cabinet met that morning, and at the start, for propaganda purposes, a television camera was allowed to pan across their faces. This recent innovation had never felt right, for Cabinet meetings are supposed to be confidential, and today it made matters worse.

While the prime minister said a few words about tax cuts, Nadine Dorries, one of his most devoted supporters, stared into the distance in a grief-stricken manner, while Jacob Rees-Mogg, also impeccably loyal, attended to the prime minister's words in a polite but pained way. Michael Gove, assassin of Johnson in 2016, ran an anxious finger quickly to and fro across his lips, as though in the grip of unbearable mental tension. Nigel Adams, a lesser known but long-standing Johnson loyalist, pursed his lips, somehow indicating that as a Yorkshireman he knew perfectly well there was nothing to be done. Chris Heaton-Harris, the chief whip, looked even more despondent than the others. They resembled a team of doctors who do not know which of them will find the courage to tell their patient he has only hours or at best days to live.

At lunchtime Angela Rayner, deputy leader of the Labour Party, asked an urgent question in the Commons 'on the mechanisms for upholding standards in public life', and more particularly about Lord McDonald's accusation that Johnson had previously been told of a specific allegation against Pincher. Michael Ellis, the Cabinet Office minister generally sent out to field such awkward enquiries, explained that 'the prime minister did not immediately recall the conversation in late

2019 about the incident'. This line sounded hopelessly implausible, for Johnson has a wonderful memory.

At six o'clock that evening, the news broke that Sajid Javid, the health secretary, had resigned from the Cabinet, followed a few minutes later by Rishi Sunak, the chancellor of the exchequer. Here were two hammer blows. Johnson tried to repair the damage by sending Steve Barclay, one of his right-hand men in Downing Street, to replace Javid, and Nadhim Zahawi, the education secretary, to replace Sunak at the Treasury. We have seen Zahawi earlier in this book predict that a Johnson premiership 'could go spectacularly badly', but on Wednesday morning he went on the *Today* programme to try to steady the ship.

The ship nevertheless continued to sink beneath the waves, with increasing numbers of passengers and crew scrambling into the lifeboats. Resignations continued at first hourly, then almost minute by minute. At noon on Wednesday, Johnson appeared for prime minister's questions, and had to turn at the dispatch box to defend himself against attack from three of his own backbenchers. The Tory tribe was all at once, and in the most public way, turning on him. Johnson himself had written in September 2006, when Tony Blair was in trouble: 'For ten years we in the Tory Party have become used to Papua New Guinea-style orgies of cannibalism and chief-killing, and so it is with a happy amazement that we watch as the madness engulfs the Labour Party.' This passage infuriated Jean L. Kekedo, Papua New Guinea's High Commissioner in London, but nobody denied it was an accurate description of the behaviour from time to time of the British Conservative Party.

Immediately after PMQs, Javid delivered his resignation statement. He spoke of the importance of integrity, said that 'treading the tightrope between loyalty and integrity has become impossible in recent months', and added that for a long time he had continued to give the PM 'the benefit of the doubt', but now he had decided 'enough is enough'.

Still Johnson tried to hang on. That afternoon he fulfilled a long-standing engagement to give evidence for two hours to the Liaison Committee, chaired by Sir Bernard Jenkin and consisting of the chairs of Commons select committees. Several of them tried to rough him up, but still he fought his corner. At the end, Sir Bernard tried to wind things up on a consensual note: 'I hope you will accept that in the end we're all dispensable.'

Johnson accepted the offer: 'That's certainly true. All flesh is grass.' Ministers were waiting for him when he returned to Downing Street. A few of them urged him to carry on, but most of them were intent on convincing him that the game was up. By the end of Wednesday, over fifty of his colleagues had resigned, but the prime minister had not. On Thursday morning, Zahawi too rebelled against him.

But that morning, the prime minister awoke in a different, more realistic frame of mind and wrote his own resignation speech. The news that he was going broke on the BBC just after nine o'clock in the morning, and at 12.30 he emerged into Downing Street to deliver a short speech. Carrie Johnson, carrying their baby daughter, Romy, in a sling, stood in a group of supporters to one side, as did Dorries, Rees-Mogg and others.

Johnson was not in the slightest bit lachrymose. He said it was 'clearly now the will of the parliamentary Conservative Party that there should be a new leader of that party and therefore a new prime minister'. He would appoint a cabinet to serve, as he himself would, until that new leader was in place. He had attempted to persuade his colleagues that 'it would be eccentric' to change governments 'when we have such a vast mandate' and are 'only a handful of points behind in the polls . . . even in mid-term after quite a few months of relentless sledging'.

But at Westminster, he remarked, 'the herd instinct is powerful, and when the herd moves it moves'. This way of describing his fellow Tory MPs was the more insulting for containing a grain of truth. At the end, they had acted with a kind of spontaneous unity. He said that 'our brilliant and Darwinian system' would produce 'another leader equally committed to taking this country forward through tough times', and whoever that leader turned out to be, 'I will give you as much support as I can'. Not a very reassuring way of putting it, for it was possible to imagine he might feel able to give the new leader no support.

Johnson did not sound broken, or even defeated. His whole demeanour said he lived to fight another day, and was living out a classical drama in which the gods set him seemingly insurmountable ordeals in order to try his courage. Fortune had turned against him, but he would not for that reason despair. He would go on fighting, like some ancient hero, and perhaps Fortune would at some unpredictable moment relent.

'A leader has got to be trusted,' Clement Attlee, prime minister from 1945 to 1951, wrote in an article published some years later. 'When men start distrusting him he stops being a leader.' That, in modern, democratic terms, was the reason for Johnson's downfall. He had not built a team of people who trusted him and would remain loyal to him. Like some brilliant insurgent who is useless at commanding regular troops, Johnson could not manage the machinery of government, or sustain others who would manage it for him. As an insurgent, he could thrive by being unpredictable, even by playing a double game. As a man of government, that was much more difficult. People felt they did not know where they stood with him and found he might at any moment change his mind, so could not, in the end, be trusted.

In January 2016, Johnson took part in a Greece versus Rome debate at the Albert Hall, with him as the champion of the Greeks and Professor Mary Beard standing up for the Romans. He began with the *Iliad*, 'the greatest poem ever composed, the fountainhead of Western literature', and found it full of 'meritocratic indignation . . . insubordination . . . you are often in the presence of rebels and satirists and debunkers . . . words that speak down the ages to anyone who does not like being bossed around'.

Johnson hates being bossed around. He was and is a rebel, a satirist, a debunker. He could believe, and encourage others to believe, that the lily-livered Establishment, unable to bring him down in an election, had resorted instead to an intrigue. But he also perhaps knew that he had done more than anyone else to blow himself up.

ACKNOWLEDGEMENTS

Celia Montague kindly allowed the reproduction on the back cover of her portrait of Johnson absorbed in the painting of a picture of himself. Craig Brown suggested, by his works on Princess Margaret and the Beatles, how to set about writing this book. Paul Goodman, my editor at ConservativeHome, has in recent years asked me to profile or interview almost every Conservative of any significance, and permitted me to draw on that work here. To all three I owe a great debt. When it comes to acknowledging the help of the many people who talked to me about Johnson, I find myself embarrassed, for I have run out of time to check whether they wish to be identified. I take refuge in a general and fervent thanks to them all.

Particular thanks are owed to my agent, Andrew Gordon, for his invariably astute advice, and at Simon & Schuster to Ian Marshall for taking on the book, and Kat Ailes for editing it.

Many friends have at various points sustained and encouraged me. They include David and Debbie Owen, Charles and Caroline Moore, Oliver and Isabel Letwin, Richard and Kate Ehrman, Noel Malcolm, Simon Gimson, David Gimson, Mando Meleagrou, Susan Clarke (maker of daily, even hourly, telephone calls), Imke Henkel, Alistair Lexden, Jan Rushton, Jules Lubbock and Esther Fitzgerald. Zewditu Gebreyohanes impelled a more rigorous study of cakeism. As in my first volume about Johnson, I have left any amount of scope for younger and fitter Johnson scholars, and also for older and less fit ones. All blunders are my own.

Andrew Gimson, Gospel Oak, July 2022

BIBLIOGRAPHY

Johnson's works, in order of publication:

Friends, Voters, Countrymen: Jottings from the stump (HarperCollins 2001)
Lend Me Your Ears (collected journalism; HarperCollins, 2003)
Seventy-Two Virgins (HarperCollins, 2004)
The Dream of Rome (HarperPress, 2006)
Life in the Fast Lane: The Johnson Guide to Cars (Harper Perennial, 2007)
The Perils of the Pushy Parents: A Cautionary Tale (HarperCollins, 2007)
Have I Got Views For You (collected journalism; HarperCollins, 2008)
Johnson's Life of London (HarperPress, 2011)
The Churchill Factor: How One Man Made History (Hodder & Stoughton, 2014)

There is as yet no collection of Johnson's speeches.

The Wit and Wisdom of Boris Johnson, introduced and edited by Harry Mount, with a preface by Lord Charles FitzRoy, is an enjoyable collection of quotations by and about Johnson (Bloomsbury, 2013)
Boris Johnson: The Irresistible Rise by Michael Cockerell, first broadcast in 2014, is a fascinating documentary

Works by members of Johnson's family:

Minding Too Much: A Charlotte Johnson Wahl Retrospective by Nell
    Butler & Charlotte Johnson Wahl (Riverdog Productions,
    2015)
The Lost Homestead by Marina Wheeler (Hodder & Stoughton,
    2020)
Alas Poor Johnny: A Memoir of Life on an Exmoor Farm by Buster
    Johnson, with foreword by Boris Johnson, edited by Birdie
    Johnson (Matador, 2015)
Rake's Progress: My Political Midlife Crisis by Rachel Johnson (Simon
    & Schuster, 2020)
Stanley I Presume by Stanley Johnson (Fourth Estate, 2009)
Stanley I Resume by Stanley Johnson (The Robson Press, 2014)

Biographies:

Boris: The Making of the Prime Minister by Andrew Gimson (Simon
    & Schuster, first published in 2006 as *Boris: The Rise of Boris
    Johnson*, updated in 2007, 2008, 2012 and 2016)
Just Boris: The Irresistible Rise of a Political Celebrity by Sonia Purnell
    (Aurum Press, 2011)
Boris Johnson: The Gambler by Tom Bower (WH Allen, 2020)
Boris Johnson: Porträt eines Störenfrieds by Jan Ross (Rowohlt,
    2020)
Boris Johnson Un Européen Contrarié by Tristan de Bourbon-Parme
    (Editions François Bourin, 2021)
Boris: Klucht of konigsdrama? by Patrick Bernhart (Prometheus,
    2017)

A few works on Tory Democracy:

Coningsby, or The New Generation by Benjamin Disraeli (first
    published 1844)
Sybil, or The Two Nations by Benjamin Disraeli (first published
    1845)
Disraeli by Robert Blake (first published 1966)
The Sayings of Disraeli edited by Robert Blake, foreword by
    Alistair Lexden (Duckworth, 2019)
Lord Randolph Churchill by Winston Churchill (first published
    1906)
A Gift from the Churchills: The Primrose League, 1883–2004 (Alistair
    Cooke, Carlton Club, 2010)

Other recent works:

Diary of an MP's Wife: Inside and Outside Power by Sasha Swire
    (Little, Brown, 2020)
In the Thick of it: The Private Diaries of a Minister by Alan Duncan
    (William Collins, 2021)
*The Assault on Truth: Boris Johnson, Donald Trump and the Emergence
    of a New Moral Barbarism* by Peter Oborne (Simon & Schuster,
    2021)
First Lady: Intrigue at the Court of Carrie and Boris Johnson by
    Michael Ashcroft (Biteback, 2022)

INDEX